History of Banking in the United States

History of Banking in the United States

(Vol. 1)

Beginning and Development

Graham W. Sumner

LM Publishers

PERIOD I - 1630 to 1780.

The Colonists Experiment with Joint Stock Banks of Issue on Land Security, and with Provincial Mortgage Loan Offices Issuing Currency.

CHAPTER I

From 1630 to 1780.

Banks the colonies

The term "bank" was used in the American colonies from the very beginning of the settlement, in the sense of a pile or heap. In a report made to the Massachusetts General Court, in 1652, reference is made to the fact that some people have been discussing a project for raising a bank, or engaging in general trade, and have been pondering on the badness of money and its fluctuations, and other things relating to the regulation of trade. The hope is expressed that these ponderings will bear fruit and that things will be "reduced to a more comfortable state than we now find." In the draft of an address to Charles II, in 1684, mention is made of the fact that before the establishment of the mint, in 1652, "for some years paper bills passed for payment of debts." Correspondence between Governor Winthrop of Connecticut and Hartlib is cited, about 1660, in which a "bank of lands and commodities" is under discussion. It is referred to as "a way of trade and bank without money," and Winthrop was

7

confident that this bank would "answer all those ends that are attained in other parts of the world by banks of ready money."

This endeavor, which we here meet with in the very earliest days of the settlement, to invent some kind of a bank on land, which could be made to work like the banks founded on money, is most interesting and important for the study of our subject, because we shall find that from that day to this the same train of thought, speculation, and effort has been repeated clear across this continent, whenever the same economic circumstances have existed. Circulating notes, which are put in the place of money, are more useful and convenient for many purposes than specie, provided their value can be assured. If they take the place of money, they become cash. They deteriorate, however, into negotiable instruments and not cash so soon as the slightest shade of difference arises between their value and that of specie. Notes issued on the security of anything but specie, or on specie, if not strictly held to the standard, are negotiable instruments. No matter how great and good the security behind them may be, it is always possible that for some reason, a divergence may arise between the paper instrument and cash. The persons who possess land in a new country are under an absolute necessity for some capital. The amount of capital that can be employed on the land is small, because no high culture would pay; but the amount of capital that is necessary for superficial culture is absolutely indispensable. On the advancing margin of new settlement, breaking the way into the wilderness all the way across the continent, the circumstances of the first settlers on the coast have been repeated. The want is capital. They always think that the want is money. Any community of people who had been educated on a money economy, and who meant to remain on it, would have money, because that would be one of its first and most fundamental needs. It would be forced to go without other things in order to get money, because the lack of money would arrest the operation of the industrial and commercial organization on which its members would depend for the supply of all needs. But new settlers, destitute of everything, begrudge the investment of capital in money, which is only a tool of exchange. They want to put all the capital they can get into the circulating capital which is turned over in every period of production and brings the full business rate of profit. If, therefore, they get any money, they part with it, as far as they possibly can, in the purchase of the real capital which they need. This is what the colonists of North America did. They got plenty of silver in commerce. They spent it all for products of civilized industry from England. They were able to do this because they gave up the money system of traffic and fell back upon barter. Then they could do without money, but when they had made arrangements to do without money, they had to do without it. It is not possible to do without it and keep it too. Their own interpretation of the facts, in consonance with such economic theories as then prevailed, was that "the balance of trade drew away all their specie." Then they thought it necessary to do something to "provide a medium," and we find them planning a bank for the purpose. Land was the one thing which they possessed in abundance and they wanted to make this a security for the notes which were to do the work of money. There was a very active speculation on banks going on in England, and many of the speculators were working at schemes for banks founded on land values, which were a very different thing in an old country from what they were in a new. It was very natural that these ideas should be taken up eagerly by the colonists.

It must be added, however, that there were circumstances of difficulty connected with the supply of money. In any such primitive agricultural community the circulation of money is extremely sluggish, because the organization is low and the households largely supply their wants from their own direct efforts. It is only at particular seasons of the year that money is more needed and that its circulation is more active. Money should therefore be drawn from commercial centers at those times and then returned to them. Otherwise the expense of maintaining money enough all the time to suffice at the times of need is really great. The distance of the colonies from England, the difficulty of communication, and the obstructive legislation which was in fashion, made it impossible that money should go to and fro with facility as wanted. Gallatin, who was a competent observer, and who lived in the midst of these primitive facts in western Pennsylvania, said of the people there: "The principle almost universally true that each country will be naturally supplied with the precious metals according to its wants did not apply to their situation."

The American colonists gave up the struggle to maintain themselves on a money system. They fell back upon barter and established a system of barter currency as their money of account. This fact is of the first importance for understanding the financial and monetary phenomena of the period.

In 1667 a pamphlet was published in Massachusetts in which the ideas which have been described were very fully set forth. The writer had perceived that, if exchanges could only be brought into coincidence, there was need of little or no money. He inferred that money itself need have no value. He wanted to provide some ultimate security in land, and in a pledge of merchandise, and he aimed to carry out the transactions by book debts, or bills of exchange, or change bills, according to the nature and size of the transactions. He also lays great stress on the advantages which would come from a more abundant supply of money. The project is like those which were put forth in England a little later by Chamberlain and Briscoe for land banks. An institution on this plan appears to have been actually started in Massachusetts, in 1671, "and was carried on in private for many months," although without issuing notes. Another similar bank was set up in 1681 which did issue notes. Nothing is known of its history.

John Blackwell and others made a proposition to the authorities of the colony, in 1686, to set up a bank to issue notes and make loans on the security of land and imperishable merchandise. The scheme was approved and authorized. "All that is known of the history of this Association, the first chartered bank in Massachusetts, is found in a brief reference to it made by the anonymous author of a pamphlet printed in 1714." "Our fathers, about twenty-eight years ago, entered into a partnership to circulate their notes founded on land security, stamped on paper, as our Province bills, which gave no offence to the government then, etc."

The first bills of credit, as they were called by a seventeenth century expression, which is said to have been applied to the goldsmiths' notes in London, were issued in 1690 by the government of Massachusetts Bay, to pay the expenses of an unsuccessful expedition to Canada. Of these bills of credit, Cotton Mather said, in a pamphlet, that they were disposed of by the first receivers at 14 or 15 shillings in the pound. He urged the impossibility of collecting them in corn "at overvalue," whereby he bears testimony to the error and mischief of the barter currency. He has heard that some individuals in New York or Connecticut have circulated notes on their credit and is indignant that these of Massachusetts, based on all the wealth of the Province, should not be sustained. "Silver in New England is like the water of a swift running river; always coming and as fast going away," but this paper currency "is an abiding cash; for no man will carry it to another country, where it will not pass, but rather use it here, where it will, or, at least ought;" etc.

A committee of the General Court, in 1701, proposed a bank, but it was negatived by the Council. Another movement for the establishment of a private bank was started, in 1714, by several gentlemen of Boston. Hutchinson says that they were "persons in difficult or involved circumstances in trade, or such as were possessed of real estates, but had little or no ready money at command, or men of no substance at all."

The scheme was that, £300,000 should be subscribed and the same amount of notes issued. The subscribers were to mortgage their estates as an ultimate security against mismanagement, etc. Each subscriber was to take out between one quarter and one half of his stock in notes and keep them out at least two years, paying interest for them. All partners agreed to take the notes at a rate equal to the bills of credit of the colony. The tenor of the notes was that all the members of the company would take them in all payments "in lieu of" so many shillings, and that they would be so received for any pawn or mortgage in the bank.

One important allegation in favor of the bank, revealing a line of thought which we shall meet with often hereafter, was that it "would sever the connection between money and might." We also find the Land Bank seeking favor by propositions of a class often met with in the nineteenth century. They proposed to give a sum annually to the use of a hospital or charity school for the poor children of Boston, provided the inhabitants, at or before their general meeting in March, 1715, would order the Treasurer to accept their bank bills in payment of town taxes and assessments.

As this project took more definite shape, it aroused great opposition, and in order to defeat it, a project was set in opposition to it for a further issue of colonial bills of credit— not for the expenses of government, but on a new scheme. The colonial government was to prepare and lend out on mortgage, in bills of credit, £50,000, repayable in five annual installments, with five per cent interest. A public meeting at Boston pronounced in favor of the public bank. All the popular arguments were on its side. The Governor and Council forbade any private company to issue bills of credit for circulation without the authority of the General Court. Nevertheless the bank proceeded to make issues. In 1716 another "public bank" was made. £100,000 "was committed to the care of the county trustees; was proportioned to each county according to its tax; secured by mortgage estates of double the value of the sum borrowed; each loan not exceeding £500 nor being under £25, for ten years, at five per cent., paid annually; the profits to help pay for expenses of government, and the bills to be returned at the end of this

13

period and burnt. Frequent litigations subsequently arose in the settlement of the mortgages for this money."

This is a specimen of the second kind of bank in the colonies, one which was adopted by all but one or two of the colonies and repeated over and over again. The sense of "bank" would be best expressed by batch, because it was applied to the mass of bills provided for and loaned out at one time, under one act of legislation. It would go beyond the limits of our subject to pursue this device as an experiment in currency. It may suffice to say that the colonists, in their issue of bills of credit, had hit upon a fact in monetary circulation which they did not understand and which is not, perhaps, fully understood yet. If they had been contented to use their bills of credit within very strict limits, to be ascertained by experiment, they might have carried on the system indefinitely, with complete success, and have conquered all their troubles from a "lack of a medium." The notion of a cheap money would, of course, have been a pure fallacy. No money can be cheap except to the issuer. If he gets it at the cost of manufacturing bits of paper, and can exchange these for commodities, in as large amounts as he could get for the coins whose names and denominations the paper bears, the currency would be cheap to him; but to those who gave the commodities for it, it would be no cheaper than the coins would have been. The paper currency in the colonies, however, might have overcome the difficulties which were due to lack of communication and transportation, and to obstructive legislation, and might have lifted the community out of barter. What actually happened was that the colonists employed this device without limitation or judgment. They pushed the bills of credit at once into their greatest abuse;

14

which is, that any paper issued at will, unlimited by the hard facts of economic supply, can be multiplied in amount indefinitely. Then, instead of facilitating intercourse, it becomes the worst barrier to intercourse. The loan offices, also, under pretense of providing the farmers with the capital which they needed, only set them to juggling with the frauds of fluctuating prices and dishonest contracts.

The colonists were not worse than their time. The mysterious and powerful functions of credit were developed in northern Europe, half by accident, in the latter half of the seventeenth century. The Land Bank scheme, Mississippi scheme, South Sea scheme, etc., were aberrations due to lack of comprehension of the nature and limits of the power which had been evoked. It was a marvelous thing to discover that a corporation, or a civil body, could emit notes and so borrow, yet win interest instead of paying interest on what it borrowed. This is what the colonies attempted to do. They were "lending" to their citizens the capital which was so much needed, and were at the same time winning an interest which paid the expenses of the State, and all at no cost but that of a little engraving and printing. The notion of credit which prevailed was that it was a way of making formulas of words do the work of capital, if only the formulas were imposing enough, or were uttered by a body having competent prestige.

As the Land Bank did not receive much encouragement, in spite of its connection with education, an alliance with internal improvements, the other great make-weight with which it was always connected for the next hundred and fifty years, was brought into its support. "Fifty thousand pounds ought to be laid out for making a bridge over the Charles river, so that workmen might be employed and currency enlarged, as well as the public accommodated; and ruin will come unless more bills of credit are emitted."

Trumbull says that nearly thirty pamphlets and tracts were printed, between 1714 and 1731, for and against a private bank or a public bank, the emission of bills of credit, and paper currency in general. One of the most notable of these is entitled: "A Word of Comfort to a Melancholy Country" and is a lamentation over the defeat of the Land Bank. Trumbull attributes it to John Wise, who, he says, has been called "the first logical and clear headed American democrat." He is chiefly concerned that a sufficient medium may be provided. The medium need not have value. It will do its work better if it has not. Coin is too costly, and blew England cannot keep it. The merchants ship it off. The bills have done great things for Massachusetts. They have built the college, etc. He preferred a private bank under government inspection to a public bank.

In the meantime, the English had been going through a mania for joint stock companies, which were a new device of credit, the limits and conditions of whose utility had yet to be learned by bitter experience. After the crisis of this speculation in England, the Bubble Act was passed which recited that many companies had, since June 24, 1718, presumed to act as corporate bodies and to make assignable shares without having legal authority so to do. After June 24, 1720, all undertakings to the prejudice of trade, and all subscriptions or cases of acting as corporations, without legal authority so to do, were to be illegal and void. Such organizations were to be deemed public nuisances, and those who made them would incur a *premunire*. Brokers were forbidden to deal in such shares. There was some doubt in law whether this statute extended to the colonies, but there was sufficient fear that it might do so to create alarm in the private bank, which had circulated notes in spite of the prohibition of the provincial authorities. The Governor was strictly enjoined by the authorities in England not to consent to any further issue of bills of credit. On this account, the treasury notes having been cut off, in 1733, "a number of merchants and others of Boston, in order to supply the deficiency of such a medium of trade, had recently engaged in a project of issuing paper to the value of £110,000. Rhode Island had also ordered a large emission of their bills, which, as usual, were expected to have their chief circulation in Massachusetts. With these facts laid before them, and concluding that by such causes their own bills would proceed from bad to worse, the General Court appointed a committee to examine them and make report." "Notified of such action, Governor Wanton replies, that the Rhode Island Assembly had enacted, in July last, to issue £100,000 loan, at five per cent. on land security. He adds, 'I do assure the General Assembly of the Province, we had an especial regard for the welfare of the public in said emission, and hope' that they 'will take care that trade may not be injured by a private emission now coming out without their sanction, as I am informed.'"

"The committee raised about the paper money in circulation make their report, which is accepted by both Houses. They state that the merchants' notes emitted by Boston gentlemen should be backed with greater security; and that his Excellency be desired to send out a proclamation, warning the people to be on their guard against taking the late bills of Rhode Island. The bills of the private bank, just mentioned, amount to £110,000, and were redeemable in ten years, with silver at 19s an ounce, then the common rate of the Province paper. Though a great and imposing effort was made to keep the Rhode Island bills out of our market, yet they soon flowed in, and became current."

"The Governor thinks it is not expedient to issue a proclamation against both of these sorts of currency, though he is decidedly opposed to them. He gives his opinion that the Merchants' Bank ought not to do business without permission from the Assembly; and that such permission should not be allowed them, because falling within the limits of his prohibitory order from the Crown, to have only £30,000 in bills circulating at the same period. Still the merchants' notes were circulated, and accounted better by 33 per cent. than Province bills."

The following year the Governor declares that "the bills of the private bank or merchants' notes, instead of preventing a further depreciation of Province bills as it was confidently said, have had a contrary effect."

Connecticut granted a charter to a society in New London, 1733, for trading. This society issued bills, "but their currency being soon at a stand, the government were obliged in justice to the possessors, to emit £50,000 on loan to enable those concerned in the society to pay off their society bills in colony bills. Their charter was vacated and a wholesome law was enacted that for any single person or society of persons to emit and pass bills for commerce, or in imitation of colony bills, penalty should be as in case of forgery, or of counterfeiting colony bills."

In 1735, a private bank was formed in New Hampshire, to which reference is made in the following: "Whereas sundry persons of New Hampshire have adopted measures the past year to issue promissory notes of a most uncertain and sinking value, as they are payable in New Hampshire, Massachusetts, Connecticut, and Rhode Island bills, or in silver, gold or hemp, at the unknown price they may be at in Portsmouth, in New Hampshire, Anno 1747, whereby his Majesty's good subjects will be great sufferers, should they part with their goods and substance for them or accept of them in payment, etc." "This was a banking speculation, which promised much advantage to its promoters, but very little to the public. The larger amount of its paper, like all such currency of that day in New England, reached Boston - the great mart for the northern colonies; but placed under the ban of the law, its market was spoiled for this Province."

The tract concerning the Colonial Currencies, which is included in the Overstone collection, was published about 1740. The author shows how the depreciated paper money hurt the wages and salaried classes, because the depreciation with respect to specie never measured the loss in purchasing power. "The shopkeepers are become, as it were, bankers between the merchants and tradesmen [mechanics], and do impose upon both egregiously. Shop notes [store-pay], that great and insufferable grievance of tradesmen, were not in use until much paper money took place." The author thinks that he can prove that the specie value of the whole currency constantly declined as greater issues were made; and he shows how little cliques of persons who were possessed of political power got the loans into their hands, in the first instance, and sold them at a premium.

19

March 19, 1740: "In continuance of the controversy between the Representatives and the Governor, he repeats his account of the Province arrearages. He says that there are £210,000 in bills now circulating, £40,000 are on loan, and the rest, £170,000, former Assemblies have promised shall be collected into the Treasury, by a tax in the several years specified, by 1742, and that this will be a heavy burden, especially as no provision is made to supply the place of paper currency. Such being the pecuniary condition and prospect of the Province, several projects are advanced by companies to supply the deficiency of money. The petitions of these associations, being laid before the Legislature, and assigned to a Committee for consideration, are reported on. One of them was John Colman and others for £150,000, to be lent in notes on land security, and payable in twenty years by various articles of merchandise. Another was Edward Hutchinson and 106 partners, for £120,000, redeemable in fifteen years, with silver at 20s an ounce, or gold *pro rata*. The latter was upon a plan similar to one before mentioned, and its bills were denominated merchants' notes. It was promoted in order to put down the other. Though the gentlemen appointed to consider them had less objection to the Specie Bank than to the Land, or as frequently called, Manufactory Bank, they give an opinion that both are inexpedient. In the Legislature, there is a diversity of opinion as to these companies. The Council express their wish that the Land Bank may be forthwith disannulled, but that the silver scheme, so called, be put over to the coming session. The Representatives, looking on the Land Bank as designed for people of moderate property as well as for the rich, manifest their desire that both suspend operations till the next

Assembly, and then be considered as to their respective claims. This was the motion agreed on, and thus the petitioners earnestly looked for a hearing."

The Land Bank of 1741 was to be for the amount of £150,000 lawful money. Estates were to be mortgaged to the company. Three per cent per annum was to be paid on loans in enumerated products of the Colony and the principal was to be repaid in twenty years (five per cent. per annum), in the same way. Mechanics, etc., might come in for not over £100 each, by giving two sureties for double the sum. [Evidently they meant to print and loan, in notes, at once to the stockholders the full amount of the stock subscribed. The mortgages carried no guarantee to the noteholders, except as they could be pursued through the company.] There were to be no dividends for five years, and after that none which should ever leave less than twice the principal paid in at the time. [They intended to trade with the products which were paid in.]

The notes were to read: "We promise for ourselves and partners to receive this 20 shilling bill of credit as so much lawful money, in all payments, trade, and business, and after the expiration of twenty years to pay the possessor the value thereof in manufactures of this Province." The projectors of this notable scheme had, probably, no intention of fraud, but their plan would have given them possession of the "manufactures of this province" to the amount of the notes issued by them, without any security or interest by them, for the term of twenty years. It was because they called it a "bank," and were "providing a medium" that their minds were obscured to the truth of the case.

At this time, the notes of the merchants, issued in 1733, were at thirty-three and one-third per cent above the Province bills, being paid in gold and silver, and the notes of the Specie Bank of 1740 were equivalent to cash, the issuers being "eminent and wealthy merchants." This seems to sound as if the notes were actually convertible and converted; but it probably should not be understood that they were so in the sense of more modern times.

Gov. Belcher took strong ground of opposition to the Land Bank which had begun operations without authorization. He published a proclamation warning the people against the notes as fraudulent, contrary to civil order, and harmful to trade. He treated the bank as rebellious, since it was unauthorized, and he tried to compel all civil and military officers to abandon it. The Specie Bank also commenced business. The government was, in fact, generally so lenient and indulgent that it was very weak when it tried to exert authority. One project led to another until there was a bank mania in a small way.

These projects led to an extension of the Bubble Act to the colonies. The act is entitled, "For restraining and preventing several unwarrantable schemes and undertakings in His Majesty's colonies and plantations in America." All clauses of the Bubble Act "did, do, and shall extend to, and are and shall be in force and carried into execution" in America.

The act went on to say that the occasion for it was the doubt whether the act of 1719 could be executed in America, because the aggrieved persons must, according to that act, bring suit in Westminster, Edinburgh, or Dublin. This act now provides that suits may be heard in any of the King's courts of record in America. Noteholders were given a right of action against each partner for the amount and interest, although by the tenor the note might not yet be due. Any person suffering harm might recover treble damages and costs; and the persons composing the company were liable to a *premunire*, according to 16 Richard II. These penalties were all to be arrested if the company should dissolve and go into liquidation before September 29, 1741. According to the fashion of the times, this enactment was met in a recalcitrant disposition. All the jargon about liberty and the charter was repeated. The irritation produced in the Colonies by the attempts of the mother country to restrain paper issues contributed more than perhaps any other one thing to produce that estrangement which resulted in the Revolution. Upon this occasion the first impulse of those interested in the Land Bank was to defy the law, and it appears that the bank produced no little demoralization of civil institutions for a year. As we shall see below, the States fought unceasingly against unchartered issuers of paper, from the Revolution to the Civil War; and the federal government, in its dealings with Territories, which are a complete analogon to Colonies, has reserved to itself the right to disallow any legislative acts of the Territories and has exercised that right, notably in respect to banks.

September 22, 1741, a committee of the General Court was appointed to meet at Milton "to examine the condition of the Land Bank. They find £49,250 of its notes are struck off and endorsed and that the Treasurer had issued them from his hands to the amount of £35,582, and that the directors employ £,4,067 of them in trade. This investigation is soon followed with heavy restrictions upon the funds of the company."

March 30, 1742: "A Committee for the settlement of the Land Bank publish a pressing call on its stockholders to settle its demands upon them. This call contains the succeeding items." "It is now nine months since the company's vote at Lynn that no more bills should be issued out of the Treasury till the next meeting, and more than six months since the vote passed at Milton to bring in and consume to ashes all the outstanding bills. By the delay of those indebted to the institution, our company is thrown into the last extremity of confusion; and without the most speedy measures are pursued in bringing in the bills, the consequence will, we fear, prove ruinous to some hundreds of the partners. The possessors of our bills are more and more uneasy every day as that part of their estates lies useless by them, and so incessant in their worries, that the directors have in their late advertisement implicitly threatened to be on the possessors' side against the delaying partners."

This bank is heard of again and again during the following twenty years. The surviving or solvent stockholders and their heirs were subject to repeated demands from the noteholders, which they seem to have evaded to the best of their ability.

There is a tradition that there was a bank in Virginia before the establishment of the Bank of North America. A special loan office was proposed there in 1765, to enable the Treasurer of the colony to make good public funds which he had loaned to his friends, but it failed. The tradition may more probably be based upon an Association referred to in an act of 1777: "Whereas divers persons have presumed upon their own private security to issue bills of credit or notes payable to the bearer in the nature of paper currency," a penalty is imposed upon those who "issue or offer in payment" any such notes without the authorization of the Commonwealth, of ten times the amount of the note, half to go the informer.

PERIOD II - 1780 to 1812.

Banks are Incorporated in the States; also a Bank of the United States on the type of the Bank of England. The Colonial Idea is continued in Banks of the States, being Institutions based either on the "Faith and Credit" of the State alone, or on a Combination of Public Funds with Private Subscriptions

CHAPTER II
From 1780 to 1812.

The earliest banks of discount, deposit, and convertible circulation.

It can cause no wonder that when the Revolution broke out, deep suspicion and prejudice were entertained against everything by the name of bank. It was only under the pressure of great fiscal necessity that the unwillingness to entertain any project under this name was overcome.

In a speech in the Pennsylvania Assembly, in, in the debate about the Bank of North America, Robert Morris said that although the proprietary government "had no idea of a bank, the commercial men of the Province had, and I, as a merchant, laid the foundation of one, and established a credit in Europe for the purpose. From the execution of this design, I was prevented only by the Revolution. Silas Dean submitted to Congress a plan for a bank with a capital of a million and a-half pounds sterling. It was suggested in the scheme of reconciliation, which the Carlisle commission brought to America, that a bank might be formed to provide for the retirement of the Continental paper currency. Alexander Hamilton was forming bank projects as early as 1779, although the plan which he then formed may never have left his own hands. April 30, 1781, he sent a paper to Robert Morris, containing a complete discussion of the financial situation, and the measures required. He wanted a national bank, the chief reason being "we have not a sufficient medium." The capital was to be £3 millions, lawful money, to be paid in landed security, specie, plate, bills of exchange, or European securities. About one-third was to be in specie. The United States and the States might subscribe not more than half of the capital. The notes under £20 were to bear no interest, the larger ones, four per cent. The bank was to buy land, from which Hamilton thought that great gains might be made because the tories would put much land on the market, and sell it cheaply. Depositors were to pay a fee for the safe keeping of their money. The bank was to lend Congress £1.2 millions at eight per cent. Taxes were to be levied, the revenue from which should be specially appropriated to pay the interest on this loan. Other revenues were also to be raised sufficient to pay the bank two per cent. on all the Continental paper outstanding, at 40 for 1; for which provision the bank was to guarantee the paper and retire it in thirty years. There were to be three auxiliary banks in Massachusetts, Pennsylvania, and Virginia. Morris replied that he was afraid to "interweave a security with the capital of this [his] bank, lest the notes should seem to be circulated on that credit, and the bank would fall if there should be a run on it."

The next step in the development of banking was independent of these projects. On the 4th of June, 1780, Thomas Paine wrote to Joseph Reed, urging that a subscription should be raised to obtain recruits and supplies for the army, which was in a very sad condition. It was expected every day that news would come of the loss of Charleston. The public were very despondent. Many members of the Pennsylvania Assembly had brought up petitions against taxation. Paine was then clerk of that body. He says that he subscribed $500, and that the next day M'Clenahan and Morris subscribed each £200 in hard money. On the 14th came the news of the loss of Charleston. On the 17th a meeting was held, at which a syndicate was formed to raise £300,000 of Pennsylvania currency, but in real money, the subscribers to execute bonds for the subscriptions and form a bank. The Board of War informed Congress of this project, and asked that a committee be appointed to confer with the subscribers. The offer of the persons who formed the so-called bank was to provide, on their own credit and by their own exertions, three million rations and three hundred hogsheads of rum, without profit to themselves; but they desired that security should be given them for their payment. The faith of the United States was pledged to them and the Board of Treasury was directed to deliver to them bills of exchange, drawn in their favor, on the Envoys in Europe, for a sum not exceeding £150,000 sterling, as a guarantee of payment within six months. Morris described this bank, some years later, as "in fact nothing more than a patriotic subscription of Continental money, ... for the purpose of purchasing provisions for a starving army." Hamilton criticised it because its purchases were made with its "stock," that is, its capital, and not with its notes; so that it was only a subscription for a single occasion, and not an institution capable of continued action.

From these statements we may infer what the plan of this bank was. Continental or State paper was brought into it as a subscription, for which the subscriber obtained the interest-bearing notes of the bank, payable in six months. The supplies were bought with the currency which the subscriber had brought in. The bills drawn on the Envoys were held as collateral security until Congress should pay for the supplies. Those bills might be negotiated, but it was the understanding that they should not be; for it was well understood that they were not drawn for value, legitimately at the disposal of the drawer, but would impose an obligation on the Envoy on whom they were drawn to borrow or beg funds to meet them, so that they would be honored or not according as he succeeded.

This institution was called the Bank of Pennsylvania, and began operations July 17, 1780, in Front street, two doors above Walnut. The last installment of the subscription was called in November 15th. The last payment in discharge of the debt of the Confederation to it was made in 1784. Some attempt seems to have been made to repeat its operations, for, November 29th, the Pennsylvania Assembly appointed a committee to confer with the directors on the practicability of an immediate supply of corn and forage for the army, on three or six months' credit, to be paid for in current money of the State, equal in value to gold and silver. In May, 1781, Reed, who was of the anti-bank party, wrote to Washington that the notes of the bank would no longer circulate; that they soon lost credit, but that the bank ruined the paper money of the State.

In May, 1781, before he had assumed the office of Financier, Robert Morris submitted to Congress a plan of a bank, which had been prepared by Gouverneur Morris. "Anticipation of taxes and funds," he wrote, "is all that ought to be expected from any system of paper credit." By this he meant that paper could only be used to anticipate the return from taxes by which the paper would be canceled. He proposed that Congress should apply to the States for power to incorporate the bank, and he hoped that the States would make its notes receivable for taxes.

May 26, 1781, Congress approved of the plan of the Bank of North America as follows: There were to be one hundred shares of $400 each, with liberty to increase the capital. The state of the cash account and circulation was to be made known to the Superintendent of Finance every evening except Sunday. The States were to make the notes, if payable on demand, receivable for duties and taxes. The Superintendent of Finance was to have access to all books and papers. The States were to make laws to punish embezzlement in the bank as felony. No director was to be paid for his services. On the question of incorporating the bank, Massachusetts voted no; Pennsylvania was divided; Madison voted no. Congress asked the States not to charter any other bank during the war, and to pass the other votes called for by the plan.

Great efforts were necessary to recommend this plan to the public. Morris was enthusiastically zealous in favor of it. "I mean to render this a principal pillar of American credit, so as to obtain the money of individuals for the benefit of the Union, and thereby bind those individuals more strongly to the general cause by the ties of private interest." In this passage he uttered one of the favorite notions of the group of public men to which he belonged; that it was wise and necessary, by various devices and institutions, to enlist the interest of capitalists in the political system which had been founded. "When once by punctual payment the notes of the bank obtain full credit, the sum in specie which will be deposited will be such that the bank will have the interest of a stock two or three times larger than that which it really possesses." A reason for establishing the bank is "that the small sums advanced by the holders of bank stock may be multiplied in the usual manner by means of their credit, so as to increase the resource which government can draw from it, and at the same time, by placing the collective mass of private credit between the lenders and borrowers, supply at once the want of ability in the one and of credit in the other." In these passages he uttered the doctrines of bank inflation, which led Gouge to call him the "father of paper money banking in the United States."

In making some historical statements about this bank, in the debates of 1786, he said that, up to September 1st, the subscriptions had not exceeded $70,000. In that month, the French man-of-war "Magicienne" arrived at Boston with $462,862 in silver, which John Laurens had obtained from the French government. This was carted overland to Philadelphia and put in the bank, but half of it was drawn out and spent before the bank commenced operations.

In June, 1781, he reported to Congress that the chief hindrance to the organization of the new bank was that the amount due to the Bank of Pennsylvania had not been paid. He thought that if it could be paid, the persons entitled to it could be persuaded to subscribe it into a new bank. Congress was not willing to sell the bills lodged as security because of the annoyance that would be occasioned to the Envoys who were the drawees. Morris asked that the bills be put at his disposal, and proposed to arrange the transfer, and use the bills, so that they would not be presented for a long time, or not at all. In this he succeeded.

A meeting was held, November 1st, to organize the new bank. It consisted of the members of the Bank of Pennsylvania and nine others. The act of incorporation was passed by Congress, December 31st, and the bank commenced business January 7, 1782, on the north side of Chestnut street, a short distance west of Third. There was a clause in the charter that "This ordinance shall be construed and taken most favorably and beneficially for said corporation." This clause was copied into State charters and became a standing feature of them in some States. Robert Morris was one of the largest stockholders, but was never a director or other officer of the bank. Thomas Willing was president. The day that the bank went into operation, Morris noted in his diary that he had paid into it $200,000 for the subscription of the United States. Gouge doubts whether there ever was any subscription to this bank except that of the government, believing that even the $70,000 above mentioned consisted of bonds transferred from the Bank of Pennsylvania. He claims to have undoubted private authority for the statement that people who were interested in the Bank of North America sent farmers and laboring men to the bank to get silver for notes. "When they went on this errand of neighborly kindness, as they thought it, they found a display of silver on the counter and men employed in raising boxes containing silver, or supposed to contain silver, from the cellar into the banking room, or lowering them from the banking room into the cellar. By contrivances like these, the bank obtained the reputation of possessing immense wealth; but its hollowness was several times nearly made apparent, especially on one occasion when one of the co-partners withdrew a deposit of some $5,000 or $6,000 when the whole specie stock of the bank did not probably exceed $20,000." It is possible that this story arose from a confusion between the Bank of North America and "an appendage of the finance office;" for Robert Morris had a bureau in his office, in which borrowed silver was laid out, in order to establish a fictitious credit for the Treasury.

In his report of his management of the Treasury Department, submitted in 1785, Morris said of the government subscription: "It was principally upon this fund that the operations of that institution were commenced, and the accounts which end on the last day of March [1782] will show that the public obtained, before that day, a loan of $300,000, being the total amount of their then capital. This loan was shortly after increased to $400,000, but the direct loans of the bank were not the only aid which it afforded. Considerable facilities were obtained by discounting the notes of individuals, and thereby anticipating the receipt of public money; and in addition to all this, it must be acknowledged that the credit and confidence which were received by means of this institution formed the basis of that system, through which the anticipations made within the bounds of the United States, had, upon the 1st day of July, 1783, exceeded $820,000. There was due also, upon that day, to the bank directly, near $130,000. If, therefore, the sum due indirectly for notes for individuals discounted and the like be taken into consideration, the total will exceed $1 million. It may then be not only asserted but demonstrated that without the establishment of the national bank, the business of the department of finance could not have been performed." He borrowed of the bank during his administration $1,247,975. He repaid this in cash, except $253,394, which was paid by surrendering the stock owned by the United States. The United States paid for interest on loans $29,719, and obtained in dividends $22,867. The date, July a 25, 1783, is given as that upon which private individuals had taken up all the shares originally subscribed by the government. It is safe to say that this, the first "specie paying, convertible bank note bank" in this country, never could have started but for the silver borrowed by the government from France and placed in its vaults.

There was much doubt about the power of Congress to pass an act of incorporation. The Virginia delegates reported to the Governor of that State that they had consented to the act on account of the utility of the bank, but that the States ought to ratify the act of Congress. The bank determined to seek a charter from Pennsylvania. Objections were made in the Assembly that the charter was perpetual; that the bank had power to hold real estate; and that the president of it had encouraged negotiations with General Howe during the war. Nevertheless the act was passed April 1, 1782. An act had been passed a fortnight earlier, in that State, making it felony to counterfeit the notes of the bank.

In 1782 a proposition was made to Robert Morris to found a bank in New Hampshire. He declined and nothing came of it.

In 1784 and 1785, the Bank of North America earned 14 per cent. In the former year it enlarged its capital by issuing 1,000 more shares at $500 each. This led to the foundation of a rival institution which was on the point of being chartered, when the new subscription was extended to 4,000 shares at $400 a share, and those who had already paid in $500 received $100 back with interest. At the same time the affairs of the bank became disordered on account of over-extension of its business in the attempt to defeat the new bank. For the safety of the community "it became absolutely necessary to drop the idea of a new bank, and to join hand in hand to relieve the old bank from the shock it had received. Gold and silver had been extracted in such amounts that discounting was stopped, and for this fortnight past not any business has been done at the bank in this way. The distress it has occasioned to those dependent on circulation and engaged in large speculations is severe; and as if their crop of misery must overflow, by the last arrival from Europe, intelligence is received that no less a sum than £60,000 sterling of Mr. Morris's bills, drawn for the Dutch loan, are under protest. It is well known that the bank, by some means or other, must provide for this sum. The child must not desert its parent in distress; and such is their connection that whatever is fatal to the one must be so to the other. ... I have had several interviews with our friend, Gouverneur Morris. He is for making the Bank of New York a branch of the Bank of North America; but we differ widely in our ideas of the benefit that would result from the connection." Disquieting rumors about the bank had been current in Holland in the previous January, where it had been reported that the bank had stopped payment on account of a great number of counterfeits in circulation.

The bank had been born of necessity, real or supposed. At the time that it was chartered many public men had felt themselves in a dilemma between the political danger and the financial exigency. As soon as the war had ended and the financial exigency seemed less obvious, their minds turned with greater submission to the fear of political danger. The mass of the people, so far as they thought of the matter at all, feared the bank as an engine of the money power, and anticipated great social and political dangers from it. This view of the matter was put forward with great energy by the class of public men who sought to be popular leaders, and also by those who were working in the interests of rival enterprises.

Petitions were presented to the Legislature, March, 1785, for the repeal of the act incorporating the bank, on account of the financial, social, and political dangers connected with it. A committee was raised "to inquire whether the bank established at Philadelphia was compatible with the public safety and that equality which ought ever to prevail between the individuals of a republic." The committee reported that the bank, as then managed, was in every way inconsistent with the public safety, and recommended that its charter be repealed. The bill for the repeal went over the session, but was taken up on the first day of the Autumn session of the same Assembly. Counsel of the bank were allowed to argue before the House, but, on the 13th of September, 1785, the charter was repealed.

The bank now fell back on its federal charter, but there were so many doubts of its validity that the attempt was made to get another State charter. February 2, 1786, Delaware gave one, which was accepted, and it was determined, if necessary, to move to some city in Delaware.

A bank war was now opened in Pennsylvania, which contained in miniature all the elements of the war that raged around banks for the next fifty years.

March 3, 1786; a memorial from 624 citizens of Philadelphia in favor of the bank was presented, in order to bring the matter up again. In the debate there were two lines of thought and argument; one in respect to the social effect of a bank on classes, and the other in respect to the political effects of a bank on democratic and republican institutions. Morris took a very prominent part in these debates and caused them to be published. We learn from his statement that, in this bank, loans upon its own stock were regarded as its most regular kind of business, and the stockholders were thought to be warranted in borrowing to the extent of their stock. The proposed re-charter of the bank was defeated in April.

At the opening of the November session it was evident that a great deal of work had been done and that a great change had been brought about. A committee reported that some amendments in the charter would make it free from objection. The bank was re-chartered March 17, 1787, for fourteen years. Its capital was limited to two million dollars.

It is stated that the Bank of North America issued penny notes about 1790.

The first and one of the most important services rendered by banks in the United States was inculcating punctuality. At the end of the Revolutionary war, Philadelphia was the only place in the country where commercial punctuality was general. Banks introduced it elsewhere. The great fault of the banks, however, was that they did not impose punctuality on themselves or each other.

The first bank chartered, after the peace, was the Bank of Massachusetts, February 7, 1784. The charter was originally perpetual, but was limited, in 1812, with the consent of the bank. Amongst the rules of this bank were: the full names of all delinquents to be posted in the bank, in order to avoid useless applications for credit; absolutely no renewals.

A scheme was published in the New York "Packet," February 12, 1784, for a Bank of the State of New York. Subscribers to the stock were to pay one-third in cash and the other two-thirds in mortgages on land in New York and New Jersey, appraised at not more than two-thirds of its value. If necessary, the directors were to borrow one-third of the value of the land. A fortnight later a meeting was called to found a bank, but on specie only. Alexander Hamilton attributed the land bank scheme to Chancellor Livingston, who, he said, had carried on a zealous propaganda in its favor. In order to defeat it, Hamilton started another scheme, and he also endeavored (as it appears, successfully,) to show the fallacies in the notion of a land bank. A constitution for the bank was drawn up, undoubtedly by Hamilton. One of the rules was that the bank should not deal in foreign exchange. There was so much eagerness to start the bank, that it began in June without a charter. The rule was adopted: "No discount will be made for longer than thirty days, nor will any note or bill be discounted to pay a former one. Payment must be made in bank notes or specie."

Loud complaints were raised against this bank as soon as it went into operation. It was charged with working in the interest of British capitalists and traders, but it is plain that the chief ground of complaint against it was the punctuality which it enforced. It will be seen, in the course of this history, that the real occasion of the unpopularity of banks, in their early history, was that they were having this effect, which produced irritation and resistance. This opposition prevented the bank from obtaining a charter. It also stimulated a paper money party which wanted a State issue, and obtained it in . The directors of the Bank of New York thereupon decided to keep two sets of accounts, and in fact they organized two banks—a "specie bank" and a "paper bank "—the latter doing business on the State paper; the former using the denomination dollars and the latter pounds. A charter was at length obtained in 1791. One clause of it was that the bank should not emit any notes or contract debts payable in the State paper.

In point of time the charter of the Bank of Maryland was earlier than that of the Bank of New York, being dated 1790. The Bank of Providence, Rhode Island, was founded in 1791; the Bank of Albany, the Bank of South Carolina, unchartered, and the Union Bank of Boston in 1792. In the last year also the Hartford Bank was founded, the State reserving the right to take forty shares within twelve months. The historian of this bank thinks that its assets, at its outset, "consisted mainly of the promissory notes of stockholders endorsed by each other, with a moderate sum of silver, a light sprinkling of gold drawn from old hoards, and possibly a few notes of the Bank of North America." One of the rules of this bank was: "What passes in the bank not to be spoke on at any other place." This expresses the mystery with which banking at this time was surrounded. Every bank was a secret society.

The Bank of Alexandria, Virginia, was founded November 23, 1792, with a capital of $150,000, increased in 1795, to $350,000. The lowest denomination of notes was five dollars. Its debts were never to exceed four times its capital. Its charter was to last ten years. It was given power for the summary collection of debts, which were not liable to the stay laws existing in the State at the time. It appears that this bank was not founded without occasioning alarm. Pope, of Kentucky, in the debate of 1811, said that the Virginians were known to be poor financiers, for they "were, a few years since, frightened at the very name of a bank. ... It required all the eloquence of [Brent of Virginia] to persuade the Legislature that the little Bank of Alexandria would not sweep away their liberties." A month later the Bank of Richmond was founded, with $400,000 capital, to last until 1804, with similar provisions. A statement is met with that from 1787 to 1804 there were no banks in Virginia, except the branch of the United States Bank at Norfolk, founded in 1799, and that the circulation was metallic.

It should be noticed that when banks began to be founded, the notion of a national bank for each State was the conception on which they were constructed. The Bank of Massachusetts was expected and intended by its founders to be the only bank in Massachusetts, and the Bank of New York was founded on that plan; whether it should be called a hope or an intention is difficult to decide. In the Southern or Southwestern States, this notion of a Bank of the State became the source of a great number of institutions which will deserve our particular attention. Such a Bank of the State might exist, like the Bank of England, or the Bank of France, although there might be any number of other banks by the side of it in the same State. One consequence, which causes very great perplexity in the case of the great Banks of the States, is that the nomenclature becomes confused. We find a Bank of South Carolina, a State Bank in South Carolina, and a Bank of the State of South Carolina; in other cases the same name was given successively to two or three institutions which succeeded one another in time, and were all called the Bank of the State of ——.

Inasmuch as the term State Banks is used for local banks, it seems desirable to speak always of Banks of the States when that particular group is intended, for they deserve a separate name.

Leaving out of account those Banks of the States in which the participation of the State was limited to the possession of some stock in the bank, and which may be better thrown out of this group altogether, we may distinguish three grades of Banks of the States. 1.—Those which had no capital at all, being "based upon the faith and credit of the State." These were paper money machines. 2.—Those in which funds belonging to the State were deposited as a capital. It was argued that the State might better "bank on" its own funds, for schools, improvements, income from lands, etc., than invest them in loans to private banks or otherwise. 3.—Those which combined with the latter arrangement, capital subscribed by private individuals.

CHAPTER III

The First Bank of the United States and its Times

The act of 1789, laying duties on imports, provided that they should be received in gold and silver only. In April of the following year, Hamilton made a report on the operation of this law, in which he construed it to mean that he might receive the notes of banks "issued on a specie fund;" and he thought that this would be advantageous to the government, the banks, and the public. Hence he had ordered bank notes to be received where banks existed, but the measure was understood to be temporary, and would be changed whenever a national bank was founded.

One of his pet ideas was a national bank. He submitted a paper to Congress, December13, 1790, to prepare the way for the proposition he wished to offer. This paper shows that he had very much developed his ideas on this subject since the earlier plans made by him, which we have already noticed. The charter of the Bank of New York, which came from his hand, became the model on which numberless charters were afterwards constructed, and the charter of the Bank of the United States, which he now proceeded to make, was taken as a model by so many others that we must attribute to his opinions on banking a predominant influence in forming the banking institutions of this country. The first great advantage which he sees in a bank is that it augments "the active or productive capital of a country."

In the explanation of this, which he gives, he entirely avoids the fallacy which would seem to be involved in the statement. He illustrates it by the case of a man who deposits a surplus while waiting to put it to use, so that it "is in a condition to administer to the wants of others, without being put out of his own reach when occasion presents." He has in view, therefore, not any creation of capital, but a more effective organization of capital, by which small and scattered amounts are so concentrated as to be made effective instead of being idle. Upon this view it would follow that when one man wanted his capital some other man would probably be desirous of making a deposit; from which it would result that some constant amount within limits could be depended upon. Unfortunately, however, Hamilton mixed up this sound and useful view of a bank with the popular misconception: "It is a well established fact that banks in good credit can circulate a far greater sum than the actual quantum of their capital in gold and silver." This is the fundamental notion of all juggling with bank issues. He here planted a germ which, as we shall see, grew to a great size and produced most evil fruit. It taught the banker to believe that his legitimate business was to carry on a kind of high class confidence operation. Next Hamilton speaks about the cases in which the operations of banking legitimately consist in setting off things against each other, which balance; but he introduces the cases as if they explained the possible inflation of bank issues, and as if they explained the transactions with actual deposits mentioned in the first place. Having mixed and confused these three things, he concludes: "This additional employment given to money, and the faculty of a bank to lend and circulate a greater sum than the amount of its stock in coin, are, to all the purposes of trade and industry, an absolute increase of capital." The confusion here introduced was important and unfortunate, especially as regards the confusion between deposits of surplus capital and the supposed increase of capital by the circulation. The gains of a bank must come either from its deposits or its circulation. Until the middle of the nineteenth century the deposits of surplus capital, even in the larger cities, were small, for the reason that capital was always in such active employment that surpluses waiting for employment were not formed. Any encouragement, therefore, which was given to the-notion already so widely current that paper issues could increase capital was directly mischievous. Hamilton went on to connect this also with 'the opinion which he said prevailed that there was a lack of a sufficient supply of money. He thought that the use of barter in remoter districts was a proof of this, and he showed that he participated in the belief that a bank could increase the amount of circulating medium in a country,—that is, not only increase the amount of capital available for employment in industry, but also increase the amount of currency acting. on prices and available to pay debts. As the confusion of these two things has been the most profound and most mischievous error in the entire currency history of the country, the fact that he shared in it and lent it his authority was most unfortunate for the subsequent history. "It is evident," he says, "that whatever enhances the quantity of circulating money adds to the ease with which every industrious member of the community may acquire that portion of it of which he stands in need, and enables him the better to pay his taxes as well as to supply other wants." This has ever been a popular notion, and his enunciation of it was

44

no doubt one of the most effective recommendations of his plan.

Answering objections made against banks, he shows that they bring about punctuality, and he answered very correctly the complaint that, if foreigners owned the stock, there would be a drain of specie to pay their dividends; but it does not appear that these arguments had any effect on public opinion. He also laid down the doctrine, which may be called the kernel of the "credit system," which was made the subject of so much debate and eloquence in the next fifty years,— namely: that banks help honest, industrious, and enterprising men by furnishing them the capital, which is the only thing they need to become very efficient producers, and that they help the same class of men's when they have met with misfortune, to recover. As to the abundance or lack of the precious metals, that seems to him to depend on the balance of trade; and he is quite sure that each state ought to have a supply of "the money of the world," and of the metals which are a "species of the most effective wealth." "Notwithstanding some hypotheses to the contrary, there are many things to induce a suspicion that the precious metals will not abound in any country which has not mines or variety of manufactures."

He condemns State issues. "Though paper emissions under a general authority [*i.e.*, federal] might have some advantages not applicable, and be free from some disadvantages which are applicable, to the like emissions by the States separately, yet they are of a nature so liable to abuse, and, it may even be affirmed, so certain of being abused, that the wisdom of the government will be shown in never trusting itself with the use of so seducing and

45

dangerous an expedient." He next points out the exact difficulty and danger of such issues, although at the same time his argument exposes the fallacy of the doctrine which he had just stated, that banks could increase the amount of circulating medium. "Among other material differences between the paper currency issued by the mere authority of government and one issued by a bank payable in coin is this: that in the first case there is no standard to which an appeal can be made as to the quantity which will only satisfy, or which will surcharge the circulation; in the last, that standard results from the demand. If more should be issued than is necessary, it will return upon the bank."

That is so, how can a bank "enhance the quantity of circulating money?" If his reasoning is correct, (and it is that which is accepted by all the best authorities), it is far more certain that there can be no deficiency below the "standard" set by the "demand;" for it would be satisfied by obtaining specie. In short, the reasoning, in order to be thrown into correct and productive order, must begin with and proceed from the notion of the requirement as the predominant and coordinating conception.

We are not without a verdict of history upon these notions of Hamilton about bank currency. The keynote of his doctrine, and the keynote of the banking system of the next fifty years is in the following passage: "Gold and silver, when they are employed merely as the instruments of exchange and alienation, have been, not improperly, denominated dead stock; but when deposited in banks to become the basis of a paper circulation, which takes their character and place as the signs or representatives of value, they then acquire life, or in other words, an active and productive quality. "The Bank

Commissioners of Ohio, in 1842, in the bitter retrospect of the previous five years, quoted these words in order to say: "The experience of more than half a century since this opinion was expressed has failed to convince the American people that gold and silver are to be regarded as dead stock, except when placed in banks as a basis for the issue of their paper. This idea that gold and silver acquire life, activity and productiveness, only when placed in banks as a basis for paper issues, rests upon the assumption that bank notes, to an indeterminate extent, may be thrown into circulation, and that a proportionate increase will be given to the commercial, manufacturing, and agricultural interests of the country." Out of the same period of sack-cloth and ashes, when delusions had been dispelled and things appeared in their naked truth, the Governor of Ohio said: "The great error which prevails on this subject [banks of issue] has its origin in the common, vague impression that we are dependent on the bank paper system for the supply of a sufficient quantity of the circulating medium, and that, without bank paper, commerce would not flourish, business would stagnate, and the country cease to advance in prosperity and improvement. This fallacy is the chief cause of that superstitious attachment to the paper system which with some has become idolatry:" "Vain indeed would be the attempt to hedge in the circulating medium of a country and pump it up to fullness by the ministry of banking institutions."

Hamilton also laid great stress on the function of banks to make loans to the government in case of financial exigency, and also to help tax payers to pay taxes. Loans to government lock up the capital of a bank and make it cease to be, as a bank. Although a bank might loan capital for the payment of duties (the case, in fact, which Hamilton puts in illustration), it certainly would not lend a man means to pay his personal taxes, which are an irrecoverable expenditure. These two points belong under the head of the political functions and benefits of a national bank. They were very prominent amongst Hamilton's motives for wanting one. Furthermore, without dilating upon it, he put into a very concise and pointed statement his view of the political philosophy of a national bank. It "is not a mere matter of private property, but a political machine of the greatest importance to the State." The history of the first Bank of the United States, and still more that of the second one, is a most instructive experiment to test the validity of this conception of such an institution under the political and social circumstances of the United States.

Finally he makes an argument against two of the pet ideas which we have already seen so active in connection with financial devices from the first settlement of the country—namely, the notion of paper issues on land security, and the notion of banking by the State, as a means of profit by which public expenditures may be provided for without taxation. His arguments on these points apparently had no effect, for we shall find that these two notions held sway for fifty years more, and were more destructive to the happiness and prosperity of one section after another than pestilence or famine.

This paper, therefore, consists of a jumble of ill-digested observations, in which correct and incorrect views are entangled with each other. In reading it, as in the case of Hamilton's other economic papers, the reader is constantly forced to think: If this writer had read Adam Smith, he would

48

have been led to just that refinement of analysis and elucidation of his ideas, which would have led them out of crude inaccuracy into exactitude and correctness. That Hamilton had perused Adam Smith's book is unquestionable. This only makes it the more remarkable that a man of his well-proved mental power, should give such evidence that Smith's book had not affected his thinking, to any ascertainable degree.

In the debate upon the charter of the first Bank of the United States, in the House of Representatives, three elements may be distinguished, the constitutionality, the social antagonism, and the sectional antagonism. The first turned upon the question whether the government of the United States, which had been created by the Constitution, was endowed with the power to pass acts of incorporation. Madison was the leader of the negative, and, both by his authority and his arguments, furnished that side with its chief strength. He affirmed that the Constitutional Convention had refused to insert amongst the powers of Congress, that to incorporate, because it had been said that this would give the power to make a bank. Inasmuch as the question of power to incorporate a bank had arisen in respect to the Bank of North America under the Confederation, the non-conferment of this power in the new Constitution was undoubtedly a pregnant omission. The advocates of the bank had no little difficulty to find a clause under which it could be implied. Hamilton, when called on by Washington to submit an argument on the objections which had been raised against the bank, put its constitutionality on the ground that the Constitution had created a sovereign state, endowed with all necessary powers for the functions which it was called upon to perform. The opponents gave to "sovereignty" its most absolute and abstruse meaning. One of their chief reasons for detesting the bank was that they thought that it would help to support the conception of the federal Union as a confederated state with sovereign powers. Thus the bank was placed from the outset in the midst of the battle of State right. They also construed the power to incorporate as an especially majestic and prerogative function of a sovereign. Hamilton met the former issue quite squarely. He construed acts of incorporation as no more awe-inspiring than other acts of legislation, and presented the bank as a pure question of legislative expediency.

The social antagonism reached little other expression than a growl of suspicion and dread that this institution was to be an engine of the money power; that it was contrary to equality; that it would benefit only the rich. This antagonism was but an incident in the great warfare inside of modern society; numbers against capital; democracy against plutocracy; the struggle to acquire against the vested interest; the caprice of the moment against the established institution. This struggle in all its phases will be seen raging around both the first and the second Bank of the United States.

The sectional antagonism included also the antagonism of city against country. The North had the free capital, because the planters could always employ more capital than they could get, on their lands. The North also had commerce and a diversified industry. The South was agricultural; it had fewer and smaller cities; its views and prejudices were strongly marked by these peculiarities. It was a special complaint of the southerners that only federal stocks were subscribable into the stock of the bank. These stocks had passed into the possession of the North, the southerners having sold them in order to use the capital on the land. Their State stocks could not be subscribed.

The first objection, that about the constitutionality of the Bank, occupied by far the most attention in the debate. It suited the temper of the time. It deserves our especial notice because it never was silenced until, in Tyler's time, it extinguished a great national bank as an American institution.

The charter passed the House, February 25, 1791, thirty-nine to twenty. There were three votes from the north of the Potomac against it, and three from the south of the Potomac for it.

There is a tradition that Washington wrote a veto of the Bank act, but that Hamilton persuaded him to sign it. No evidence can be found to support this tradition.

The Bank was chartered for twenty years; to be located at Philadelphia; to issue no notes under $10; to have twenty-five directors; only stockholders residents of the United States might vote by proxy; seven directors were to constitute a quorum; no foreigner was to be a director; the directors were to elect the president, who was to be compensated while the directors were not to be compensated; one quarter of the directors were to be elected each year; one share was to have one vote, three shares two votes, five shares three votes, and so on until one hundred shares had twenty votes. The Bank was to report to the Secretary of the Treasury at his demand not oftener than weekly, and that officer might inspect the books except private accounts. The notes of the Bank were to be receivable for dues to the Treasury of the United States. The Bank was to hold no land or buildings except for its own use or by foreclosure. It was not to buy or sell goods except forfeited collateral. It might sell but not buy public stocks. The rate of interest was limited to six per cent. The Bank was not to loan the United States over $100,000 without an act of Congress, nor any State more than $50,000, nor any foreign potentate anything. Congress was to charter no other bank. The capital was to be $10,000,000 in shares of $400 each, $8,000,000 of which was to be subscribed by individuals, and $2,000,000 by the United States. The private subscriptions were payable in four installments, the first at the time of subscription, the second six months later, the third one year later, and the fourth after eighteen months. One quarter of each installment was to be paid in gold or silver, and three-quarters in public stocks; the six per cents at par and the three per cents at fifty. No private subscription was to exceed a thousand shares. The Bank might go into operation when $400,000 had been paid in gold and silver.

A provision was inserted against Hamilton's plan and judgment, providing for branches. Sooner or later such were organized at Boston, New York, Baltimore, Washington, Norfolk, Charleston, Savannah, and New Orleans. For the fiscal operations of the government, the branches were very useful, and we have no information that any evils were produced by them in the first Bank; but later experience with branches in the United States has been almost uniformly bad.

Hamilton's Bank, created by this charter, fell in with the notion of a bank which then and long afterwards prevailed in this country. "What is that," said Daniel Webster, "without which any institution is not a bank and with which it is a bank? It is a power to issue promissory notes with a view to their circulation as money. Our ideas of banking have been derived principally from the act constituting the first Bank of the United States, the organization and powers of which were imitated from the Bank of England." "Banking in America," said Gallatin, "always implies the right and practice of issuing paper money as a substitute for a specie currency." The free banking law of New York, in 1838, first defined a bank without any reference to the function of note issue.

Let it be permitted to introduce at this point what it seems necessary to say in regard to the nature and functions of a bank.

The inconvenience of barter consists in the lack of coincidence between the persons who desire to exchange, with respect to the commodities, amounts, and qualities. Money overcomes this, but it is stiff and angular in its operation. Every step must be taken and no cross cuts are possible. What we call credit, in connection with currency, introduces harmony and rythm. By combination of steps, an accelerated movement, and abbreviated operations, many processes which are necessary in the use of money may be omitted in the use of credit. They are understood, or taken for granted, or are simply recorded until they are cancelled by some subsequent operation. These are the facts which led to the invention of banking, and to the devices by which it is carried on. Various paper instruments have been devised for convenience in these processes. It is a most mischievous mistake to include them in the definition of money. That introduces confusion at the first step and leads to fallacies at every step of deduction. The paper instruments abbreviate the processes and avoid the need of money.

A bank intervenes between lenders and borrowers and itself performs both operations. It gathers up capital from the lenders and distributes it to borrowers. Then it collects it again from the borrowers and returns it to the lenders. The pulsations of this movement are the life phenomena of a bank. When the pulsations are high, sharp, and well accentuated, the vitality of the bank is high and its efficiency in rendering all the capital in existence as efficient as possible is very great. When the pulsations drag, are broken, and unpronounced, the efficiency of the bank is low. It tends to rest and idleness. The latter case is what is commonly called a lock-up of capital. It is a negation of the sense and activity of the institution. It is only banks whose movement is at the highest pitch of energy which can maintain a bank note circulation under the free control of the banker, and then the circulation will be involved in the business risks attending the discount and deposit operations.

The stockholders are also lenders of their own capital which is amalgamated with what they borrow to lend again. Banks hold an auxiliary or ancillary position in the economic organization. They hold a certain amount of capital free, which, since it is free, is in the form of money, which they bring to bear, now at one point, now at another, in the operations of the industrial system, as it is wanted, especially to bridge over intervals of time. They thus prevent any arrest in the operations; keep up the certainty of the movements of the market, and sustain the rythmical movement by virtue of which it is possible to calculate on the future. They prevent loss and waste, and maintain the efficiency of all parts of the system. They produce nothing at all directly. They are operative, not creative.

It follows that of course it is a question of organization how great the amount and proportion of bank capital should be. It is a part of the total capital which is set off to this auxiliary function. The total organization is more efficient by virtue of it, but it can easily enough be out of proportion either way. The question how great it ought to be in a given case can never be answered except by experiment.

In the supplementary charter of the Bank of England that institution is given the sole right to "borrow, owe or take up any sum or sums of money on their notes or bills payable at demand," etc. There was no delusion there about the difference between bank notes and money, nor about the fact that what a bank does, when it issues notes, is that it borrows and takes up money and therefore owes it. Anyone who issues notes takes a corresponding amount of specie out of the circulation, which is there or would be there, but for this interference. It is proper to approach the matter by conceiving of the community as provided with specie enough to do its business with, according to the ratio of its business to that of the commercial world taken on the total amount of money metal in existence. The note issuers take this away and put their notes in its place; or, they obtain the possession of an equivalent capital which is imported when the displaced metal is sold abroad for real capital. This is the capital which they lend, and the one which produces the interest which they obtain on their notes. As there are four or five steps, and they are all out of sight, at least so far as their connection with the operation of the bank is concerned, there is room for a great number of partial and fallacious interpretations. It comes to be believed that bank notes have a substantive existence, that they, on which interest is obtained, are not like the notes of individuals, on which interest is paid; in short, that they are money, perhaps even capital.

The view of notes as supplanting specie to an exactly equal amount is what is called the "currency principle." According to it the note issuers have a monopoly privilege and strive with each other for shares in a quantum of gain which cannot be surpassed.

A very large class of credit operations, however, consists in what we might call suspended exchanges. Half the exchange operation is performed but the other half is delayed under a promise or contract of later delivery. A bank steps between. It fulfills the contract at once and does the waiting. If no defalcation occurs, all the givings and takings will be equal, plus a commission for waiting. If, therefore, a bank could intervene in all the cases of suspended exchange which occur in the market, it could keep an account of debit and credit with all the parties. At the end of a certain time all the entries would balance, except for the commission which would fall to the bank as reward for its services, and all the transactions would be closed. If, therefore, the bank could get all the transactions into its hands, and promise to pay everybody, it would need to pay nobody. The whole would be resolved into a book-keeping transaction. If, moreover, all those who had money would carry it to the banker for safe keeping, it is with this money that he would pay in the few cases in which for any reason the use of money was actually called for.

In these last observations lie the magic and mystery of banking. If only the requisite prestige ("credit;" "confidence") can be won to set the institution in operation, it is self-acting, and all that the happy manager has to do is to take toll from its operations. The legitimate way to win the prestige is by offering guarantees of capital and character. Another way is to impose by inflated words and pompous parade upon the credulity of the bystanders. This history will show the difference between the two.

We can go one step further. It would be a great additional advantage if the transactions were not only recorded on the books of the bank, but if also evidence of them was transcribed on portable records, which could be shown and transferred by the parties in the market as their interests in further transactions might render desirable. The bank therefore "issues" paper evidences of the existing contracts which may take any convenient form. Bank notes are one form. Their great convenience is that they are entirely impersonal, and betray nothing of the mode or occasion of the contract by which their possessor obtained them from the bank, while they enable him to divide his credit as he sees fit and to buy what he wants without further guarantee. Since all the transactions will cancel within a brief period, all the paper evidences will return to the bank within that period. It will then be found that the bank has only "furnished a medium" for all the transactions. We have here a striking illustration of the way in which phrases, in this domain, alter their meaning before the man who uses them is aware of it. To "furnish a medium," on the currency principle, means to provide the community with a currency, in the belief that, but for this provision, it would have none, while in fact the bank takes away specie to give paper. On the banking principle, the bank does, in a legitimate sense, furnish a medium of credit in operations in which money is dispensed with, and a kind of barter of a higher grade is reintroduced, money being used as a standard of reference for the terms of the barter. All the persons in the market may find themselves in a snarl of debts which would hinder them all from moving, but there would be a thread of mutual or consecutive obligations which, if it could be found and drawn out, would absolve them all. The bank operations effect this.

This latter set of facts is the one on which the "banking principle" is based. Both principles are true, but no one has yet succeeded in defining their spheres or their relation to each other. The only line which can be drawn between them is a vague and empirical one; that the small notes are under the currency principle, and the large notes under the banking principle. The latter are used in the greater transactions of business; the former in expenditures for consumption. Hence the earnest attempt of the banks, which we shall see in this history, to get the right of emitting small notes, and also the constantly repeated effort of currency reformers to forbid the same. The small notes, under the currency principle, were a permanent loan obtained by the banks from the public, but they also compelled simple and uneducated people to hold a stake in the prosperity of the bank with which they had nothing to do, and on which stake they might lose but never could gain.

It will be seen that the bank projectors of the th and tl centuries mentioned above, Chapter 1, had won a vague and imperfect perception of the facts underlying the banking principle. They were trying to enunciate its doctrines and devise an institution to operate upon them.

The arguments in favor of bank note currency in this country have always been made from the standpoint of the "banking principle." That currency was always on the currency principle: The banking principle fails entirely when loans are made on accommodation paper, or on land, or on long contracts of any kind. Hence in the history of American banking, the banking principle appears to have been a delusion.

In the paper in which he first laid before Congress the arguments for a Bank and the outline of his plan, Hamilton made a special explanation and defence of two features in it. The first was the provision that shares in the public debt might be subscribed into the capital. The purpose of this was "to enable the creation of a capital sufficiently large to be the basis of an extensive circulation, and an adequate security for it." He wanted to make a large issue; he thought it impossible to collect a large amount of specie; he had rejected the notion of an issue based on land security; therefore, taking his model from the Bank of England, he based the issue on debt. The best writers on banking, in the third decade of the nineteenth century, had generally reached the conviction that the capital of a bank ought to be invested in some permanent security, and that the operations should be carried on with the notes. Evidently, if a bank should be formed by an association of capitalists who should buy bonds with the capital and carry on the business with the notes; or if they should be already owners of government bonds, which they subscribed as capital, printing notes for use in banking; or if they should lend their capital to the government as a book debt and obtain the franchise of note issue with which to do banking, as the Bank of England did in the first place; or if they should organize, as our national banks now do, it would all amount to the same thing. When the first Bank of the United States was organized, the government did not need to borrow and did not obtain any loan by the subscription of the public stock into the capital. That arrangement never had any proper cause or excuse, and only served to give occasion for some clamor against the Bank, as a piece of jobbery and favoritism to the bondholder.

The other point which Hamilton felt it necessary to apologize for was that the government was to take shares in the Bank. The government possessed no capital and the Treasury had no surplus. What right had it to take shares in the Bank? Hamilton said: "The main design of this is to enlarge the specie fund of the Bank, and to enable it to give a more early extension to its operations." This is unintelligible. The government put bills of exchange on Holland into the Bank in payment for the stock; then it borrowed the bills of exchange out again, and gave its note at five per cent. for the amount. This was called a "simultaneous transaction;" a phrase of ill-omen for an ill-devised operation. The government had simply given a stock note and set the example, which impecunious and bankrupt individuals adopted and repeated during the next fifty years, in hundreds of cases, with the most disastrous consequences. It was bound to pay $200,000 annually on this note, which, as Hamilton said, would "operate as an actual investment of so much specie." He added another reason for this arrangement, which was the real one: that the government would thus share in the profits of the institution. He had, however, well argued against State banking for profit, in the same document. This arrangement was unnecessary and mischievous. It was right that the government should participate in the profits of the Bank either by a bonus or by taxes, but this device put the government in the wrong on the most fundamental and farreaching difference which can exist in regard to the conception and organization of a bank. If the stockholders of

60

a bank are debtors to it and not creditors of it, it is a swindle. They take something out where they have put nothing in. They are not lending a surplus of their own; they are using an engine by which they can get possession of other people's capital. They print notes which have no security and make the public use them as money. They bear no risk of their own operations, but throw all the risk on others while taking all the gain. The government had no more right to subscribe stock when it possessed nothing, and put nothing in, than an individual would have to do the same thing.

The stock of this Bank and four thousand shares more were subscribed in two hours. It went into operation December 12, 1791. A very active speculation in the scrip sprang up as soon as the first installment was paid, and it was run up to a premium. This contributed largely to the financial crisis in the winter of 1791-2, "with distress for money unequaled in this country." A story is told that the son of the president of the Massachusetts Bank, and two others, borrowed the funds of the bank to such an extent that it stopped discounting for six or eight weeks, while they went to New York and speculated in government paper. They sold out to Duer. The next day the stocks fell 20 or 30 per cent., and he was ruined. He had high credit and had taken on deposit the savings of small people. He was put in jail, where he remained five years. Threats were made of lynching him.

The belief at the time, and subsequently, was that no more than the specie part of the first installment ever was paid into the Bank in specie.

In managing the relation of banks to each other, Hamilton set some precedents which deserve careful attention on account of the momentous consequences which afterwards followed from them. He naturally had a tender feeling for the Bank of New York, and one reason why he opposed branches for the national bank was that he foresaw a collision of interests. As soon as the charter was passed he wrote to reassure the Bank of New York, saying that he had explicitly directed the Treasurer not to draw upon it without special directions from himself. He declared his intention in lhe public interest to protect that bank against speculators.

In November, 1791, he assured the cashier that, although it would be his duty to put the public deposits in the branch, he would precipitate nothing, but would conduct the transfer so as not to embarrass or disturb that institution. In the commercial crisis of 1791-2 he ordered the Bank of New York to buy government bonds, in order to sustain their value and relieve the money market. In fact he followed the course of the panic with such interference as he judged would be useful. In May, 1792, he encouraged the Bank of New York to make loans to manufacturing companies on easy terms, giving the assurance that the bank should suffer no diminution of its pecuniary facilities by so doing. In March of that year, the Bank of the United States and the Bank of New York had agreed upon a policy of co-operation, but, in 1796, the president of the Bank of the United States having directed the New York branch to demand payment of an amount due from the Bank of New York, the latter was forced to contract, producing alarm. Thereupon Hamilton wrote to his successor, Wolcott, asking him to interfere to produce a mitigation of this order. He thinks that this will be good policy, the weakness of the New York Bank being due to its loans to the government. Wolcott replied: "I will thank you to inform the president of the New York Bank or any other confidential person that they may rest assured of as full and cordial assistance in any pressure of their affairs as shall be in my power. I think, however, that they must principally rely on sales of stock, and in my opinion any sacrifice ought to be preferred to a continuance of temporary expedients." In the same letter he also said: "These institutions have all been mismanaged. I look upon them with terror. They are at present the curse, and I fear they will prove the ruin of the government. Immense operations depend on a trifling capital, fluctuating between the coffers of the different banks." The significant facts in these proceedings are: the interference of the Secretary of the Treasury in the collision of interests between different banks, and the function of mediator or arbitrator which he assumes. His interference in the money market, although noticeable, was not nearly so important.

Wolcott wrote to Hamilton in 1795: "Banks are multiplying like mushrooms. The prices of all our exports are impaired by improper negotiations and unfounded projects, so that no foreign market will indemnify the shippers." And again: "It would astonish you to know how far the capital of this country has been placed in the power of France by speculations to that country and the excessive use of credit during the last season. If we have a good crop and the ardor of speculation can be checked so as to allow a loss which I know to be inevitable to fall gradually upon us, the merchants will struggle through; but if we proceed in our present course until a sudden revulsion takes place, the consequences may be serious." These fears were speedily realized in the financial crisis of 1796, which was connected, no doubt, with the financial crisis in Europe which produced suspension of specie payments by the Bank of England.

Early in 1796, before these troubles came on, John Adams wrote to his wife, in view of his approaching accession to the presidency, that the paper money of the country was the worst evil he saw. In 1799 he declared:

"Public credit [*i.e.*, general mercantile credit, not the credit of the government], can never be steady and really solid without a fixed medium of commerce. That we have not such a medium, you know, has been my opinion for several years. The fluctuations of our circulating medium have committed greater depredations upon the property of honest men than all the French piracies. To what greater lengths this evil may be carried I know not. The Massachusetts Legislature are authorizing a number of new banks. The cry is the immense advantage to agriculture. Credit cannot be solid when a man is liable to be paid a debt, contracted to any, by one-half the value a year hence." The rise of a bank mania in Massachusetts, to which he here alludes, produced consequences which we shall soon have to notice.

In 1797, a federal tax was laid on all notes of banks, not exceeding $50, of six mills on a dollar, and lower rates on higher denominations. These taxes might be commuted at one per cent. on dividends. In 1798, an act of Congress made it felony to counterfeit notes of the Bank. In 1807, passing counterfeit notes was included. This latter was made necessary by a decision that the former law was inconsistent with itself, and void, so that it would not support an indictment for knowingly uttering as true a forged paper.

Under Gallatin's administration of the Treasury we find one case of "arbitration" between banks, and we find proofs of Jefferson's ideas of the proper relations between those institutions and the federal government. In 1802, the Bank of

Pennsylvania applied to Gallatin for help. It fell one hundred thousand dollars per week in debt to the Bank of the United States. Upon this Gallatin comments: "They have extended their discounts too far." On an application of the Bank of Baltimore for a share of the federal deposits, Jefferson commented favorably, because he said that the stock of the Bank of the United States was almost all owned by foreigners.[19] Jefferson wrote to Gallatin, July 12, 1803: "As to the patronage of the republican bank at Providence, I am decidedly in favor of making all the banks republican by sharing deposits amongst them in proportion to the dispositions they show. If the law now forbids it, we should not permit another session of Congress to pass without amending it."May 3, 1804, Gallatin reported to Jefferson that there was a great drain of dollars out of the country.

"There are not at present one hundred thousand dollars in Philadelphia, New York and Boston put together. More than three millions of dollars have been exported in six months from the vaults of the Bank of the United States alone."

The banks which were in existence at the end of the century were paying from eight to fifteen per cent. dividends. This stimulated a movement for the creation of more of them.

The first bank mania, with inflation and collapse, after the introduction of convertible note banking, took place in New England, and the rest of the country came to look on that section as sunk in the follies and vagaries of paper money.

MASSACHUSETTS.— In 1799 a law was passed making it unlawful to join any association to do banking of any kind unless authorized by law. The penalty was $1,000; the notes were void. All such associations then existing were to dissolve by March, 1800. The period was one of great

65

prosperity in New England, but in 1800 we hear that, "the tide of wealth which had flowed so long has considerably ebbed, and the effect of this change has become visible in everything. Property has fallen in price. Real estates especially are not worth so much by 20 per cent. as three months ago."

Although nearly every charter for a bank in Massachusetts required the bank to report annually or semi-annually, "few seem to have paid any attention to these provisions." A general act of 1803 led to systematic reports. A law of 1799 in that State had made it illegal to emit notes for less than $5, but in 1805 they were allowed for $1, $2, and $3. This measure was in obedience to a popular demand and was to be temporary only. Besides the branch of the United States Bank, there were then twenty-one associations for banking in Massachusetts, which were privileged to issue $13 millions.

In the first years of the century there was a great multiplication of country banks in Massachusetts, Maine, and New Hampshire. Their notes all flowed into Boston and displaced the circulation of the Boston banks. A double currency was thus introduced, one called foreign money or current money, and the other Boston money, differing by about one per cent. which was construed as a premium on Boston money. The brokers dealt in these currencies, reserving a quarter of one per cent. commission. The country issue then became excessive and the brokers sent it home. Hence it came about that a bank was profitable in proportion to its distance from Boston and the difficulty of access to it. The favorite locations became remote parts of Maine and New Hampshire. In order to equalize and extend the circulation of foreign bank notes the Boston Exchange Office was incorporated in 1804, its capital consisting of such notes and its business being done with them. It was not very successful. The brokers sent home the bills of the nearer banks and the discount on the currency continued to increase as the bills of the more distant banks predominated. Andrew Dexter, having studied the operations of the Exchange Bank, undertook the control and monopoly of the circulating medium of New England. He bought up at a great premium nearly the whole stock of the Exchange Office and of several distant banks in Maine, Berkshire, and Rhode Island. With these funds he bought real estate and built the "enormous pile, since destroyed by fire, known by the name of the Boston Exchange Coffee House." This immobilized his capital. The discount on country bank notes increased and the country banks invented ingenious ways of defeating and delaying payment.

In the autumn of 1808 the Boston merchants raised a fund for the purpose of sending home the country notes for redemption. The discount was from two to five per cent. This caused a crisis, and in 1809, "the greater part of the country banks in Massachusetts, Maine, and New Hampshire, having any considerable amount of bills in circulation, stopped payment. Some of them recovered, but a great number proved irredeemably insolvent. It would probably be a moderate estimate to put the losses by the bank failures of that period at $1 million. In the following year, a law of Massachusetts imposed a penalty of two per cent. per month on any bank which refused or delayed payment of its notes. A Boston firm writing to Matthew Carey, says: "We have heard that a bank mania is raging in your State. If this is true we wish your legislators could see some of the fatal effects resulting from a too free incorporation of banks in this quarter of the Union, and learn wisdom from our misfortune."

The most famous case which occurred was that of the Farmer's Exchange Bank of Gloucester, Rhode Island. It was incorporated in February, 1804, with a capital of $100,000, payable in gold and silver, in seven installments stretching over three years. The directors paid the first installment in specie, but in a few days borrowed of the bank the same amount without security, and gave their notes without endorsers for the first five installments; on the two last they made no payment whatever. The shares were gradually bought in with the property of the bank. Each director was allowed to take $200 in notes in order to exchange the same for specie, and the bills of other banks, as these could be found in the circulation.

This became one of the favorite devices. A grocer who was interested in a bank, or who was induced by a commission, took a quantity of its notes to exchange. He paid them out at every opportunity in "change" and retained the notes of other banks which he brought back to the bank. This provided that bank with "specie funds" without further trouble or expense. Hence arose also a fraud in the term "specie paying" banks. Two, neither of which had any specie, but each of which held a quantity of the other's notes, became thereby "specie paying;" because each returned its stock of notes of the other as "specie funds," or "cash items." Gouge, Raguet, and other writers of Jackson's time refer to the period before the second war as one in which there had been some sound, honorable, and high principled banking. Investigation does not verify this. Sometimes there was a certain *naïveté* and simplicity about the way of behaving, but these earlier bankers invented nearly all the later abuses, and they set about the exploitation or them with less reserve than their successors. Perhaps they and their contemporaries had not yet learned how mischievous the abuses might become. If so, that is the most which yet can be said for them; for they did not show any greater scrupulosity than their successors. The fact is that what New England did in the first decade of the century is what the Middle States did in the second, and the Southwest in the fourth, and the Ohio States in the sixth.

In 1808 Andrew Dexter bought up all the outstanding shares of the Farmers' Exchange Bank, giving for them his own notes or notes which were the property of the bank. He then put in a new set of directors. During January, 1809, he was writing constant letters from Boston to urge the cashier to sign notes as rapidly as possible and send them to him in great quantities, with complete secrecy. He also gave orders that notes should be redeemed only by drafts on Boston, or with vexatious delays. When at last the attention of the Legislature was drawn to the matter, Dexter tried to persuade the cashier to pay no heed to its summons. The Committee of Investigation found in the bank $86.48 in specie. The books were in such confusion that the actual outstanding circulation could not be definitely ascertained, but it was thought to be $580,000. "It is impossible for us to picture the ruin and distress that followed, the effects of which are still remaining. It is said, and we presume correctly, that in one county of this State there were $100,000 of the bills of the Farmers' Exchange Bank in circulation at the time it failed, and probably in the State there were $400,000 or $500,000, all of which, after being bartered at various discounts, became a total loss to the last holders, which, in most instances, were the poorer and less informed parts of the community. There is no doubt that thousands of farmers will be ruined, and leave their families in poverty, in consequence of the facility with which they obtained money at the banks by mortgaging their estates."

It was in the name of the Boston Exchange Office that Dexter first approached the Farmers' Exchange Bank. He had seen how the notes of one bank could be played off against those of another, especially if they were at a distance from each other. The second bank with which he was operating was the Berkshire Bank at Pittsfield. If a bank issued its own notes in very great quantities, they would become very abundant in the country around it. This would excite attention, and they would be brought in for redemption; but if the Berkshire Bank issued notes of a Rhode Island bank, and *vice versa*, and if they were widely scattered, these dangers could be averted. The Boston Exchange Office in fact accomplished this on a large scale for its constituents. It is also noticeable that amongst the notes which Dexter sent to the Farmers' Exchange Bank, in order to strengthen it, were notes of the Marietta Bank, Ohio. He thought them quite available, because there was such a demand for remittance to Ohio. We learn from other facts that the circulation of bank notes from one end of the Union to the other was, at that time, wide and easy, far beyond what one would have believed possible.

In 1814 the New England Bank adopted the plan of receiving the bills of all the banks in New England at a discount varying according to distance, but in no case exceeding one per cent., and on condition of a sufficient permanent deposit being maintained, they were returned to the banks at the price at which they were bought. The bills of banks which did not keep a deposit were sent home for payment. The other banks competed with the New England Bank for these deposits, and thus diminished the discount.

In the story of the early Massachusetts banks we see the first development of the antagonism between commercial banking and agricultural banking. In the larger towns of that State city industries were beginning. They could support banks of discount and deposit with short paper. Persons who were fitting out ships or tilling land could not use ninety day paper. Loans to farmers always had the character of accommodation paper with renewals, although a mortgage would give ultimate security. The Bank Commissioners of Connecticut, in 1841, expressed the opinion that "the practice of some banks to confine their discounts exclusively to business paper or paper that is subject to no renewal, is a great innovation, and denies to a worthy class of borrowers those facilities and advantages to which they are entitled in common with those of more various and extended business." True bank note circulation could not be maintained by the country banks, but if they could get a distant circulation they could live on an abuse of issue-banking. The jealousy of the rural population in respect to banks led them to insist on inserting in bank charters a provision that a certain fraction of the capital should be loaned on mortgage of land. We shall presently see the antagonism, which here arose between parts of the same State, marking the relations of parts of the Union.

We observe that a bank was conceived of primarily as a means of creating wealth. Everyone wanted a share in its beneficent operation. If the Legislature created it, all the people ought to participate in its blessings. To do justice to this notion we must not forget that the banks then existing had been organized very generally on stock notes, and if they succeeded, were mines of wealth to their owners. A generation later, as we shall see below, people came to say that banks were a curse to all agricultural interests and persons. We shall see that, in the history of banks in this country it has been a question of paramount importance: What is the utility of banks to farmers and how is it to be realized? From the standpoint of commercial banking with ninety day paper, a loan to a farmer for a year with a stipulated renewal was bad banking, but, on the other hand, such a loan could never answer the purpose of a farmer. Repayment within a year is, for him, vexatious and impracticable. He needs loans for years or for an unlimited period. Never until modern institutions of credit suited to the necessities of the case grew up did this antagonism of facts, interests, and institutions pass away.

The incident of the Farmers' Exchange Bank led the Legislature of Rhode Island to pass a law, fining any officer of a bank $50 for every check, note, or bill signed by him, for a less sum than $50, payable at any place out of the State. A fine of $5 was also imposed on any one who should pass a note for less than $5 issued by a bank out of the State.

The banks of Rhode Island had a peculiar "bank remedy" or "bank process" against delinquent debtors, according to which execution issued directly without previous process and finding of judgment. The bank process was abolished in 1836, on the recommendation of a committee of the Legislature, who found that it was liable to abuse, and that the remedies provided for other people were also sufficient for the banks.

72

In VERMONT, in 1803, two bank acts were vetoed, on the ground that banks demoralize the people by gambling, concentrate wealth in the hands of the few, and are useless to the many since they give credit only to the rich. Here now we meet with the first great State paper money machine. It was first proposed in o 5, and rejected; but November 10, 1806, it was adopted. It was to be called the Vermont State Bank; to have two branches; to be the property of the State; to be controlled by the State, and all the profits to go to the State. The directors were to be chosen by the Legislature, six for each branch. Each branch had a great degree of independent life and action. The directors of each branch were to borrow specie from time to time for that branch and on its credit, not issuing more notes than the actual specie on hand until that amounted to $25,000. After that they might put in circulation three times the amount of specie, provided that the last should never exceed $300,000. Five hundred dollars were appropriated to procure plates and paper, and the Legislature might appropriate money in the Treasury to fill the coffers of the bank. The directors were authorized to purchase, hold and transfer real or personal property, as it might be necessary to protect the interests of the State in the proposed operations. The next year the directors reported that, on September 30, 1807, there was due the bank, $139,757. The notes were of the denomination of fifty cents, seventy-five cents, one dollar, a dollar and a quarter, a dollar and a half, a dollar and seventy-five cents, two dollars, and three dollars. These had been printed and issued on mortgage loans. The institution was reported prosperous and successful, and in order that the State might win the expected profits it made a monopoly of its bank, just like the other banks, by enacting that no notes

73

issued by any bank out of the State should be brought into the State to be loaned there.

The next year the trouble begins. It is charged that noteholders cannot get notes redeemed without paying a discount of one per cent. or two per cent. or taking a draft on a distant bank, payable after thirty or sixty days. The defense was that this rule was made only for defense against speculators or persons unfriendly to the bank, and it seems to have been held good. These, however, were the familiar tricks of banks formed by selfish private capitalists. The notes in circulation were now over half a million; the State was creditor of the bank for about $80,000, and the latter had cash assets, $187,000. In 1809, the banking crisis having taken place in the adjacent States, the Governor declared that although he had not favored the State Bank originally, he thought that the people, but for it, would now have been in possession of the worthless paper of the broken banks. The House replied that they valued the institution as a source of revenue; considered "the final redemption of the bills already guaranteed by the honor and wealth of the State," and that they were ready to do anything to remove real or imaginary obstacles to the prosperity of the institution. The accounts of the bank now showed a net gain to the State of $22,412. A committee of the House thought that all the loans were good, each note having two or more endorsers; but they are obliged to add: "Although causes unforeseen to the president and directors have produced a temporary suspension of punctual payment at the bank, yet it does not appear that this state of things will long continue." It is also very significant that two or three laws were passed at the same session to enforce the collection of debts due the bank. A summary process of execution, like the Rhode Island "bank process," was provided. The next year it is enacted that the directors shall give a list of all who are in arrears to the bank, annually to the Legislature; and a similar list of delinquents is to be published in the newspapers. In 1811 the legislative committee hoped that if the bills were called in, as they had been during the last year, very few of them would, in another year, remain in circulation. They recommended the appointment of a committee with power to make a full examination of the bank during the recess. No notes were to be put in circulation until the specie equalled half the debts; and the loans were to be called in as rapidly as possible. A year later the report showed the bank in possession of lands taken on execution to the amount of $11,062; the loans outstanding were $95,418, of which half were in suit. The Bank held notes of broken banks, $3,052; the notes in circulation were $78,431; a balance unaccounted for was $13,680.

In 1812, laws were passed to wind up the institution. The State Treasurer was to give to noteholders treasury notes payable, half in one year, and half in two years, with interest at six per cent. In 1822, the State Bank owned lands taken on execution to the value of $21,685. The State redeemed all the outstanding obligations by receiving them for taxes, and in 1825, distributed the avails of the property which it had received from the bank amongst the towns for schools. The affairs of the bank were settled up in 1845. The loss by it never could be exactly ascertained. A tax of one cent per acre was levied in 1812 in order to retire the notes. It brought in $100,000 of them. There were in the State Treasury $130,000 received otherwise. The assets of the bank produced about

$30,000, leaving the loss about $200,000. One Durkee of Boston, who demanded specie of this bank, was arrested, in 1808, and an indictment drawn against him; but the bill was not found.

CONNECTICUT.—The bonds of the United States owned by the State having been paid, in 1803, the Legislature voted to put the amount in banks which would receive it as stock-deposit; that is; it was to be deposited, but to get the rate of dividend instead of the rate of interest, be withdrawable, but not transferable as stock.

The shareholders of the Hartford Bank voted, in 1806, that they would receive subscriptions from religious societies or school corporations on similar terms to those here provided for the State. The following year the Legislature authorized an increase of the capital stock of this bank to one million dollars, with the provision that "the bank should be open at all times to subscriptions of shares from the funds of schools, ecclesiastical societies, or other incorporations for charitable purposes in the State, without any advance thereon, and with the right, on the part of the privileged associations, to withdraw their moneys on giving six months' notice. Whenever the holdings of any favored society reached $50,000, the full capital of one million dollars having been otherwise filled, it was entitled at the annual meetings to the choice of a director. These shares were not transferable." In 1809 the bank petitioned the Legislature to relieve it from the necessity of receiving these subscriptions. In 1816 it had $212,800 of such non-transferable shares. This arrangement became customary in Connecticut, and was introduced into nearly all the bank charters which were granted before the civil war. The Connecticut charters, also, as a rule, did not run for a prescribed length of time, but they contained a clause allowing the Legislature to amend or repeal them.

NEW YORK.—In 1799 the Manhattan Water Company was chartered in New York City with a capital of two million dollars, and with power to use any part of the capital not required for water-works in any way "not inconsistent with the laws and Constitution of the United States or of the State of New York." Aaron Burr is mentioned as the inventor and chief promoter of this charter. When the bill came before the Council of Revision, the Chief Justice objected that, under the clause quoted, the corporation might engage in trade. No one seems to have noticed that the corporation might engage in banking, which was the real intention. In excuse of this subterfuge it was alleged that no Charter for a republican bank could then have been obtained. The charter was perpetual, but in 1808 the company was allowed to sell or lease its water-works to the city, and to use all its capital for banking. The charter was to expire thirty years from the date of such sale or lease. The State might subscribe for one thousand shares of the stock, and the Recorder of the City of New York was made a director *ex officio*. The right of this company to do a banking business was tried and affirmed by the Supreme Court of the State.

The next measure of this kind was the charter of the New York State Bank at Albany, which was petitioned for on the express ground that the bank already existing at Albany was federalist. This republican bank petitioned for an exclusive grant of the salt springs for sixty years. This request was not granted, but Hammond gives a description of the lobbying devices by which the charter was carried. "The company, before their petition was presented, had agreed on a dividend of stock between themselves, and reserved the surplus to be distributed among the members of the Legislature. It appears from the affidavit of Luther Rich, a member from the county of Otsego, and several other affidavits, that assurances were given that those members who voted for the bill should have stock, with a further assurance that the stock would be above par." A modified statement in regard to this, intended to excuse it, is to the effect "that the applicants founded their claim to a charter upon the ground that it should be a republican bank, and with a view, as was pretended, to insure it that character, they agreed that each republican member should be entitled to subscribe for a given number of shares, and that this privilege was secured to every republican member, whether he voted for or against the bill."

In 1804, two unincorporated partnerships doing a banking business, one in New York City and the other in Albany, tried to get charters, but the Legislature passed instead a restraining law forbidding all unincorporated companies from banking, and compelling these companies to go into liquidation. As Hammond says, this law established a monopoly of the issue of notes in the existing banks. In the following year the Merchants' Bank, one of the above-mentioned companies, renewed their application for a charter. They were opposed by the persons interested in the banks already chartered, some of whom, as DeWitt Clinton, John Taylor, and Judge Spencer, were among the most powerful politicians in the State. One of the strongest grounds of opposition which they openly alleged was that "the granting of the application would be injurious to the republican party." The petitioners were denounced as federalists and tories.

They thereupon had recourse to lobbying and bribery. The whole affair constituted a great political scandal.

The charter of the Bank of America, in 1812, was an occasion of bribery and corruption. John Martin, a preacher and sub-agent of the bank, was convicted of attempting to bribe members of the Legislature, and was sentenced to confinement in the State prison. There was a Legislative investigation and a great political scandal. In April, 3, certain bank charters were extended until June, 1832. Among them was that of the Bank of New York. Certain colleges were allowed to subscribe a specified amount of stock in these banks, at the original price. The trustees of Hamilton College sold to the Bank of New York their right of subscription at $126 per share.

PENNSYLVANA.—The Bank of Pennsylvania was incorporated March 30, 1793, for twenty years. Its charter was renewed in 1810 for twenty years longer. At one time it had four branches, but they were not all maintained. In 1796, the State obtained from this bank, as dividends on the shares owned by it, about $100,000 per annum, which paid nearly all the State expenses.

In 1796, a defalcation was discovered in this bank, amounting to $111,000, and overdrafts for $100,000 more. This was a republican bank, some of the leading republican politicians of Pennsylvania being in control of it. As all banks in this period had a political character, their doings and fortunes were discussed in the partisan newspapers just as the personal qualifications of candidates were discussed. In the financial distress of 1796, Madison thought that the banks were powerful to persuade people to sign petitions in favor of

Jay's treaty, on account of the general dependence on bank accommodation.

The Philadelphia Bank was chartered March 5, 1804, having previously been in operation as a partnership. Its first period was ten years; renewed in 1806 for ten more; in 1809 it was authorized to institute branches, of which it established four, but not all were maintained. At this time the farmers had come to believe that the prosperity of cities was largely due to banks. In 1810, the Farmers' Bank was established in the county of Lancaster, and others in other parts of the State. March 19, 1810, unincorporated associations were forbidden to issue notes; but they continued to do so, and circulating notes were emitted by bridge and turnpike companies. The Farmers' Bank of Lancaster made such large issues that it paid dividends of more than 12 per cent. per annum. This greatly stimulated the desire for banks.

In 1810, the State of Pennsylvania owned $1 million in the Bank of Pennsylvania, $523,300 in the Bank of Philadelphia, and $75,000 in the Farmers' Bank, which had just been chartered. It also had shares in the Mechanics' Bank. In 1810 it subscribed $396,920 to the Bank of Pennsylvania, whose capital was then raised to $2.5 millions. Perhaps the most influential publication on financial matters during this period was Blodgett's Economica, 1805. It favored an increase in banks, the use of public securities as money, land security for bank notes, etc.

The Farmers' Bank of DELAWARE was chartered February 3, 1807, with a capital of $500,000, of which the State took one-fifth. It was to be the State bank, but was free from fantastic features.

VIRGINIA.—The Bank of Virginia was incorporated January 30, 1804, to last until 1818. It was to have $1.5 millions capital, of which the State subscribed $300,000, borrowing that amount from the bank at four per cent. The lowest denomination of notes was $5. In the following year it was made unlawful to pass a note of an unchartered bank. The next bank chartered by that State was the Farmers' Bank of Virginia, incorporated February 13, 1812, with a capital of $2 millions. Of the shares 3,334 were reserved for the State, if it should choose to take them. It was to last until 1827 and have four branches. It might not own more than two and two-third times its capital, nor owe more than three times its capital besides deposits, unless authorized by the State. By a subsequent law it was allowed for two years to make loans to the United States, in view of the impending war. It was forbidden to buy any stock but its own.

The banking history of NORTH CAROLINA begins with the Mutual Fire Insurance Company, incorporated in 1803, which appears to have issued notes, although this is not certain. In the following year the Newbern Marine Insurance Company was incorporated, of which the same may be said. The president and directors were authorized to "direct the issuing of policies, notes, and all and every instrument in writing that may be necessary and proper in the transaction of the affairs of the company." In the same act a bank was established at Newbern, with a capital of $200,000, to last until 1820; $50,000 to be raised at once; the debts, exclusive of deposits, never to exceed three times the capital. In the earlier part of the century this ratio was the usual one in the southern States. The State reserved the right to subscribe $25,000. If it did so, the note issue might be increased in proportion. In the same year the Bank of Cape Fear was established at Wilmington, as was said, on account of increasing population and commerce, to last until 1820; capital, $250,000. The State might subscribe, within three years, $25,000. This bank might become a branch of the Bank of the State, if one should be founded.

A legislative Committee of Investigation, in 1828-9, reported: "It is in evidence to the undersigned that soon after they [these two banks] went into operation, they contrived to get possession of nearly all the paper money which had been issued on the faith of the State, which, being at the time a legal tender, enabled them to evade demands for specie, which they did by thrusting this ragged paper at those who presented their notes for specie." In 1814, the two banks were authorized to increase their capital to $800,000 each; which increase, this same committee said, was taken in the stock notes of favored individuals.

The State Bank of North Carolina was first incorporated in 1805. It was repealed in the following year, and is therefore important only as showing the trend of ideas at the time. The most peculiar provision was that the bank might open an account with any farmer, mechanic or manufacturer, for any sum between $100 and $1,000, on which he might draw or deposit not less than $50 at a time, paying interest on debit balances and receiving interest on credit balances. He must give security of land or other property satisfactory to the bank, and not over one-fifth of the capital of any bank or branch might be in these accounts at one time.

In 1807 the Treasurer was authorized to subscribe for the shares which had been reserved for the State in the Cape Fear and Newbern Banks, paying in three annual installments, with four per cent. interest. After paying the last installment, he might borrow the same amount from each bank "until the dividends received be sufficient to pay off the sum borrowed." A law of 1809 seems to show dissatisfaction with the Banks of Newbern and Cape Fear. As they were forbidden to issue notes under $1, it must be inferred that they had done so. The Governor was ordered to appoint State directors, according to the power reserved in the charters, in virtue of the State subscription. Annual reports were to be made of the outstanding circulation. If notes were issued beyond the lawful limit, the charters were to be forfeited. The banks were not to issue notes on account of their deposits beyond the minimum amount of them in the previous year. In the same year £5 penalty was imposed for passing any note under 10 shillings, because, as the preamble states, "the circulation of promisory notes or due-bills, by individuals, for small sums, has become so general in some parts of the State as to be very inconvenient and injurious to travellers and others."

At the following session, it is ordered that the banks be proceeded against for the tax laid on them in 1809, as delinquent sheriffs are proceeded against, and the State directors are ordered to examine the cash in the vaults of the banks as often as they think proper, and to report to the Legislature annually, whether the published statements are correct.

In 1810 it was enacted that a bank should be established "in the State." It was to have $1.6 millions capital, of which the State might subscribe $250,000; three-fourths of the subscriptions were to be in gold and silver, and one-fourth in the paper currency emitted by the State in 1783 and 1785,

83

which was not afterwards to be a tender either to or from the bank. All judgments for and against the bank were to be in gold and silver. The State dividends were to go to redeem the paper currency. The State was to pay its subscriptions in United States stocks or in specie. There were to be six branches; it was to last until 1830, and no other bank was to be chartered during that time. It seemed to be hoped that it would absorb the two existing banks, for their stockholders were allowed a priority in subscribing to the stock of the Bank of the State. They did not avail themselves of it. The State Bank was to issue no notes under $1.

The subscriptions to this bank disappointed expectations, and the paper currency could not be retired. Accordingly at the next session greater inducements were offered; four per cent. might be reserved from the dividends due to the State, and the charter, with monopoly, was extended to 1835, if the bank would redeem the State paper by 1817, giving either its own notes or specie, at the option of the holder, and at the rate of $1 for 10 shillings. When this was accomplished the Governor was to make proclamation that the State paper was no longer a tender, and it was to cease to be such except to the bank; but if the funds did not prove sufficient to redeem it all before the bank expired, it was to be once more a good tender. Dividends accruing to the State were to be appropriated to pay the notes of the State held by the bank. In the loose and inconsistent wording of the clauses about this State paper money, we can see the play of opposing factions in the Legislature, which interjected amendments to preserve the State paper currency, or guard it against what was considered invidious action. This bank was not to be liable to taxation.

The attempt to retire the State paper proved vain, and similar stipulations were repeated three years later.

SOUTH CAROLINA.—By a law of December 21, 1799, it was peremptorily forbidden, under a fine of $10,000, to issue and re-issue bank notes founded on the paper currency of the State.

The Bank of South Carolina and the State Bank were chartered December 19, 1801, both being already in existence as partnership associations. They were chartered until 1823, the capital being undefined, the former being charged to pay, as a preliminary, into the State Treasury $15,000. The State might subscribe $300,000 to the State Bank in six per cent. bonds, which were not to be sold by the bank unless in the last necessity, upon the consent of the Comptroller; and the bank was not to have the interest on these bonds. Three directors were to be appointed by the Legislature. The State Bank refused to accept this charter, and a new one was enacted December 18, 1802, the capital to be $800,000, of which the State might subscribe $300,000 in certificates of indebtedness, at six per cent., saleable, and the interest paid quarterly; the bank to be free of taxes; to have the public deposits; to issue no note under $5 (which is enacted as to all banks), and to discount the Comptroller's warrants at seven per cent. for not more than $140,000, in order to retire the State paper money.

The State Bank at Charleston and the Manhattan at New York wanted to make an arrangement to redeem each other's post notes, but the Legislature of South Carolina forbade the former bank to give credit to any bank outside of the State. The terms were so wide that the prohibition prevented the State Bank from becoming a federal deposit bank.

85

The Union Bank of South Carolina was chartered December 20, 1810, but seems to have been previously in existence. Langdon Cheves was an incorporator. The capital is not fixed. Limit of property, $3 millions; duration, twenty-one years; bonus, $20,000; notes receivable by the State. On the same day the Planters' and Mechanics' Bank was chartered, with branches, until 1832; capital $1 million; limit of property, $3 millions; not to be taxed; to give the State 800 shares, at $25 each, which was the par amount. By an amendment, the following year, this bank and the Union Bank were allowed to deal in exchange. E.S. Thomas tells us in his "Reminiscences," that he was piqued because the State Bank threw out his notes, in 1810, and so he got up the Planters' and Mechanics' Bank. He subscribed as attorney for a great number of shares and sold them for double; that is, no doubt, on the first installment paid.

The first bank founded in GEORGIA was the Planters' Bank, December 5, 1807, with a capital of $1 million, increasable to $3 millions, but to begin when $300,000 were paid in in gold and silver. The president and directors were to have no favors over others in respect to loans. December 19, 1810, this charter was repealed. Apparently no action ever was taken under it, because the required amount of capital was never subscribed. A new charter was now enacted, the capital being $1 million, and shares being reserved for the State until January 1, 1812. It was to last until 1840. At the following session, however, another law shows that subscriptions had not been obtained; for the old subscribers were all released, and it was provided that it might begin when $30,000 were paid in in specie. December 6, 1810, the Bank of Augusta, which already existed as a free association, was chartered until 1830. The capital was $300,000, increasable to $600,000; the State might take $50,000 of this at any time before January 1, 1812, and if the capital was increased the State reserved the right to take one-sixth of the increase. A year later the Governor was directed to subscribe the amount reserved.

We may now gather together such meagre information as can be obtained about the history of the first Bank of the United States.

In 1804, it was authorized "to establish offices of discount and deposit in any part of the territories or dependencies of the United States." This is the act under which the branch at New Orleans was established. It was signed by Jefferson under the persuasion of Gallatin, and was afterwards held by the friends of the Bank to be a waiver, by Jefferson and his adherents, of their scruples about the constitutionality of the Bank.

In 1805, Georgia passed a law to tax the Bank. It refused to pay. The State officers entered the Bank and seized two boxes of silver worth $2,004. The bank brought an action for trespass in the Circuit Court of the United States for the District of Georgia, where the decision was for the defendant on a demurrer. On appeal to the Supreme Court of the United States the case became involved in technicalities. Georgia desisted from the attempt to tax the Bank until it should be decided whether it was to be rechartered.

The charter of the Bank was to expire March 4, 1811. As this time approached, a loud and somewhat angry discussion was raised over the question of renewing it. When the question of founding the New Orleans branch was pending, Gallatin was led to make a statement of the advantages of the

Bank to the Federal Treasury. They were: safe deposit of the public money; prompt transmission of the same from one end of the Union to the other; and facility in the collection of the revenue. March 2, 1809, he made an elaborate and very favorable report on the Bank, in which he endeavored to meet the current objections. He was very much afraid of the financial effects of the multiplication of small banks. He gave a statement of the operations of the Bank in round numbers, which was intended to show what was the general magnitude and proportion of the different factors in its operations. We possess but one other statement of the affairs of this Bank. According to its charter, it was bound to report to the Secretary of the Treasury, at his demand, not oftener than weekly. Upon the question, how often it did report, history throws no light whatever. The fact that a law imposed some duty on a bank, at that period, raises but a limited presumption that it ever did it. In a communication of January 24, 1811, Gallatin said that the charter of the Bank called only for "general statements" of the leading facts in regard to its condition; that only such had been required, and only such had been furnished. In view of the prevalent notions about the mystery and secrecy proper to a bank, we may well believe that this bank was very reluctant to make statements, and we may doubt if the Secretary called for them very often. If any were made, who should have been in a position to use them, if not the man who had been Secretary of the Treasury for ten years? If they ever existed they have been burned; so that the question whether they ever existed or not is open to easy and unprofitable speculation. According to the detailed report of January, 1811, the bank held private deposits, $6 millions; public deposits, $2 millions; bank deposits, $600,000. It had

$5 millions circulation; $14.5 millions discounts; had lent the United States $2.7 millions; was a creditor of other banks for $900,000 and held their notes for $400,000. It had $5 millions in specie. In looking to the future, Gallatin regarded the Bank as essential to the fiscal affairs of the federal government, especially if there should be a war. He proposed that, in renewing the charter, the Bank should be called on to pay interest on the public deposits; that itshould have some government directors; that its capital should be made $30 millions; and that the States should be allowed to subscribe a part of the capital and to appoint some of the directors.

The 5,000 shares in the Bank owned by the United States were sold as follows: 2,493 shares, in 1796-7, at 125; 187 shares, in 1797, at 120; 2,200 shares, in 1802, at 145. As the stock was paid for in ten annual installments, some of this was sold before it had been paid for. The total premium obtained was $671,860; the amount of dividends received by the United States, while it held the stock, was $1,101,720. The sale, in 1802, was to Sir Francis Baring, who re-sold in England at 150. Carey argued that it would disgrace American credit not to re-charter the bank after selling the stock at this rate. He also argued that the Bank of the United States was no longer a "national" bank, since these government shares had been sold, and therefore that all the allegations of danger on account of the connection between the government and the Bank had now fallen to the ground. He attributed the stringency in the money market, in 1810, which the "Aurora" and other opponents of the Bank charged to its willful and malicious action, to the multiplication of branch banks in Pennsylvania, and the necessity imposed on the mother banks by an act of the Legislature to receive the branch notes in payments. He complained very much that he could not obtain the information which was necessary for the defense of the Bank, and of "the obligation of secrecy in banking transactions which precludes a writer who undertakes the defense of such an institution from the use of many of the most important documents on which the whole of his reasoning may depend." The Bank had not taken the notes of its branches in payment from its customers, which was a ground of complaint the justice of which Carey conceded. His chief argument for renewal was the terrible calamity that would occur to the business of the country if the bank should wind up, and he quoted Atwater of New Haven, with horror, because Atwater thought that it would be a good thing to have all banks, bank paper, and bank charters burned up together.

Bollmann held that the winding up of the Bank would force the winding up of all the other banks, and hence would retire $55 millions of circulation. The "Aurora" was the organ of the opposition party. November 8, 1810, it offered twenty reasons why the Bank should not be re-chartered. The one which was reiterated the most frequently and in the greatest number of different forms was that it was foreign, or was owned by foreigners. In fact about two-thirds of the stock was owned abroad. The ninth reason was "because its influence has been exercised in our local elections," and because it was a political engine to favor "such as would abandon the interests of popular representative government." There were declared to be great abuses in the Bank, above all at Charleston and New Orleans, and its patronage was declared to be hostile to American interests. The most original reason for winding it up, however, was in order to find out whether it had been useful or not.

In regard to the political influence, we find a specification, in the same paper, January 9, 1811, in which it is stated that the cashier of the Charleston branch went "upon the election ground," and threatened curtailment of discounts as a punishment for voting for those who were "hostile to English domination." "From that day [of its origin] to this, the whole force of this all-corrupting Bank has been directed with an uniformity unsurpassed to the service and use of England, to the injury and abuse of this nation." The bank was intended to create a "money interest, which was to supersede and occupy the place of those interests which were solemnly promulgated in the Declaration of Independence." The "Aurora" had a story that the branch at New York had endeavored to punish Astor, for not being a sufficiently good federalist, by refusing him discounts, and that the clique surrounding it had given information to the English cruisers so that they might catch his ships. The arguments of these newspaper disputants were full of emphatic denunciation, but we can glean from them nothing more in regard to the history. The "Aurora" often hinted that it had a project of its own in reserve, which would be far better, and it denounced Gallatin as a traitor for defending the Bank. Its ideas were those which had already begun to find expression in the great banks of the States. "To any banking institution not founded on the landed security o the United States, we are hostile."

Atwater's pamphlet echoes the same notions and prejudices, of which the strongest is the hostility to foreigners. "Think of the locusts of Egypt. These were to the people precisely what banks are to our farmers." The Bank is aristocratic and federal. "One bank like that of the United States will destroy the industrious habits of a thousand families annually." Niles, in his reminiscences of political history, says that the federalists regarded the first Bank of the United States as their "sheet-anchor," and the democrats "deprecated it as an oppression, unconstitutional in its organization, and pernicious in its operation." "The time has been that a man, who did not wear a black cockade might as well have offered up his prayers to the father of mischief for a benefit {as some savages do) as have asked an accommodation of the Bank of the United States."

The Legislature of Virginia, at the session of 1810-11, instructed their Senators and requested their Representatives to vote against the renewal, because the use of the power to pass an act of incorporation by Congress was unconstitutional and "an encroachment on the sovereignty of the States. The Pennnsylvania House of Representatives adopted resolutions against the Bank, December 13, 1810, which were based on the doctrine of the Virginia and Kentucky resolutions of 1798. In the debate on these resolutions, Nicholas Biddle took a most prominent part. All these expressions taken together show the social and political animosities which were awakened and developed in connection with this institution; but we have very little means of learning what truth there was in the assertions. In a speech in the House of Representatives, in January, 1834, Horace Binney, who had, as a young man, been a director of the Bank, in the last years of its existence, spoke with great feeling and eloquence in defense of the men who had at that time been directors, and against the old imputations against the first Bank, which had been renewed in the war against the second: "The directors of the parent

Bank were a body of as honorable men, as impartial, and as faithful to their trust, as any men that ever lived. There was not a politician at their board, nor a man who gave himself up to anything but the performance of duty to his trust."

The debate in Congress on the renewal of the charter added very little to these arguments. The petition of the Bank for a renewal was presented March 26, 1808, but no action was taken upon it. December 4, 1809, Nicholas of Va. moved that "provision be made by law for a general national establishment of banks throughout the United States, and that the profits arising from the same, together with such surplusses of revenue as may accrue, be appropriated for the general welfare, in the construction of public roads and canals, and the establishment of seminaries for education throughout the United States." This outcropping of the notions which entered into all the big banks of the States schemes is worthy of notice. The plan was to have the federal state carry out the same operation with the States, as the State, in all those schemes, did with the counties, and the proposition came from the core of the State rights group who were fighting the Bank. The very men and the very school of opinion who were hostile to banks altogether on the federal arena, invented and established the big State paper money machines.

Love of Virginia reported, April 2, 1810, an elaborate plan of a national bank, to have its seat at Washington, and branches in such States as consented. The States were to subscribe shares which were allotted to them. It was something between the proposed Bank of the United States and the big banks of the States. April 7th, a bill was introduced to continue for twenty years the existing Bank of the Unit States with the modifications which Gallatin had suggested. A bonus of $1.25 millions was to be paid within the year; the Bank was to loan the government not more than $5,000,000, at not more than six per cent., and it was to pay three per cent. on the minimum annual balance of the public deposits in excess of $3 millions. April 13th, this bill was debated in Committee of the Whole, but the House never gave the Committee of the Whole permission to debate it further.

Although the Bank had presented the subject in 1808, it never was really considered in Congress until January, 1811, three months before the charter was to expire. Perhaps the most representative speech against the Bank was that of Dasha, of Kentucky. He said that the question was: "Whether we will foster a viper in the bosom of our country that will spread its deadly venom over the land, and finally affect the vitals of your republican institutions; or whether we will, as it is our duty, apply the proper antidote by a refusal to renew the charter, thereby checking the cankering poison, the importation and dissemination of foreign influence, that has already brought our government to the brink of ruin." He had no doubt that George III was a stockholder in the Bank. He viewed all banks as hostile to the principles of our government. Commerce was but little better, yet he was not hostile to it, but wanted it kept "within the pale of reason." The large foreign capital in this Bank, he said, gave the tone to elections in New York until Burr checked it with the Manhattan Company. He was sufficiently familiar with banks to be convinced that "they are systems of speculation, calculated to suit the speculatory and mercantile class at the expense of those who are the support and sheet-anchor of

94

your government." He referred with scorn to the broken banks of New England. The information of the speculations and swindlings in the East had made the West shun "the possibility of being engulfed in a similar vortex." The Bank "will further the views of federalism by increasing their power, and assist them in overturning the present system of government, on the ruins of which they will count upon raising one more congenial to their purposes." Not only the British capital in the Bank, but the British possessions in North America were a menace to us. It was high time to find out whether this Bank was solid or a fraud. Wright of Maryland, gave specifications of the alleged political influence of the Bank. Merchants of Philadelphia had signed petitions for Jay's treaty, against their convictions, and had excused themselves by saying that, if they did not do so, they could get no more bank accommodation. In Maryland, bank directors had been thrown out of office because they voted for Smith. Evan Jones had been elected president of the branch at New Orleans to succeed a good republican, although Jones was a refugee tory and was suspected of being one of Burr's men.

In answer to the argument about the constitutionality, it was pointed out that the State Constitutions did not expressly grant to the States the power to pass acts of incorporation. Nobody noticed that banks had already been incorporated by the territorial governments of the Mississippi Valley, the strongest case of all being that of the Bank of Louisiana, which was incorporated before there was even an organized territorial government.

Nicholson, of New York, stated that the charter could have been carried a year before by a majority of nearly thirty.

The destruction of the Bank was a part of the programme of the young democrats, who wanted a war with England, in order to conquer Canada. Clay was a representative and leader amongst them. In his speech against the Bank, he complained that an act of Congress, after being passed according to the prescriptions of the Constitution, must be submitted to the president and directors of the Bank for approval. This referred to the provision that the Bank should explicitly accept the new charter if it was passed. He also said that we might be on the brink of war with England, and added, "Should such an event occur, do you apprehend that the English premier would experience any difficulty in obtaining the entire control of this institution?" The fact was often pointed out in the debate, which lay upon the face of the bill, that no foreigner could vote in the Bank. Of the 25,000 shares, 18,000 were owned abroad; the other 7,000 shares ruled the Bank. Therefore it was plain that the foreign stockholders, instead of gaining, through the Bank, any power to act upon American interests, had, by taking stock in it, put their own interests at the mercy of Americans.

Leaving aside all the subtleties about "sovereignty," the question was whether the Constitution had constituted a State, with a complete structure, adequate functions, and sufficient powers to fulfill all the duties of civil life for the welfare of the people. The opponents of the Bank argued that the State banks could perform all the services required by the government just as well as the national bank, but, as they were answered in the debate, this was admitting that some bank was "necessary," in the sense of the Constitution, for the purposes of the government. In truth, however, the gravest question in the political order of the United States was then, how much integration the Constitution had given to the Union. The conception of a federal State was passionately hated and resisted by a majority of the people. They felt the discipline, order, method and punctuality of the great empire as an irksome restriction on the loose and shiftless habits of former times which they called liberty. It was true that there was such an advancing constraint. The Bank, by its symbolism, and by its functions, was the only great institution which was helping on the work of social and political integration. That was exactly the reason why it was hated by the State rights men and anti-federalists.

Testimony to this action of the Bank was given in the debate. "I ask the question: Will a bank in North Carolina trust a bank in New Hampshire? No! but the State and every individual in it would trust the Bank of the United States. You could not establish a connection between North Carolina and New Hampshire, so that either would trust the other. The establishment of the Bank of the United States affords, in this case, a facility useful and absolutely necessary to carry on the measures of the government." It had a corresponding effect on commercial affairs. Before 1800 the collectors at the different ports kept the duty bonds in their own custody. After that time, by a new law, the bonds were deposited in the Bank for collection. They thus became bank debts, and although, as Smith of Maryland argued, trying to break the force of this fact, the coercion to pay was not in the Bank but in the custom house, nevertheless, in practice, it was the Bank usage which set the standard. Crawford said: "It is impossible to resist the conviction that the prompt and secure collection of our revenue is principally owing to the influence of the Bank." These facts, however, furnish the reasons why the

Bank was hated by large classes of business men and politicians. The republicans felt sure that it never would be an ally of theirs, and therefore they thought it the simplest dictate of political policy to destroy it while they could. In vain the fact was pointed out to them that the federalists, although they had, as the opponents said, had this tremendous engine in their hands for twenty years, had been ousted by the opponents, and that the only three out and out federal States, besides Massachusetts, had no branch of the Bank, while the States in which there were branches, with the same exception, were either wholly or in large part republican.

In the House of Representatives the renewal of the charter was indefinitely postponed January 24, 1811, by a vote of 65 to 64. In the Senate it was lost by the casting vote of the Vice-President, George Clinton, February 20th.

After the re-charter was defeated, the Bank asked for an extension of the powers requisite for winding up. This was refused. In a report on it by Clay, to the Senate, it was said: "The injurious effects of a dissolution of the corporation will be found to consist in an accelerated disclosure of the actual condition of those who have been supported by the credit of others; but whose insolvent or tottering situation, known to the Bank, has been concealed from the public at large."

March 19, 1812, the receivability of the notes of the Bank for dues to the United States was repealed, the Circuit Court of Virginia having just before decided that those notes were still everywhere a good tender for duties.

As soon as the re-charter was definitely defeated, the Bank applied to the Legislature of Pennsylvania for a charter, to retain all its capital, and to be allowed to do business in such States as might permit it. The application was defeated, but renewed the next year, with an offer to subscribe $500,000 to public works, and to lend the State, at any time during the charter period, the same sum at five per cent.

Charles Biddle, who was then in the State Senate, thought that it would be a great advantage to the State. His son, Nicholas, was in the State House of Representatives, and made a speech in favor of it. The objection which weighed most was that the stock was owned by foreigners.

Between March 1st and September 1st, the Bank paid the public and private deposits, and redeemed $3.5 millions worth of bank notes—in all $9.2 millions, and its specie fell only $335,175. In the first year of liquidation it paid $11.6 millions, and the specie stock increased $1.2 millions. Gallatin said that the public deposits were removed within a week before the expiration of the charter, and no harm was done. He takes no note of the fact that the Bank was a creditor of the Treasury for a sum about equal to the government deposit. In his report on the selected banks, January 8, 1812, he stated that the public deposits were gradually withdrawn and that the account of the Treasury with the Bank was closed, September 2, 1811, except that $70,000 were still at the credit of the disbursing officers at New Orleans. The credits of the disbursing officers always cause ambiguity as to the public deposits. During the existence of this Bank the public deposits were not placed in it exclusively even on the Atlantic coast. The principal disbursing officers were directed by law, in 1809, to keep the public money in their hands, whenever possible, in some incorporated bank to be designated by the President. A treasury report of January 9, 1811, shows that one-third of the public deposits were, at that time, in eleven State banks, of which only three were west of the Alleghanies.

As soon as it was certain that the Bank would not be re-chartered, local banks were selected at the chief ports of entry, in which the collectors were ordered to place the duty bonds for collection. The only condition imposed on the selected banks was, that they should give a preference in discounts to persons who had duty bonds to pay. Within a year, the cash balance in the Treasury was divided in deposits between twenty-one banks. As to the currency receivable for dues to the Treasury, the law of 1789, modified by Hamilton's orders, came into force again, but by the Act of June 30, 1812, Treasury notes were made a good tender to the Treasury, and the first of them were issued in October.

The dividends of the Bank, down to January, 1809, inclusive, averaged eight and thirteen thirty-fourths per cent. The highest point the stock ever reached was 150. It is stated that at one time the stock of specie in the New York branch was reduced to $10,000. It is also stated that the average loss per annum by bad debts, during the twenty years of its existence, was sixty-one one-hundreths of one per cent. No financial disturbance whatever occurred upon the winding up of this bank. Carey's apprehensions proved entirely groundless.

Its stock was liquidated at one hundred and nine dollars, one and a-quarter cents for one hundred dollars paid in. The last such payment which has been found, is mentioned in Niles' Register for September 13, 1834. Raguet calculated that ifthe dividends were regarded as deferred payments, compounded semi-annually, the return was equal to 97, on the day the charter expired. The amount of its notes which had not been presented, in 1823, was $205,000. The court then released the commissioners from liability for them, $5,000 being reserved to meet any cases of special hardship. Eleven hundred dollars only were afterwards presented, most of it by an old Revolutionary soldier, in 1825.

In 1854, the city council of Philadelphia appointed a committee to inquire into the best means of closing the trust of the old Bank of the United States, in order that they might get possession of the house which had been bequeathed to the city by Girard, but which was then "in tenure" of the cashier of Girard's bank without rent. The report of this committee showed that Girard bought the banking house of the old Bank and a house in Chestnut street belonging to it, which was the one in question. The banking house had already passed to the city and was leased to the Girard Bank. It was stated that the Bank trust held at that time, $22,564 of unclaimed dividends, and had just declared a dividend of $51,250. There were some debts not collected. The city desired to take over the trust, to be administered by the Commissioners of the Girard estate. It is inferred that this was done.

It is very desirable to form, if possible, a notion of the point of departure from which the country entered on the inflation of the following period. Blodget's figures represent the amount of specie in the currency as exceeding the paper in the first years of the century. In the debate on the renewal of the charter, however, the statements made show a very different state of things. "Specie has been almost banished from circulation by paper." Only notes of the Bank of the United States are current everywhere. "You can outride in twenty-four hours the credit of any other bank in the

101

country." The paper of some of the banks is depreciated. That of others is current but a short distance.

CHAPTER IV.

The Earliest Banks in the Mississippi Valley

It no place and at no time has the history of banking ever been so varied, so bold, and so rich in experience, as it was in the Mississippi Valley in the first thirty years of this century. It was intertwined there with a number of the matters which touch the interests of men and excite their passions in the highest degree. It was thus linked with the political interests which were connected with the growth of the United States into a federal State; with the questions of constitutional law concerning the inviolability of contracts and the independence of the judiciary; with the question of disputed title to land, which of course affected every man in the community; and with the system of execution for the collection of debts.

The Governor of Kentucky, in his message of 1800, complained of a lack of revenue and of the economic situation which he described as "almost destitute of specie." The exports would not pay for the imports. He proposed an effort to open trade down the Mississippi. The notion was that the eastern trade drew off specie because the exchange of commodities was not mutually advantageous. Here we see a recurrence of the ideas and of the misinterpretation of facts which we noticed on the Atlantic coast in the colonial days, in regard to the trade with England. It has been stated that silver ceased to come up the Mississippi Valley after the peace between Spain and England in 1801, but this is certainly a mistake, for that movement of silver continued to be large and important for twenty-five or thirty years more, and it would be difficult to say when it stopped.

By an Act of December 6, 1802, the Kentucky Insurance Company was chartered until January 1, 1818. The purpose was to insure boats and cargoes on their way down the river. This company was not explicitly authorized to issue notes for circulation, but it was incidentally provided that its notes payable to bearer should pass by delivery only. On reading the section of the charter it is difficult to say whether it was very craftily or very carelessly drawn. Butler says in regard to the institution that "it began in fraud and ended in bankruptcy." "The political party which then controlled Kentucky held banks in horror and never would have passed the bill had they understood its provisions."

December 27, 1806, the Bank of Kentucky at Frankfort was chartered, to last until December 3, 1821. The capital was to be $1 million, half of it to be subscribed by the State. It was to begin when $20,000 were subscribed. All the debts, exclusive of deposits, were not to exceed three times the capital. It was to loan only to Kentuckians; no director might borrow over $5,000 or be an endorser for more than $10,000 in the bank. It might have branches in the State for discount and deposit only. It was to make weekly reports to the Governor, and its notes "payable on demand in current money" were to be received by the State. The debt to the State from the settlers on the vacant lands was relied upon to pay the State's subscription. The Legislature had the power to elect the president and six directors. "The political majority, when times of excitement arose, drove the bank on the shoals of party and ultimately shipwrecked the institution. The

104

power of branching the bank became a subject of local and party contention, and the influence of the Legislature, through its election of the majority of the directory, was brought to bear upon the decision. The extension of the bank then ceased to be a mere fiscal or mercantile question to be governed by the interests of the corporation, but was converted into one of political influence."

OHIO.—The Miami Exporting Company was incorporated in April, 1803, with "banking privileges." February 10, 1808, the Bank of Marietta asked for a charter until 1818, from which it appears that it was an already existing association. The limit of the capital was set at $500,000, besides such shares as the State might take. The State might subscribe one share for every five subscribed by individuals. It was to have one year's credit in paying for them, but was to receive dividends on them as if paid for. There was no clause providing for specie payment and no penalty for suspension; but the bank was forbidden to issue notes or contract debts "payable in the bills of credit emitted by the laws of this State." A week later the Bank of Chillicothe was incorporated, with a capital not to exceed $100,000. The State subscription and the prohibition against dealing in State notes were the same as in the case of the former bank. It was provided that this act "shall be construed in all courts and places benignly and favorably for any beneficial purposes thereby intended." At the same time the Bank of Steubenville was incorporated with all the same features. Three other banks were incorporated in 1812 and 1813. At the session of 1813-1814 a number of manufacturing companies and companies to make canals and harbors were incorporated, but they were expressly forbidden to engage in banking.

105

In the Territory of MICHIGAN, the Governor and three Judges constituted the Legislative Council. They passed an act "Concerning the Bank of Detroit," September 19, 1806; which act was disallowed by Congress March 3, 1807. An act of November 4, 1815, imposed a penalty on any proprietor or member of an unincorporated bank. The first bank was the Bank of Michigan, chartered December 19, 1817. The power of the Territorial authority to charter it was affirmed by the Court in 1831.

TENNESSEE.—Hugh L. White, in a speech in the Senate, March 24, 1838, described the currency of the State of Franklin in eastern Tennessee, in the years following the Revolution. The salaries of the Governor, Chief-Justice and other great officers were paid in deer skins; those of the inferior officers in raccoon skins. The tax collectors cheated the Treasurer, who was not an expert in furs, by putting raccoon tails on opossum skins, and paying them in instead of the raccoon furs which they had collected.

The Nashville Bank was chartered in 1807, to last until 1818. A copy of its charter has not been accessible, November 20, 1811, the Bank of the State of Tennessee at Knoxville was incorporated, with a capital of $400,000. The shares were apportioned amongst the counties, and there were to be commissioners in each to receive the subscriptions. It was to begin when $25,000 were paid in in specie, and the State might subscribe not more than $40,000 of the total proposed capital. It was not to owe, exclusive of deposits, more than twice its capital, and was to issue no notes under $5. It was to last thirty years; to report to the Treasurer of East Tennessee annually, and to establish branches if thought expedient. The Nashville Bank might unite with it and

106

become a branch of it. November 19, 1811, the charter of the Nashville Bank was extended until 1828, and November 16, 1813, it was extended until 1838, the capital being increased from $200,000 to $400,000.

The Legislative Council of the MISSISSIPPI TERRITORY enacted, December 24, 1807, that taxes should be receivable in "any territorial paper, duly and legally issued by the Auditor of public accounts." All the civil organizations in the Valley seem to have used auditor's certificates as a currency from their earliest organization. In this Territory it was also necessary to provide against the malfeasance of the sheriffs, collectors, and clerks of court, by providing that they must pay in the currency which they received, whether it was specie or auditor's warrants; from which it is inferable that the latter were not at par of specie. December 23, 1809, the Legislative Council of the Territory incorporated the Bank of Mississippi at Natchez, with a capital of $500,000, as a limit; $50,000 to be raised at once; to last until 1848. A supplementary act, February 6, 1818, changed the name of the bank to the Bank of the State of Mississippi. The Governor was to subscribe, on behalf of the State, one share for every four subscribed by individuals, and to appoint five directors. The capital was raised to $3 millions; it was to last until 1840. It might have branches; was to report to the Governor at his demand, not more frequently than monthly; its notes. were to be receivable by the State; no other bank was to be chartered so long as it lasted.

ALABAMA.—The Planters' and Mechanics' Bank at Huntsville was chartered by the Legislative Council of the Mississippi Territory December 11, 1816; with $50,000 capital; to last until 1837; never to owe more than three times its capital, deposits being left out of account; to issue no note under $1; five hundred shares to be reserved for the Territory for ten years. February 13, 1818, its name was changed to the Planters' and Merchants' Bank. On the last date, the Tombeckbee Bank, at St. Stephens, was chartered, to last until 1838, with $500,000 capital, with the same limit on its debts, and the denomination of its notes; two-fifths of the capital to be reserved for the Territory for ten years. The Bank of Mobile was chartered November 20, 1818, with a capital of $500,000, payable in gold and silver (a specification which had not been included in the former charters), to last until 1818. One-fifth of the shares were reserved for the Territory for ten years. As soon as the State government was formed, in the following year, we find it borrowing from these banks. In the Constitution of the State, it was provided that one State bank might be established, with such branches as the Assembly might deem expedient. No branch and no bank charter was to be renewed, except by a two-thirds vote of both Houses, and only one bank or branch might be chartered or renewed at the same session of the General Assembly. At least one-fifth of the shares of every bank must be reserved for the State, which was also to have a number of directors in proportion. The State and the stockholders were to be liable for the debts of any bank in the proportion in which they shared the stock. Remedies for the collection of debts were to be reciprocal for and against banks. No bank was to begin until half its capital was paid in in gold and silver. Twelve per cent. penalty was imposed for a failure to redeem bank notes in specie, unless the suspension should be sanctioned by the Assembly. Whenever a State bank should be founded, the existing banks might become branches of it.

When LOUISIANA was bought by the United States, the movement of silver thither from Mexico was arrested for a time, and there was a complaint of lack of currency, although Spain had a quantity of paper money called "liberanzas" afloat, which were not redeemed at once. One of the first acts of Governor Claiborne was to found the Bank of Louisiana. The non-American population was extremely displeased at this, regarding a bank as an instrument of robbery, and fearing more paper money.

In 1811, two banks were chartered—the Planters' Bank and the Bank of Orleans. The former was an already existing association. The capital was to be $600,000, payable in specie. It was to last fifteen years. The Bank of Orleans was to have a capital of $500,000, to last for fifteen years, and the subscriptions were made payable in money or "notes payable to the directors." This and the following are the only cases in which we have found, in a charter, an explicit provision for what appear to be stock notes. It may be added here that the charter of this bank was extended March 26, 1823, until 1847, it being provided that a bonus of $25,000 should be paid, and that the old notes should be replaced by new. The Louisiana State Bank was chartered March 14, 1818, with a capital of $2 millions. One-fifth of the subscription was to be paid at once "in cash or notes payable to the directors," endorsed to the satisfaction of the managers, who might also accept mortgages. One-quarter of the capital was reserved for the State, which was to subscribe $100,000 at once, and appoint six directors out of eighteen. The bank was to last until 1870; to organize when $500,000 had been subscribed by private individuals; to establish five branches within six months; and to pay a bonus of $100,000. No provision was made in any of these charters for the case of suspension.

March 3, 1819, the Louisiana Bank was ordered to liquidate before March 12, 1822.

MISSOURI.—The Bank of St. Louis was chartered August 21, 1813, to last until 1838, with a capital of $150,000. The Territorial government might take one-tenth of its shares; it might have branches in the Missouri Territory, and could carry on a lombard business with fur, lead, or other commodities deposited in the control of the bank. Not more than one-quarter of the capital might be sold out of the Missouri and Illinois Territories.

The Bank of Missouri was incorporated, existing already as an association, January 31, 1817, with a capital of $250,000. It might have branches. The Territory reserved an option for ten years to subscribe 1,000 shares. It was to last until 1838, and must pay specie or forfeit five per cent. per month during refusal. Unauthorized issues were forbidden December 12, 1820, and it was forbidden to pass them. Notes of incorporated banks of other States, if not under $1, were not included.

The earliest State Constitution which contained any mention of banks was that of Indiana, of 1816, in which it was forbidden that any corporation should be created to issue "bills of credit or bills payable to order or bearer," but a State bank with branches might be established. The Mississippi constitution of 1817 provided that no bank should be incorporated in which one-fourth of the stock was not reserved for the State, with the power to appoint a proportionate number of the directors. The provision on this

110

subject in the Constitution of Missouri, 1820, was: "The General Assembly may incorporate one banking company, and no more, to be in operation at the same time."

PERIOD III - 1812 to 1829-32.

Local Banks are Multiplied to Replace the Bank of the United States. Their Issues are Stimulated by their Fiscal Functions, soon Intensified by War Financiering. Commercial Crisis is Produced with a Prolonged Liquidation, Attended by Various Experiments in Bank Issues and Stay Laws for Relief. A Banking System is Created Consisting of Local Banks Co-ordinated Around a Bank of the United States, as a Regulator of the Currency, and Fiscal Agent of the Government.

CHAPTER V.

Inflation on the Atlantic Coast

The war of 1812 was undertaken in the belief that it could be conducted by loans, and without the necessity of taxation. Gallatin was relied upon as a competent financier, but the role which had been assigned to him he was not willing to undertake. He accepted an appointment as one of the Peace Commissioners, and departed to Europe. As soon as the attempt was made to obtain resources by loans, the fact was developed that they could be obtained only in the Middle States. The New England States were strongly opposed to the war. In the South there was no superfluous capital. The Middle States were enthusiastic for the war as a continuation of the embargo system, and a "protection to domestic industry." The stringent measures which were taken to prevent importations, as a war measure, cut off the revenue. The loans met with only slight success, and the real financial resource consisted in treasury notes, bearing five and two-fifths per cent. interest. These at once stimulated banking issues in the Middle States. Campbell, Secretary of the Treasury, in 1813, wanted the exportation of specie forbidden, believing the banks would then loan to the government more freely, and the President recommended it in a message, but Congress would not adopt it.

In order to supply the place of one bank with $10 millions capital, 120 banks with $30 millions capital were created, according to the best statistics we have, between 1811 and 1815. A few banks in Maine suspended early in 1814, and the three banks of New Orleans in April. The English having invaded the District of Columbia and burned Washington, in August, the District banks suspended. Those of Philadelphia followed on the 30th, and the other banks of the Middle States immediately afterward. In explanation of this action of the banks, it is stated that a large amount of English government bills had been sold here at a very heavy discount. In his report of February 12, 1820, in which he reviewed the financial history of the last eight years, Secretary Crawford attributed the suspension to bank inflation, small notes banishing specie, and accommodation paper. Isaac Bronson attributed it to the anomalous state of things produced by the war, cutting off intercourse, so that inflation produced no demand for export.

From the time of this suspension the banks of the Middle States entered upon a career of reckless increase of their issues stimulated by the public loans. "It is impossible," said

Crawford, "to imagine a currency more vicious than that which depends upon the will of nearly four hundred banks, entirely independent of each other, when released from all restraint against excessive issues."

The banks of New York City agreed to take each others' notes and pay interest on debtor balances monthly. No bank was to increase its loans unless bound to lend to the State, and the debtor banks were to diminish their discounts when the general committee of the banks should recommend that this be done.

The notes of the Connecticut banks disappeared from circulation and those of the suspended banks further south took their place. "At a special session, January, 1815, the General Assembly [of Connecticut] empowered each incorporated bank in the State to issue bills to the amount of one-half the actually paid capital, receivable for all debts due the same, and payable in specie on demand two years after the close of the war. Presidents and cashiers were to make statements semi-annually to the General Assembly of the amounts outstanding at the time of such returns. In October, 1814, the General Assembly had authorized them to issue promisory notes of less denomination than $1 for the payment of money only."

"Our banks now put out bills under two forms, the first promising to pay the bearer —— dollars in notes of New York banks, on demand at the —— bank in New York, or in specie two years after the war; and the second promising to pay the bearer —— dollars two years after the war. Both were receivable for all debts due the several institutions issuing the same. The public named them 'facilities.' Fractional notes ranging from six and a quarter to fifty cents

114

were also freely injected into the currency. Individuals and corporations, barbers and bartenders, as well as manufacturers and capitalists, the solvent and the insolvent, further variegated the assortment of 'shinplasters' by liberal contributions, some professing to call for money and others for services."

"At the May session of 1815 the power granted to the banks to emit post-notes payable two years after the end of the war was made to cease and determine from the first day of January, 1816. The issue by any unauthorized person, persons, or corporation of paper intended to pass in lieu of money was prohibited under heavy penalties."

The southwestern part of New England did not, therefore, escape the contagion.

The currencies of the various parts of the Union at once began to fall to different stages of depreciation, and the internal exchanges were thrown into confusion because the quotation contained the depreciation.

In some respects the period on the study of which we are now entering is without a parallel. The question uppermost in a man's mind in regard to whatever is offered as a circulating medium is: Will it pass? That means: is it the money of account, in which prices and contracts are set, so that it will be accepted as cash, without discount, dispute, or delay? If the money of account is specie, paper notes may still be cash; namely, if they are at once exchangeable for the coins whose name they bear. If they are not so exchangeable, they degenerate at once into negotiable instruments, and are not cash. If they fall to a uniform discount, as negotiable instruments, they may become the money of account, superseding specie. Then they are cash again. The discount is

115

included and accounted for in the prices and terms of contract. People who are unfamiliar with affairs then do not know that there is any discount or any negotiation. If the discount of the paper. varies, an insurance rate is included in the prices, etc., but, as it is uniform, it is unnoticed. These latter suppositions were fulfilled in the case of our paper money after the civil war. It was our money of account, or "current funds," and was cash. This is why people came to think that it was money and lost the sense of its relation to money. In 1814 the notes of each bank were at a different rate of discount. Each town or county accepted some one kind as its local money of account. Others in the same place and groups of them in other districts were quoted with reference to that one, but the great characteristic of the period was, that the varieties were so great, and the badness of all was so extreme, that there was no money of account. The state of things is very difficult to understand and realize, and is almost incredible. It was the *differences* at the same time between the existing media of exchange which produced the result that there was no medium. Exchanges were made by barter of such paper as one had for the goods which the other had.

Specie became very scarce in the Middle States and remittances could hardly be made. We are told, however, that the places where the currency was worst were the best places at which to import foreign commodities; no doubt because there was a double transaction in converting the currency obtained, and bringing home the proceeds in specie or in government securities.

The Treasury, as we have seen, after the expiration of the charter of the Bank of the United States, received duties in the bank notes of the port at which the goods were entered. Consequently there was a further advantage to import commodities at the port of entry where the currency was most depreciated. Hence Philadelphia and Baltimore enjoyed a period of great apparent prosperity, for, in July, 1815, New York paper was at 14 per cent. discount, and Baltimore paper at 16 per cent. discount, compared with Boston paper or silver. The discount on southern and western paper, at that time, was small.

The government suffered the greatest loss and embarrassment from the derangement of the currency. Boston was the money market of the country, and there were heavy disbursements there, which must all be made at specie par; but there was no revenue there, all being obtained further south in depreciated notes. If anyone had payments to make at Boston to the Treasury, he bought notes of the suspended banks to the southward with which to do it. Hence Secretary Crawford stated that "until the resumption of specie payments in the early part of 1817, treasury notes, and the notes of the banks which had suspended payment, formed the great mass of circulation in the eastern parts of the Union. Specie, or the notes of banks which continued to pay specie, formed no part of the receipts of the government in Boston, and the districts east of that town, until about the close of the year 1816."

June 15, 1815, the Secretary of the Treasury gave notice that he would not receive the notes of any non-specie paying banks which did not take treasury notes at par with their own notes. If the notes of any bank stood higher than treasury notes, it refused to receive the latter at par. Such banks were in general the creditor banks, and the best ones, and the Secretary's rule led him to refuse their notes while he

117

accepted those of the worse banks. August 15th he published a list of the banks whose notes he would no longer receive. He said that the proposition which he had made to the banks had been generally acceded to by them "*with the exception of those which pay their own notes on demand, in gold or silver,* and those who are specified in the subjoined list." The specie paying banks of New England so far as they received treasury notes, suffered for it, and were afterwards petitioners for redress.

Advertisements were made by the Secretary for subscriptions to a public loan, March 10th, the object of which was to fund treasury notes and get a "supply of the local currencies of different places in some proportion to the probable amount of the local demand." Up to April 19th, he received no bids over 89, and some as low as 75. "Upon this experiment," he says, in his report for 1815, "it was seen at once that the new situation of the Treasury required a new course of proceeding, and that neither the justice due to the equal rights of the public creditors, nor a fair estimate of the value of the public property, nor an honorable regard for the public credit would permit the loan to assume the shape and character of a scramble, subservient to the speculations which create what is called a market price, and shifting in every town and village of every State, according to the arbitrary fluctuations of what is called the difference of exchange." He, therefore, fixed the price of his stocks at 95, not specifying in what, and he gives a table of the subscriptions received at different places, distinguishing subscriptions in money (*i.e.* the bank note currency of the place) from subscriptions in treasury notes. The table shows how little "arbitrary" was the difference of exchange. The quotations on the 19th of August were as follows: at Boston, treasury notes, fourteen and fourteen and one-half discount, local currency at par of specie; at New York, treasury notes, par; specie 12 per cent. premium in local currency; at Philadelphia, treasury notes, par, specie 15 per cent. premium; at Baltimore, treasury notes three and four premium, Boston notes premium, Philadelphia notes two premium, New York notes seven premium, specie 16 premium; at Washington about the same as at Baltimore. Turning now to the Secretary's table, we find that he received his largest subscriptions at Washington, Baltimore, and Philadelphia, and less and less further East. At Washington, only one-eighth of the subscriptions were paid in treasury notes, the rest in the local currency. At Baltimore not quite one-third were paid in treasury notes, the rest in currency. At Philadelphia nearly one-half were paid in treasury notes. At New York very nearly all were paid in treasury notes. Elsewhere nothing but treasury notes were received. The case is a remarkably good one to prove how absolutely certain the facts of value are to vindicate themselves against any attempt to juggle with them.

It must be added that, as between different bank notes, the Treasury received the worst. In a Treasury report of February 12, 1821, it was stated that there were then $818,590 to the credit of the Treasury, as special deposits in suspended banks. The Treasury also held $482 in counterfeits. In a report of February 1, 1838, it was stated that the amount of bank notes received between 1814 and 1817, and still on hand in 1838, amounted to $178,470, and that "the direct loss to the United States on bills that were depreciated but were still received and paid out again on public account probably equaled five or six millions of dollars."

119

In December, 1816, before the Bank of the United States went into operation, the Secretary had to borrow $500,000 from it, with which to pay interest at Boston. In his report for 1816, he complained that he could not tell which notes were at par and which not. The depositories would only accept the notes which he had received, as special deposits, and he was obliged to keep four accounts, "cash," (*i.e.* local currency, special deposits, treasury notes bearing interest, and treasury notes not bearing interest. He too had no money of account.

The financial exigencies had become so great, even in 1813, that the minds of men began to turn once more to a national bank. There were fears about the proceedings of the local banks. The very men who had so jauntily declared, in the debate on the renewal of the charter of the United States Bank, that the fiscal affairs of the government could be carried on quite as well by the local banks, saw already grave reason to doubt whether that would prove to be true. The old dilemma was renewed between the social sentiments and political opinions hostile to the bank on the one side, and the financial exigency on the other. It was not at all on account of a change of political opinion about a bank in the administration party that the project of a national bank was taken up again; but, against their will, and with deep misgiving and dissatisfaction, they turned back to that device.

The subject of a national bank was brought up in Congress, January 4, 1814, by a petition from New York City, but nothing was done at that session except to appoint a Select Committee. As soon as Congress re-assembled in September, the subject was taken up again, the finances being in a desperate condition. Secretary Dallas proposed a national bank, October 14th, the leading motive being to obtain financial resources. In order to serve this purpose in the way desired by the administration, the proposed bank must be a non-specie-paying bank. One bill was completed and brought to a vote in the House, January 2, 1815, when it was defeated by the double vote of the Speaker, Cheves. Then, having been re-moulded, it was passed, 120 to 38, containing a provision against suspension. The Senate restored the provision for suspension, but afterwards receded and the bill was passed on the 20th, for a bank which might not make loans to the government and might not suspend; that is to say, it created a national bank of a general and permanent character, suitable for peace times, and not such a machine for war finance as the administration wanted.

President Madison vetoed the bill, because the bank, as provided for, "cannot be relied on during the war to provide a circulating medium or loans or anticipations of revenue," on account of the clauses forbidding it to make loans or suspend. In this history we have seen Madison vote against the Bank of North America, furnish the leading argument against the constitutionality of a Bank of the United States, in 1791, and the one which was most relied on by the opponents of the re-charter in 1811. Now, as President of the United States, in the midst of a war, his action must be taken to mean that he not only thought a bank constitutional if it was a sound institution, but even if it was to begin under a suspension of specie payments. The only excuse was that such an institution was "necessary" to the purposes of the State—that is, that it was constitutional in such form as the Legislature or the administration, under the circumstances, might find necessary. The position of the Senate had been that the chief reason for wanting the bank was to get loans from it for the war. If these were obtained, it could not maintain specie payments. Why, then, make it at all without a provision for suspension? This leaves us face to face with the fact that the mismanagement of the war finances was forcing the federal government to set up a paper money machine.

February 6th, another bill was introduced in the Senate for a bank with $50 millions capital, $20 millions in treasury notes, fundable in six per cent. stock, $15 millions in six per cent. stock, $5 millions in specie, $10 millions by the government in four per cent. stock. It was not to pay its notes in specie until the last installment on the capital was paid. There were to be five equal installments, the first payable April 1st, and the four others quarterly thereafter. Congress might at any time authorize a suspension of specie payments on petition of the directors. February 10th, the Senate refused to strike out the last provision and passed the bill. February 17th, the day on which the news of the signing of the treaty of Ghent arrived, and as it appears, under some premonitions of that news, the bill was indefirotely postponed in the House. Jacob Barker, who had a great speculation on this project, was in Washington at the time. He says that the bill had passed both Houses, and lay on the clerk's table for assent to be given by the Senate to a change in respect to the date of organization, "when an express on its way to Alexandria for a speculation in flour passed through Washington with the news of peace, which so elated Congress that the members left their seats without waiting for an adjournment, and they could not again be induced to consider the question of a national bank during that session. This bill was framed with a view to induce moneyed men to subscribe to its stock. It was the best ever devised. It did not impose any bonus, and if it had then become a law would have worked wonders." ... "Had the news been delayed a single hour, the bill would have passed and its stock would have been worth 100 per cent. premium."

At this point, then, all demand for a national bank as a means of war finance ceased, but a new demand arose for it to regulate the currency, which had now fallen into great disorder. We lay emphasis here on the story of the legislative birth of the second Bank of the United States, the circumstances which led to it, the motives which impelled the actors, and the necessities which gave the controlling ideas, because this is all-important with respect to the character of the institution which was produced. This has been sufficiently apparent already in the struggle over the question whether the bank, for war finance, should suspend or not. We shall hear no more of any suggestion that the bank, if created, should contemplate suspension as a possibility. It was as a regulator of the currency above everything else that a bank was now called for, and the motive for it was weariness, contempt, and disgust, in regard to the local banks and the currency provided by them.

One of the chief reasons given by the opponents of the old Bank of the United States for winding it up was to find out whether it had been useful or not. In 1815 it was almost universally believed that this question had been fully answered by experience, and that the experience had been costly.

During the year 1815, the bank note currency became worse and worse. The story is told of a "little Frenchman and his bank notes," who entered the country at Savannah with specie and travelled up the coast to Boston. He found his "money" all the time melting away. His American adviser told him that if he would begin at Boston and go back again, he could recover it all. The Frenchman, "holding up a parcel of ragged, dirty bills, pregnant with filth and disease," said: "Voila! it's like making a difference between the rags of one beggar and the rags of another."

Another traveller gives his own experience: "Such was the state of the currency that, in New Jersey, I met with an instance where a one dollar note I had taken in change, which was current on one side of a turnpike gate, would not pass at an hundred yards' distance on the other side."

The following case illustrates the difficulty of enforcing rights against a bank: A gentleman of Richmond wanted to enforce the payment of ten notes for $100 each against the Bank of Virginia, in 1815, but he could not get a lawyer to take his case until the following year. The president refused to obey the summons of the Court. The Sheriff brought him by force to Court, and, as the bank still refused to pay, the Sheriff closed its doors. The bank then brought suit for damages against the plaintiff, and instituted proceedings against the Sheriff. It re-opened its doors and went on with its business. No means were found to make it amenable to law. The "Richmond Enquirer" said that it was perfectly sound and able to resume, but held its opinion that it was not expedient to do so until others did.

Another cause of irritation with the banks was that they were held to have failed completely as agents for the fiscal operations of the federal government. Gouge quotes a statement from a pamphlet by "A Friendly Monitor," attributed to W. Jones, first president of the Bank of the United States, that the State banks, depositories of the public money, refused to make the necessary transfers for the government expenditures, and finally refused to pay the balances due by them, except in the ordinary course of public expenditure at the places in which they were, claiming indulgence on various pretexts, while they held the paper of the other banks, which had come to them in payment of the public deposits, and prevented those banks from resuming.

The President, in his message for 1815, urged Congress to provide for a "uniform" currency, either by a national bank or by government issues. The Committee on Currency asked Secretary Dallas, December 23d, for his opinion as to the amount of capital, the form of government, the privileges, and the organization of a national bank, and as to the amount of bonus which the bank ought to pay and the measures by which it might be aided in restoring specie payments. He replied the next day by a sketch of the bank as subsequently established. As to resumption, he thought that the best way to assist it, would be for the Treasury to refuse to receive notes of any bank which did not pay specie after December 31, 1816. He declared resumption impossible without a "contraction" of the existing issues.

The charter of the Bank of the United States became a law April 10, 1816. It passed the House, 80 to 71, and the Senate, 22 to 12. The federalist opposition at this session was due to the fact that the Bank would be in the hands of the opposite party. An amendment to establish the Bank in New York City was passed, but Dallas obtained a reconsideration. The New York members held a conference to secure its location at New York or its defeat; but one of the New York City members said that he had promised the administration to vote for the Bank and that he should do so. Upon this the effort was abandoned.

It was chartered for twenty years. Its capital was to be $35 millions, $7 millions in specie, $7 millions by the United States in five per cent. stock, and the rest in specie or public stocks of the United States. It was to pay a bonus of $1,5 millions in three installments after two, three, and four years. It was not to issue notes under $5, and was not to suspend specie payments under a penalty of 12 per cent. There were to be twenty directors chosen by the stockholders, and five, being stockholders, appointed by the Presidefit of the United States. No person might subscribe over 3,000 shares, unless the total subscription should be less than $28 millions. In that case, one person might subscribe the deficiency. The subscriptions were to be paid in three installments: 1—At the time of subscribing, $5 in specie and $25 in specie or stock; 2—Six months afterwards, $10 in specie and $25 in specie or stock; 3—Six months later, $10 in specie and $25 in specie or stock. The Secretary of the Treasury might at any time redeem the public stocks in the capital of the Bank at the rates at which it was provided that they should be received in subscription; namely, the six per cents at par; three per cents at 65; seven per cents at 106.51, and accrued interest. He might also redeem the five per cent. stock to be given by the government for its subscription. The directors were to be chosen annually and no one of them might be a director in any other bank. The Bank was to commence operations when the second installment was paid. The stockholders were to have one vote for one share or two shares; one vote for every two shares above two and not above 10; one vote for every four shares above 10 and not exceeding 30; one vote for

126

every six shares above 30 and not exceeding 60; one vote for every eight shares above 60 and not exceeding 100; or one vote for every 10 shares above 100; but no one was to have over thirty votes. Stockholders actually resident in the United States and none other might vote by proxy. Five of the elected directors and one of the appointed directors were to go out each year, and no one might be a director more than three years out of four, except the president. The Bank might not buy public stocks nor take over six per cent. for loans. It was forbidden to loan the United States more than $500,000, or any State more than $50,000, or any foreign prince or state anything. It was bound to transfer public funds from place to place at the demand of the Secretary, without charging for difference in exchange. Congress was to charter no other bank during the period of this charter. The Bank was to give to the Secretary of the Treasury, reports of its condition as often as he should require them, "not exceeding once a week." It was allowed to issue post notes for not less than $100, having not more than sixty days to run. The directors of the parent Bank appointed the officers of the branches, and fixed their compensation, and established by-laws for them. It might accept deposits of specie, paying not more than one-half of one per cent. for them. It was bound to keep in separate books the accounts of the government and of private individuals. The total amount of its debts, exclusive of cash deposited, was limited to the amount of its capital, unless Congress should otherwise allow.

This charter was evidently imitated from Hamilton's charter of the first Bank as nearly as personal and party pride would allow. The best criticism on it will be its history, but there are two or three points in regard to it, which produced immediate consequences. The country was suffering from excessive banking, upon which this Bank was to act as a check. It began with a very large capital which it was forced to employ. In the course of events the Secretary found the revenues of 1817 so large that he was able to redeem $13 millions of the public debt in the capital of the Bank during that year. The Bank was therefore forced to employ this large sum actively, even if it had been content otherwise to leave it quiescent in government stocks. At the same time, it became the creditor of the State banks for the vast amount of their notes, with which the Secretary accomplished that redemption. This put it in the power of the Bank, it is true, to exercise the great function, for which it had been created, of regulating the currency, by exerting great pressure on the State banks. It could force them to retire their issues and resume specie payments; but it was sure to arouse angry opposition and complaint. The banks had no desire whatever to be regulated.

In the second place, if the plan of putting public stocks in the capital had had very little ground in the first Bank, it had none in the second, after the war was over. The construction of the Bank on this plan gave unnecessary occasion for cavil at the favor shown to holders of government bonds.

In the third place, there was no reason why the nation should hold any stock in the Bank. The government itself, being destitute of capital and involved in the difficulties of disordered finance, although it was no longer compelled to find means for heavy war expenditures, the example of creating a great stock note with which to buy bank stock, repeating the operation which it had performed with great profit, as we have seen, in the first Bank. it made a note at five per cent., interest payable quarterly, to take stock in a bank which could not be expected to pay over seven per cent. semi-annually. When the troubles came and the Bank paid no dividend, its enemies were fond of figuring up how much the public paid annually for the privilege of being a stockholder.

This, however, only touched upon the profit or loss of the arrangement, not on its propriety. When the government gained by the Bank, as it did later, private individuals naturally asked themselves why they might not, by associating themselves, do the same. Ten men who, individually, could not have borrowed ten dollars apiece, associated themselves into a "bank" and by circulation and deposits borrowed $100,000.

In the fourth place, the arrangement about voting on stock in the Bank, although it was universal and had been borrowed from England, proved mischievous. Some gentlemen at Baltimore who had had great experience in organizing financial institutions had devised the plan of subscribing by attorney. George Williams a government director took 1,172 shares as attorney in the name of 1,172 different persons. In his testimony before the Committee of 1819, he declared that this was a common procedure, which indeed it was, and that the market price of proxies was eleven pence. Baltimore took in all 40,141 shares on 15,628 names, and got 22,137 votes out of 77,759, which was the total number of votes which all the stockholders were entitled to under the rule, taking the subscriptions as they were actually made. The clique at that place thus took less than one-seventh of the shares and got over one-fourth of the votes. At Philadelphia, where one-third of the shares were taken, only two-ninths of the votes where held.

We must also notice that the public expected of the Bank faultless performance of two functions. It was to provide a uniform currency or equalize the exchanges, and it was to collect and pay, on behalf of the Treasury of the United States, at all points and without delay. Under the former head, it was expected not only to furnish notes of its own at a uniform value everywhere, but also to force the local banks to come to an equality by coming to the same standard. The notion of equalizing the exchanges, or making a uniform currency is elusive and illusory. What people meant was that they wanted to be able to put a note in a letter at one place and have it current at par of specie at any place to which it might be sent. In the discussions which arose it was often unclear whether it was expected that all notes should be equally valuable at all places, or at all times, or all equal to each other. The only realizable equality was that all should be brought up to specie at the place of issue and redemption, and in that sense, be equal to each other. The more intelligent demand on the Bank was that it should make its own notes a universal currency, and force the local banks everywhere to keep theirs up to par with those of the Bank.

There was also a very general popular expectation that it would do more than this, and would do away with any rates of exchange, properly speaking, between different points. Great fault was found with it for charging for drafts. It is very clear that too much was expected of it under this head. Considering the immense extent of territory over which its nineteen branches were scattered, and the difficulty, delay, and expense, of transportation and communication, it was not possible, in the early years of its existence, that it should do what was expected of it under either of these heads.

The Bank had also to contend with clamorous demands for branches at a great number of points, with all the familiar phenomena of local jealousy and ambition.

The only measure which was at once adopted, which was calculated to enforce specie payment, was a rule in regard to the currency which the government would receive for its dues. Dallas wrote to Calhoun, March 19, 1816, urging that Congress should designate specie or its equivalent as the only currency which might be accepted at the Treasury; also that it should forbid the deposit of public funds in non-specie-paying banks, and should lay a very heavy tax on any bank notes which were not redeemed in specie on demand. The bank interest in Congress was too strong to allow any such stringent measure to be passed. The result was the resolution of April 29, 1816, that the Secretary should take measures, as soon as may be, to secure payment in specie or United States Bank notes, or treasury notes, or notes of specie paying banks, and that nothing else ought to be received after February 20, 1817. This took from the Secretary the power, after the nominal resumption of specie payments, to reject the notes of banks which pretended to pay specie. The history of the years 1817 to 1819, as far as the interests of the federal Treasury were concerned, would have been quite different if Dallas's recommendation had been adopted. Matthew Carey objected earnestly to this resolution, with the resumption of specie payments which it contemplated. He declared that there was not specie enough on hand or to be had to maintain the system proposed. He wanted specie notes to be used only in part, and for the rest credit notes, by which the bank should pledge itself to receive the notes for specified sums in the payment of debts to itself.

This period was, considering the circumstances, one of active literary discussion on topics of currency, and Carey was one of the most active writers. In a public letter to Calhoun on resumption, he objected to it until the balance of trade should come around so as to protect the specie stock. He objected to the stamp tax, which, as we have seen, Dallas had proposed to be laid on non-resuming banks, because the specie stock was quite inadequate to sustain a general resumption. In his Letters to the Bank Directors of Philadelphia, he described the great prosperity of 1816. It was the golden age of Philadelphia. An immense business was done with great profit, upon bank credit, the banks being very liberal. Superficial observers have blamed them for too free loans, over-issues, and over-trading. These charges were highly unjust. They were only to be blamed for too great loans to some individuals, and for curtailing their loans in order to invest in government securities. He expected the national bank to emancipate men from slavish dependence upon the local banks for loans.

One of the current notions of the time, which always recurs under similar circumstances, was that it was the specie which had advanced and not the paper which had depreciated; and another was that by the advance of civilization and its arts, paper had superseded specie as money. These notions were very wide-spread in England at the time, under the suspension of specie payments by the Bank of England, and they can be traced in the writings of the American pamphleteers. Of the former notion, Raguet said that it was beginning to be abandoned in 1816. Both these doctrines were most ably expounded by Dr. Bollmann in his "Plan of Money Concerns." In this "Plan" he maintained that

132

the general government ought to agree to pay the interest of the public debt in coin, and that the notes of the national bank ought to be payable on demand in six per cent. stock at par, or in specie at the option of the institution. The national bank ought to have no branches, but to be the bank of the banks. The notes of all the banks in any one State should be made convertible on demand in the notes of one designated central bank, and the notes of these chief State banks ought to be redeemable in notes of the national bank. There should be no notes of the national bank under $5, and said notes should be made legal tender. The charter of the Bank of the United States was published in time for him to notice it in a postcript. He was extremely displeased with it. "A volume might be written on this ill-judged scheme."

Carey pronounced Dr. Boilmann's plan a magnificent one, and said: "It would be a sovereign remedy for all the financial difficulties of the country." That plan seems to have influenced the minds of the persons who invented the Pennsylvania "relief" system of 1841.

An anonymous writer of 1819 ridicules the notion of a lack of circulating medium urged in favor of banks of circulation. "Everyone ought to, and will, receive of the circulating medium that quantity which he is entitled to by his property or industry, unless it is diverted from its natural channels by the knavery of banking Legislatures, which is the case in this country." He regarded note-issuers as robbers.

Dallas issued a circular July 22, 1816, in which he called upon the banks, especially those of the Middle States, to meet the Treasury in an effort to put the resolution of April 29th into effect. He proposed that the banks should agree to the publication by the Secretary of a notice that he would not receive, after October 1st, any notes of any bank which did not pay its notes for five dollars or less in specie, and that, after February 20, 1817, the joint resolution should be the rule of the Department. August 6th, a meeting of representatives of the New York, Philadelphia, and Baltimore banks was held at Philadelphia, at which it was voted not to approve of any such notification by the Secretary, and to express to him the opinion that resumption ought not to be attempted before July 1, 1817. It being thus clear that nothing could be obtained from the banks in the way of voluntary co-operation, the Secretary published a notice, September 12th, that the Department would receive after February 20, 1817, only the currency approved in the joint resolution of April 29th. The fact was that there was no authority which could deal with the banks. W.H. Crawford, of Georgia, became Secretary of the Treasury, October 22, 1816. There were at this time 89 banks of deposit. In a letter to the Senate, in 1823, Crawford says that, when he took office, the Treasury had $11 millions in the State banks. Urging them to join the Bank of the United States in resuming, he offered not to draw on them before July 1, 1817, unless his receipts should prove less than his expenditures, which there was no reason to apprehend, and that then he would only draw gradually and not in favor of the Bank of the United States, unless it should be necessary in order to protect that bank against the State banks. They refused. Here certainly there was very dainty action with regard to the "removal of the deposits." His further correspondence with them shows the same disposition on their part, and the same lack of authority on his side. No such insubordination was ever manifested by either Bank of the United States as characterized the State banks in the dealings of the government with them.

Subscriptions for the stock of the Bank of the United States were opened at various points July 1, 1816. When the reports were received, it was found that the subscriptions fell short of the $28 millions open to the public by $3,038,300. Stephen Girard subscribed this sum. The Secretary of the Treasury informed the Commissioners at Philadelphia, August 16th, that the stock had been subscribed, and recommended them to proceed with the necessary preparations for opening the bank.

It has been said above that the public conception of the way in which this bank was to bring about resumption and "equalization of the exchanges" was very vague; but the fear in the State banks that in some way or other it would force resumption was also vague, and their reduction of their liabilities, with an improvement in the exchanges, commenced from the time that the bank stock was subscribed. The banks held large amounts of public stock, as we have seen. These they were unwilling to dispose of for the reduction of their issues, and some complaints arose that they confined their reductions entirely to their discounts. Some of them had lost on public stocks in 1814, and as those securities were now rising, it was a good investment to hold them. These bank contractions arrested the speculations which were in progress, which accounts for Carey's complaint. Others complained far louder than he. Virginia tried to force resumption by a State law, but the opposition prevailed to secure a postponement of the day set and, subsequently, a return to inflation. However, in the latter part of 1816, no crisis or panic at all occurred. No evidence of distress in the business of the country appeared. The exchanges steadily improved down to the day fixed for resumption. At the end of July, specie was at par at Boston, at five per cent. premium at New York, at eleven or twelve per cent. premium at Philadelphia, at fourteen or fifteen per cent. premium at Baltimore. Southern and western notes were generally at a discount of about the cost of shipping specie from the place at which they were issued to the place at which the quotation was made. In September, it was announced that the New York banks were paying specie.

In November, the comparative quotations of public stock show that the currency of Boston and Charleston was at par, that of New York, at one and a-half per cent. discount, that of Philadelphia at six per cent. discount, and that of Baltimore at nine per cent. discount. A Treasury circular was issued January 28, 1817, to the banks of Pennsylvania, Delaware, and Maryland, stating that the Bank of the United States had been authorized to receive the public deposits in those banks, the manner of transfer being left to that Bank. February 1, 1817, the banks of New York, Philadelphia, and Baltimore agreed to resume on the 20th of February, the day which the Treasury Department had proposed and always adhered to, the Bank of the United States promising not to call on them for balances until after it should have discounted for individuals at New York $2 millions, at Philadelphia $2 millions, at Baltimore $1.5 millions and in Virginia $500,000. February 22nd, the quotations of the exchanges were at New York, in the local currency, Boston one premium; Philadelphia par to one-quarter discount; Baltimore three-quarters discount; Virginia and North Carolina one-half discount; South Carolina and Georgia par; New Orleans two discount.

During the whole of the Fall and Winter, the foreign exchanges were favorable and silver was imported in great amount. It must be remembered that irredeemable paper was in use at this time nearly all over Europe, except in France. The English bank notes were depreciated from six per cent. to ten per cent., although rapidly improving during this year by the destruction of large numbers of country banks. This depreciation abroad made it easier to draw specie to America.

The important point now, for our purpose, is, that on the day appointed for resumption, February 20, 1817, the currency had been, in fact, brought to specie par all over the country. To secure resumption it was only necessary to still further withdraw bank notes, which would have been replaced by silver, and would have been no contraction.

The Bank of the United States was organized November 1, 1816. Ten of the elected directors were federalists and ten republicans. The President appointed five republicans. November 28th, Niles's Register reported: "United States Bank scrip has sold at Philadelphia for $42.50 on the original installment. Speculation is the order of the day." Such indeed was the fact. Stock jobbing with the shares of the Bank began from the first subscription and was carried on most vigorously by the officers and directors of the Bank.

The second installment was due January 1, 1817. Ten dollars per share would then become due in specie. Specie, however, was then still at six per cent. premium in Philadelphia. At a directors' meeting December 18th, it was voted to make loans on stock in order to facilitate the payment of the specie portion of this second installment.

December 27th, other votes were passed, in form restricting these loans somewhat, but really only limiting the advantage to a few. Measures were taken to buy and import specie for the account of the Bank. During the two years, 1817 and 1818, the Bank imported $7,311,750 in specie, at an expense of $525,297. Upon the inquiry which was subsequently made, the bank officers declared that they could not distinguish in their accounts so as to tell how much specie had been paid in at the second installment. The amount of specie in the Bank, in January, 1817, was $1,724,109, which was only $324,109 more than the specie part of the first installment, and the latter sum is therefore the utmost which could have been paid in on the second installment, when it was intended and expected that $2.8 millions would be paid in specie. Checks on the Bank and on other banks which claimed to pay specie, as well as notes of the latter, were taken as equivalent to specie. Everyone who was acquainted with the methods of banking of the time declared that no specie would be added to the stock of the Bank by the second or third installment. Crawford, in 1820, showed that such was the usual practice in organizing banks. "The reason why a bank of $35 millions could be created in 1816, was simply that there was then a large amount of funded debt of the United States incorporated in the capital, rendering it necessary for the subscribers to raise less than $5,000,000 in specie before the Bank went into operation."

The measures which had been adopted in the Bank encouraged the stock jobbing. The discounts were not even restrained to the coin part of the second installment, but, in some favored cases, reached the total amount of the first two installments. After February 20th, this became the general rule, although the second installment, in many cases, had not yet been paid.

"The discounts, the payment of the second installment, the payment of the price to the owner, the transfer, and the pledge of the stock were, as it is termed, simultaneous acts." At the end of December, 1816, the stock was at 41 7-8 for 30 paid; in April at 81, and in May at 98 for 65 paid; August 20th, at 144 for 100 paid; and August 30th, at 156 1-2, where it stood for a few days.

Some suspicion of the proceedings in the Bank was aroused in the public mind, and strong criticism was provoked. January 6, 1817, Forsyth introduced in the House of Representatives, a resolution of inquiry whether the payment of the specie part of the second installment had been avoided. The Committee on Currency addressed an inquiry to Mr. Lloyd, a director of the Bank, who chanced to be in Washington. He replied, on the 9th, admitting that discounts had been made to facilitate the second payment, but excusing it on the ground that the payments would not otherwise have been made. The only penalty for non-payment was to lose any dividend which might be declared, and this, he said, was not sufficient. In fact, the discounts did not cause the installments to be paid, but enabled the stock to be carried until it could be sold at an advance. The Committee transmitted Lloyd's letter in answer to Forsyth's resolution, whereupon Forsyth introduced another resolution, January 13th, that the bank should not be allowed to go into operation, or to receive public deposits, until the second installment was paid, according to the charter. This resolution was not acted on until the end of the session, when it was indefinitely postponed for want of time, on Forsyth's own motion.

January 30, 1817, the directors of the Bank voted to issue post notes at sixty days for loans granted.

Thus it was that the great Bank, instead of acting as a check to inflation, adopted all the worst methods of bank organization of the time, and joined in the career of inflation. "The Bank did not exercise with sufficient energy the power which it possessed and might have retained, but rather afforded inducements to the State Banks to extend the amount of their circulating notes, and thus increased one of the evils it was intended to correct." From the very brink of resumption the great Bank carried the whole country back into the slough of inflation and depreciation.

Its notes, being redeemable at any branch, became at once a good and cheap remittance. Boston was then the money market of the country, and the Middle States were in the debtor relation to the East. Notes of the Baltimore branch were advertised for sale at Boston a few days after the branch at the latter place went into operation. The Boston and New York branches were busy redeeming the notes issued by the Baltimore branch, and the parent Bank had to send them continually new supplies of silver. From March, 1817, to December, 1818, $1,622,800 in specie were sent to Boston and $6,293,192 to New York. During the latter half of the year 1818, the sum sent to Boston was small, because treasury drafts were issued to the Baltimore branch on the northern branches, drawing to it the public deposits. First, therefore, the Baltimore branch drew to itself the capital of the Boston branch, and then it drew to itself the public deposits. January 3, 1818, the Baltimore branch owed the other branches $9.5 millions. The silver paid out by the northern branches was shipped to India and China, for which fact the merchants in that trade were denounced as enemies of their country. The banks of Massachusetts resisted the payment of deposits to the Bank of the United States, because they held specie paid in by the people of Massachusetts, and wanted the same or their own notes paid out to them. It seemed that the Middle States, which had gone so deeply into the paper system, had now organized a big bank to draw the specie which the Eastern States had kept during the war, giving United States bank notes for it. Here, then, we find that in the East the operation of the Bank was to draw into the paper system this section which had thus far kept out of it. In 1814, the Boston banks had circulation and deposits to the amount of $1.66 for every $1 in specie they possessed; in 1815, $2,07; in 1816, $3.45; in 1817, $4.08; in 1818, $5.78. The ratio then improved until 1821, when it was $2.58. Silver was at seven per cent. premium in Boston, October 17, 1818.

If we now turn our attention to the Western States, we find that the notes issued by the branches there were obtained on easy credit and remitted East in purchase of commodities. The cashier of the branch at Lexington, Kentucky, being alarmed at this remittance of his notes to be redeemed at Philadelphia, thought best to use the notes of the State banks, and to restrict his own circulation. For this he received a rebuke of extraordinary severity from the president of the parent Bank, who instructed him that his business was to issue and circulate his own notes, and directed him to sell drafts at a low enough rate to hinder the shipment of his notes, and to buy drafts when he could get them. This drew out a remonstrance from Crawford, who warned the Bank that the public, who had been pleased at the apparent success of the Bank in equalizing the exchanges [that is, the improvement of the exchanges up to February 20, 1817], would be very much dissatisfied if it should now appear that the Bank and its branches were about to establish a system of internal exchanges, "without reference to the commercial relation which exists between the two places." In fact this arrangement made little difference in respect to the operation of the Bank on the western country. The loans were repaid in local notes, which accumulated in the branch until they were presented for redemption; then the silver obtained for them was shipped eastward. At the same time the notes of the United States Bank and the local banks together increased to occupy the space left, and then to become redundant and depreciate. Therefore in this section also the operation of the Bank was mischievous, and we find it drawing into the inflation another section which had not yet taken part in it. In the South it had very much the same effect, although that effect was not developed until somewhat later.

The Bank had scarcely gone into operation before it began to make difficulties about paying specie for its notes without reference to the place of issue. Jones wrote that it would furnish weapons for its own destruction by so doing. He illustrates this as follows: "During the existence of the late compact between the Bank of the United States and the State banks [that the former would not demand balances of the latter until it had discounted to a certain amount in the large cities], it became necessary to level the exchange from Washington to Boston, whatever might be the cost or hazard of the undertaking, inasmuch as the Bank of the United States had engaged to receive on deposit, and of course to pay in specie, the paper of all the contracting banks, and to permit them to check on each other for the liquidation of the public balances, the payment of which was suspended. The consequence was that each check impaired the value of the debt due to the Bank of the United States by substituting paper less valuable than that of the original debtor. It was soon discovered that this practice was not confined to the liquidation of the public balances, but was made to embrace the current business between the banks of the respective cities. The banks in New York discounted paper payable in Philadelphia, and those in Philadelphia discounted paper payable in New York. The Bank of the United States and its offices were made the instruments to place the amount of these transactions in specie wherever money was most in demand."

The pretended resumption of 1817 was unreal. It never was accomplished. In 1820, Secretary Crawford said that, for most of the time since resumption, the convertibility of bank notes into specie had been rather nominal than real in the great portion of the Union.

By May, 1817, complaints began to be heard that the resumption was only nominal. May 17th, Niles said: "Though our banks ostensibly pay specie, it is almost as rare as it was some months ago to see a dollar."

The third installment of the capital of the Bank became due July 1st. Little notice was taken of it, and it seems to have been paid much as the subscribers chose. No specie was paid in, although $2.8 millions should now have been paid, according to the charter, and as public stocks had risen above the rates at which they were receivable in the capital, and as the amount of public stocks held by the Bank was subsequently found to be deficient, it appears that a large part of this installment was paid in bank notes or by stock notes. July 25th, the directors voted that the branches might make loans on pledge of Bank stock. August 26th, they voted to make loans on the stock of the Bank at 125, giving as a reason that it had been taken as collateral for loans at that rate in New York. The Committee of 1819 could not find that this was true. An endorser was at first required for the amount above par, but later this was not insisted on. September 30th, the president and cashier were authorized to renew notes discounted on pledges of stock. The president and some of the directors were deeply engaged in the stock jobbing. The former had a very large interest, on which he suffered a loss. The stock began to decline at the end of September, and in December, 1818, was at 110.

October 11, 1817, Niles said: "Though the Bank of the United States and its branches has had a considerable effect to equalize the exchange of moneys between different places, being assisted in its operation by the natural courses of trade, still the people are inundated with paper called bank notes at almost every depreciated rate, one-half to seventy-five per cent."

The important incidents of the period of inflation; in the banking history of the several States, were as follows:

The Legislature of MASSACHUSETTS, in 1812, tried to reduce the number of banks by refusing to renew the charters which expired in that year. The New England Bank was chartered June 6, 1813. It constituted another attempt to deal with the circulation of the country notes in Boston, on which the discount was then from three per cent. to five per cent. It undertook to send home these foreign bills, as they were

144

called, to the banks which issued them, at the cost of the operation. This rapidly reduced the discount on the country notes. In January, 1814, it sent certain New York bank notes home for redemption to the amount of $138,874. "This silver Was put into three wagons, which proceeded on their way hither as far as Chester, 14 miles. There they were seized by order of the Collector of New York, commanded back, and the money deposited in the vaults of the Manhattan Bank, of which he was a director. Though a protest was handed to him against such a course as illegal, by the agent, yet he declined to alter his purpose. He assigned as a reason for this procedure that he suspected such cash was going to Canada. Many this way supposed that he was chiefly actuated by dislike to the frequency with which the New England Bank dispatched large sums of the New York bills which flooded Massachusetts, to be redeemed with dollars. On being made acquainted with these facts, the General Court resolved that the conduct of the collector in this respect is a violation of his duty and an infringement on the rights of the New England Bank. They also decided to have the matter laid before the President of the United States, with the expression of their judgment, that the collector had committed an outrage on one of their corporations, ought to relinquish the deposit, and be dismissed from his office. Such application so far succeeded as to have the money restored."

During the war, the banks would not lend to the State, at the risk of increasing their issues. February 6, 1816, an act was passed to compel them to do so when necessity might arise. In the summer of that year, the Dedham Bank issued a quantity of paper in the form of drafts on a bank at Middletown, Connecticut, payable to bearer, which led to an act of December 13, 1816, which enacted that all the notes and obligations of banking institutions should be payable in specie at their own counters. The Court in King *vs.* the Dedham Bank, held that this law was void as to issues made before its passage. Before that, therefore, these Massachusetts banks had been able to issue drafts which were used as currency. In 1817, notes for less than $1 became very abundant. They were forbidden February 3, 1818.

NEW YORK.—Credit notes, by their tenor only receivable by a bank for dues to itself, were, by a law of 1816, made recoverable in money, and banks were forbidden to issue any notes payable otherwise than in money.

The law of this State forbade any unauthorized association to issue notes. In 1818, this prohibition was extended to persons, and both persons and associations were forbidden to do any kind of banking unless chartered so to do. Jacob Barker's Exchange Bank was excepted for three years. The act was called for on account of the mass of fractional notes which had been issued by all kinds of persons and corporations.

PENNSYLVANIA.—At the session of 1812 and 1813, twenty-five banks were chartered by the Legislature in one bill. The total capital was $9,525,000. The bill passed both Houses by a majority of only one vote in each and was vetoed by the Governor. "At the following session the subject was renewed with increased ardor and a bill authorizing the incorporation of forty-one banking institutions, with capitals amounting to upwards of $17 millions was passed by a large majority." It was vetoed by the Governor, but passed by the constitutional majority and became a law March 21, 1814.

146

Under it thirty-seven banks were organized; four of them in Philadelphia.

VIRGINIA.—The Bank of Virginia and the Farmers' Bank were authorized October 19, 1814, to issue one's, two's and three's, but not to increase their total circulation, until six months after the peace.

February 19, 1816, perhaps with some reference to the incident narrated on page 70, provision was made by law for suits against corporations including banks, and for writs of execution against them; service to be on the chief officers; levy might be made on the current money as well as on the goods and chattels. February 23d, a summary proceeding was provided against any bank which did not pay specie after the 15th of the following November, six per cent. interest being imposed and a levy on property of the bank anywhere in the State being authorized. This remedy was not given to any bank or its agent. This appeared to commit Virginia to a resolute policy of resumption; but on November 14th following, this act was suspended for a month, and then for six months, although banks which did not pay specie for their notes under $1 after January 10, 1817, were excepted from the indulgence.

All unchartered banks were made illegal, February 26, 1816. If any such issued notes, the officers and partners were liable to fine. Such notes were null and void. The fine for signing was threefold the amount of notes signed. Such a company could not recover in any court in the State. Such illegal notes under $1 being in circulation, the holder of one of them may recover $5 from the issuer or signer. November 15th, this act was suspended as to ten enumerated companies and banks until August 31, 1817, in order to give them more

147

time to wind up. On the following day this extension was granted for four more. January 5, 1816 a long report on banks, resumption, etc., was presented to the House of Delegates. It ended with a proposition to establish fourteen banks in various counties up and down the State. This committee stated that, before the war, the notes of eastern banks were at a premium of two or three per cent. in the West. During the war those of the western banks came to bear about the same premium in the East. Since the war the former state of things had returned. This no doubt refers especially to Virginia and Kentucky, and it may be only a reminiscence of the effects of the rising tide of inflation in the two sections at different times.

The Northwestern Bank of Virginia was chartered February 5, 1817, at Wheeling; capital not less than $400,000 nor more than $600,000; to be paid in in coin. A peculiar provision was here introduced that 15 per cent. of the capital should be created in additional stock to be given to the State as a fund for internal improvements. It was to be paid for "by charging an equal proportion of the amount thereof on each share disposed of to subscribers."

This amount was to be paid in in thirty semi-annual installments, the first one on the day of the first dividend, out of which such installment was to be retained, if the dividend sufficed for it; if not, the shares were to be assessed and any stockholder who did not pay the assessment was to forfeit his stock. Three branches were provided for. It was to last until 1834. Evidently the payment to be made by each stockholder on his stock, in order to pay for that given to the State, was one-half of one per cent. each six months, which was to come out of his dividend if it exceeded that amount. This bank was

148

to make no loan for longer than 120 days; to issue no notes under $5; and to have three State directors. In the same act the Bank of the Valley in Virginia was chartered with similar details throughout. The State might sell its stock in each at will, and 15 per cent. penalty was imposed, with forfeiture of the charter, for failure to redeem.

The complaints about the unauthorized note issuers came up again in 1820, for they continued their operations. New penalties were imposed, including imprisonment from one to twelve months for individuals, and a fine of $50 on corporations. A fine between $10 and $100 was imposed on bringing such notes into the State with intent to circulate them, and a fine of $10 for offering to pay or pass them.

The Northwestern Bank did not pay the contributions to the State stock promptly. Therefore an act of January 7, 1822, provided that the notes of the Northwestern Bank and the Valley Bank should be receivable for taxes as long as they pay specie, and if the former pays up its arrears on the State stock. The charter of the Farmers' Bank was extended March 6, 1824, for fifteen years, and it was brought under the same law of penalty for suspension, etc., as the Northwestern Bank. A bonus of $50,000 was exacted for internal improvements, which sum must be paid out of dividends on the stock not owned by the State.

NORTH CAROLINA.—The charter of the Banks of Cape Fear and Newbern were extended, in 1814, until 1835; the capital of the former might be increased $525,000; that of the latter, $575,000. Each bank was bound to lend to the State not more than one-tenth of its capital at not more than six per cent. An option was reserved for the State on 1,000 shares in each, of which 180 shares were to be given to the State as a

149

bonus, and the State might pay for the 410 shares with its own treasury notes. The remaining 410 shares were to be paid for at the convenience of the State. The debts of either bank might not exceed all cash deposits by more than $2,400,000. The State paper was not to be a legal tender to either of these banks, but only to the Bank of the State after January 1, 1816. No notes were to be issued under $1. Treasury notes were to be issued for the sum of $82,000 in denominations of five cents, ten cents, twenty cents, etc., all of which were to be paid over to the two banks in payment of the first installment ($10 per share) on 410 shares in each. They were to bear no interest; were to be issued by the banks and redeemed by the Treasurer; to be re-issued by him. If the Bank of the State should be voluntarily dissolved before December 18, 1816, these banks were to take up the State paper with their own paper, at the rate of $1 for 10 shillings. If this was done, the Governor was to proclaim that the State notes were not a legal tender, except to these banks until their charters expire, after which, if State notes are still out, they were to be legal tender again; but the dividends on the stock owned by the State were to be employed in redeeming them.

A Committee of the Legislature in 1828-9 reported, in regard to the banks of Cape Fear and Newbern, that the increase of their capital in 1814 was paid for by stock notes of favored individuals. "It follows that the whole amount of the interest drawn from the people on the loans made on this fictitious capital was a foul and illegal extortion. * * * Taking the issues made on this fabricated capital, to be in proportion with those made on the former capital, they must have put into circulation on the faith of the assumed stock, between $3 millions and $4 millions of notes, and thus a parcel of individuals under the name of stockholders, but who in fact held no stock, contrived to exchange their notes without interest to the amount of $3 millions or $4 millions for the notes of the people bearing an interest of more than six per cent., and while the property of the people was pledged for the payment of the notes they had given to the stockholders, there was not a dollar or an atom of property pledged to them for the payment of the notes they had received *from* the stockholders."

This State passed a law against due bills and small promissory notes in 1816, declaring that the abuse was increasing and was very detrimental to the true interests of the State. It appears that schools and academies were making such issues. "It shall not be lawful for any person or persons to pass or receive any check or checks drawn for less than $1 on the State Bank, the Banks of Newbern or Cape Fear, or the various branches or agencies thereof, for the benefit of any academy, school, or corporation, or company of private citizens, or any check or checks drawn on any person or persons whatever." The penalty was £10, half to the prosecutor. Issuing notes without authority was punishable with a fine of £100 and imprisonment for six months. At the same session so much of an act to incorporate a school, and of another act to incorporate a manufacturing company, as might by construction authorize either of them to issue notes was repealed. If they did not pay on demand, the holder might recover, as the law expresses it, 100 per cent. on the principal sum. An alteration was also made in the charter of the Bank of the State, providing that the Treasurer should cause $80,000 to be printed in treasury notes, in denominations from five cents to seventy-five cents, redeemable and re-issuable by the Treasurer, to be in part payment of the debt of the State to the bank.

In regard to the Bank of the State, the committee of 1828-9 said that: In 1818, the proportion between its notes and circulation, was one to twelve; in that year $424,000 of stock unsold was sold for their own notes, in order to reduce the amount of them. This the committee calls a "scribbling process." While this operation was pending, the three banks entered into a formal agreement, July, 1819, not to pay specie, and their notes fell at once to 85. Up to this time there had been inflation and prosperity. "A scene of extortion and usury ensued which has no parallel in the annals of avarice; the strange spectacle of moneyed institutions exacting specie in exchange for their notes, which they themselves refused to redeem with specie."

SOUTH CAROLINA.—The Bank of the State of South Carolina was chartered, December 19, 1812, as a measure of relief after the sufferings from the embargo, and the preamble of the charter stated that it was "deemed expedient and beneficial, both to the State and the citizens thereof, to establish a bank on the funds of the State, for the purpose of discounting paper and making loans for longer periods than have heretofore been customary, and on security different from what has hitherto been required." All stock of the United States, loan office bonds, bank shares, and credits belonging to the State are to be put in this bank, and the faith of the State is pledged to make good any deficiencies; public deposits to be placed in it; to lend on two-name paper and on real and personal property, the borrower giving power of attorney to confess judgment; no loan to run more than a year; no renewal to be granted unless the next year's interest is paid in advance; no loan to one person to exceed $2,000; one-tenth of each loan to be called in in each year; prompt execution to be enforced against defaulters; the Legislature to elect a president and twelve directors; to issue no note under $1; to be called the Bank of the State of South Carolina; to be situated at Charleston, with a branch at Columbia. The loans on mortgage were to be apportioned between the election districts; all stock owned by the State in other banks might be sold and the proceeds turned into this one. The State might issue $300,000 of six per cent. stock, the proceeds to go into the funds of this bank. The notes were to be receivable by the State. Five commissioners were to be appointed in each district to appraise the lands on which loans were wanted. In an explanatory act, a year later, it was enacted that no other bank should issue notes under $5, which gave this bank a monopoly of small notes. December 21, 1814, the Bank of the State was required to issue notes under $1, and no one but the chartered banks was to be allowed to issue circulating paper. The city of Charleston was given until January 1, 1816, to call in its bills of credit. The Bank of the State was authorized to deal in inland exchange, December 15, 1815. At this time, also, the connection of the State with the old "State Bank" was dissolved, except by virtue of the stock which it still held. The Bank of the State was charged, December 17, 1816, with the liquidation of the old loan office of the State, which was still dragging along a load of bad debts. It was to sell the land which had been mortgaged to that office, but was not to call up in any one year more than one-third of the debt. The effect of the war finance is seen in an act of December 17, 1817, that all the banks in the State may invest not over half their capital in stocks of the State or the United States.

In 1819, October 1st, the directors of the Bank of the State of South Carolina published an anti-bullionist argument against resumption. It did not resume until 1823. The United States Bank at Charleston used its paper.

GEORGIA.—The Bank of the State of Georgia was chartered December 16, 1815, with a capital of $1,500,000, $600,000 of which was to be reserved for the State until January 1, 1817; the State to appoint six out of fifteen directors; to organize when $250,000 in specie paid in; the circulation never to exceed three times the capital; to last until 1835. The Governor was at once authorized to act upon the right reserved to the State. He was to make the subscription as well as he could, so as to give the next Legislature a chance to appropriate for it. The Governor in his message of 1816, tells how this bank was organized. It was forbidden to go into operation until $250,000 were on hand in specie. The State had to come forward and subscribe the requisite amount from its own part of the capital. This it did in notes of the Augusta and Planters' Banks. Instead of presenting these for redemption, the Governor entered into a negotiation with those banks to "advance" the specie on "a deposit of their own notes." No doubt therefore this bank was organized after the fashion of others at the time, by borrowing specie long enough to defeat the law.

December 18, 1816, the Governor was ordered to assign to the branch of the Bank of the State at Milledgeville a room in the State-house, to be used as its banking office. December 19th, it was enacted that no unincorporated association should thereafter issue a note for $2 and above. In case of violation, the holder might recover one hundred and twenty-five per cent. of the note. If anyone but an incorporated bank

154

should issue notes for less than $2, the noteholder might recover three times the value. Twenty per cent. tax was laid on such unauthorized notes already in circulation. The banks of Georgia were ordered to resume when the Bank of the United States and the banks of the neighboring States should begin specie payment. After that time, any noteholder might recover twenty-five per cent. until the notes were paid in specie. Two years later another very stringent act was passed against unlicensed banking.

The Bank of Darien began a very checkered career December 15, 1818. Its capital was to be $1,000,000, half of which was reserved for the State until January 1, 1820. It was to last until 1837, and its charter was to be forfeited if it did not pay specie on demand.

CHAPTER VI.

Inflation in the Mississippi Valley

The inflation in the Mississippi Valley began at the end of 1815. The president of the Bank of the United States stated to the Committee of 1819 that when the Bank stock was subscribed, specie was at six per cent. premium in the West, and at fourteen per cent. premium at New York, Philadelphia and Baltimore. The inflation advanced rapidly during 1816 in Kentucky and Tennessee, and spread in that and the following years to Indiana, Illinois and Missouri.

KENTUCKY.—The popular party had now fallen under the dominion of a mania for banks, as the institutions which could make everybody rich. Clamorous demands were made for a share in the blessings which the Bank of the United States was expected to shower upon the country, and two branches were established as soon as the Bank was organized—one at Lexington and one at Louisville. Prices immediately began to rise, specie was exported, and contracts were entered into, in the expectation of further advance. All hastened to get into debt, especially for the purchase of land, which, in a country of new settlement, always offers a tempting chance for those who have already settled to make profits out of the new comers. "Deeds in old books of record show the to us astonishing fact that town lots on the back streets of the suburbs of Shepherdsville brought prices on time that would now [1882] be esteemed great for the best property in Louisville. ... Every salt lick and sulphur well

156

was marked as a fountain of prospective wealth, and eagerly bargained for at astonishing values. ... The most active speculators were those whose means were small."

February 4, 1815, the capital of the Bank of Kentucky was increased to $2 millions, half the increase to be taken by the State. The bank and branches might deal in exchange, United States treasury notes and bonds, and might lend to non-residents and to the United States not more than $500,000 for not more than two years. There were two significant features in this law. First, it tried to construe more strictly the limit set by the original charter on the amount of loans which a director might have; and second, it enacted that the notes of the bank and its branches should be current at all branches and receivable for debts to them all. This bank suspended in 1815, as we learn from resolutions of the Legislature, approving of that action. A committee of the Legislature examined the bank, and its report was printed, with a letter of the president, giving the reasons for suspension. We have a statement of the condition of this bank in February, 1817, according to which it had a capital of $2 millions, loans $4 millions, cash deposits $1.3 millions, circulation $1.9 millions, cash $1.2 millions.

The circulation of notes by persons or associations not authorized by law was forbidden January 28, 1817, under a penalty of ten times the amount. Everyone who passed such a note was required to endorse it, and was liable to the same penalty. The law was not applicable to notes over $2, and was limited to February 1, 1818.

The State was not able to take the shares in the Bank of Kentucky which had been reserved for it. It was ordered, February 3, 1817, that the same should be sold for not less than 102, in order to increase the active capital. By the same act, the limitation on loans to directors was relaxed in respect to bills of exchange created by the exportation of products of the State; but this was not to be construed to warrant dealing in bills "founded on a speculative system of acceptances." The obligation to receive all notes at all branches was also limited to the payment of debts to the bank.

January 26, 1818, the act was passed which stood first amongst the great and fateful acts of legislation of this period of infatuation. At first twenty-four banks were established at the more important points up and down the State, with an aggregate capital of $5,870,000; then the act starts off again and provides for four more with a total capital of $400,000; then twelve more are provided for, with a total capital of $1,650,000, so that there were forty in all with $8 millions of capital. The capital was to be paid in in current money, notes of the Bank of the United States, or of the Bank of Kentucky, in five installments. The president and directors might extend the time for the three last installments as they should see fit. The banks were incorporated until 1837; were to begin when one-fifth of the capital was paid in; were never to owe, exclusive of deposits, more than three times the capital; to pay the State one-half of one per cent. on each share annually; and any one of them was to cease to exist if it did not redeem its issues in specie, United States Bank notes, or Bank of Kentucky notes. Any bank whose stock was not sold within eighteen months was not to be organized. February 3d, a supplementary act was passed, providing for six more banks which seem to have been forgotten, with a capital of $9 millions. On the same day with the last act, the corporate powers of the old Kentucky Insurance Company were extended for two years in order to wind up. It was forbidden to issue notes after January 1, 1818.

TENNESSEE.—The neighboring States were also now well started on the road of inflation. The State Bank of Tennessee was authorized to issue notes down to $1, by an act of October 3, 1815. November 17th three banks were incorporated, each with a capital of $200,000, of which $15,000 was subscribed by the State. November 26th, the Bank of the State and Nashville Bank were authorized to unite and to absorb either of the others. The Bank of Nashville had suspended in July or August, in'connection with the suspensions in the East.

In 1815, OHIO commenced a war which she carried on longer and more vigorously, because apparently with less success, than any other State, against unauthorized bank notes. She also tried to impose taxation on her banks, and her first steps in this direction are especially noteworthy because they show that her attempt to tax the Bank of the United States, a few years later, was not an isolated act against that Bank. February 10, 1815, it was enacted that every banking company in the State should pay annually four per cent. on its dividends. If any bank failed to report, the Auditor was to levy one per cent. on the nominal capital of the bank. The Sheriff was to present the bill of the Auditor to the bank and if it was not paid at once, with four per cent. additional for the Sheriff's fees, he was to levy on the specie and notes. If he could not obtain enough of these, he was to seize any other property of the bank, advertise, and sell it. All contracts with persons or firms issuing notes, without being authorized by law so to do, were to be void. Signing or issuing such notes was made punishable by imprisonment for one year and a

159

fine not exceeding $5,000. The act was not to affect unincorporated banks which began before January 1, 1815, until after January 1, 1818.

February 14th, the Governor was authorized to borrow of the banks $155,000 for one year, at six per cent., in order to make up the State's quota of the direct tax.

At the next session another war was begun against persons acting as agents of any bank of issue chartered by the laws of another State. A law of January 27, 1816, imposed a fine of $1,000 for each offense. The use of the Courts and of the processes of justice were forbidden to all such agencies. Anyone interested in such a bank was made personally liable to any noteholder. Such banks or agencies were allowed until January 1, 1817, to wind up, and a half dozen banks which were named were allowed to go on one year longer. February 23d, six banks were incorporated in one act, each to have a capital of $100,000, and to last until 1843. Seven of the unincorporated companies with which the State had been at war were also incorporated by the same act. Each bank was to "set off" to the State one share in twenty-five before beginning, and so afterwards for any increase. The certificates for these shares were to go to the Auditor, and they were to draw dividends like tho others. Each bank was to save from its profits a sum which at the expiration of the charter would pay to the State the capital value of shares so set off to it. The State was to re-invest the dividends from each bank in shares of that bank, until it should own one-sixth of the capital. The bank, if necessary, was to make new shares to meet this provision. All former charters were extended to 1843, if the banks should respectively accept this act. When the State should own one-sixth of a bank, the dividends were to go into the available revenue of the treasury. Banks which came into this scheme were not to be taxed. Any bank which violated it was to forfeit its charter. The act was to be construed "benignly and favorably." For some years afterwards this act was treated as a general banking law.

In 1816 and 1817 bank charters were rapidly multiplied. In that of the Bank of Hamilton it is first provided that the capital shall be paid up in "money of the United States;" in that of Galipolis it is first provided that the Governor shall send a commissioner to see that $20,000 is actually in hand, half in specie and half in United States Bank notes, before it may begin.

The Farmers' and Mechanics' Bank of INDIANA was incorporated September 6, 1814, and the Bank of Vincennes, September 10th. The following mysterious paragraph from a law of December 26, 1815, seems to show that the Territory was infested by persons who were issuing notes without authority. "If any person or persons in this Territory shall sign, issue, pass, exchange, or circulate any due bill, promissory note, bank note, or instrument of writing for the payment of any money or property, or performance of any covenant or contract, purporting to be the act of any bank, company, secret society, or set of men in this Territory other than is or are expressed by name, upon the face of such due bill, promissory note, bank note, or instrument of writing, so as to gain a credit and trust in some unknown person, company, or set of men, to the holder of such note, due bill, or instrument of writing, besides the signer or signers thereof," he shall be fined three times the sum in the note and be liable to the noteholder for the amount. This is not to

161

affect any bank chartered by this Territory, and any one may recover what he can in payment of "bank notes of any secret company or set of men" or of any other paper; but it applies to the bank notes of the Indiana Manufacturing Company at Lexington, Indiana. Passing any counterfeit bank note knowingly was to be punished by a fine of three times the value, and twenty-five to fifty lashes on his or her bare back.

The Bank of Vincennes was adopted as the State Bank of Indiana, until October 1, 1835, by a law of January 1, 1817. An additional capital of $1 million was to be raised, of which $375,000 was reserved for the State. Arrangements were made for receiving subscriptions all over the State. Branches were to be established. The Farmers' and Mechanics' Bank might become a branch. Three State directors were to be elected by the Legislature, and a greater number when the State should subscribe more, but never more than five out of fifteen. The greatest amount which it might be called upon to lend the State was $50,000 for five years. No director might borrow more than $5,000 at one time, or have endorsements in the bank for more than $10,000. December 31st, the State renounced its right to subscribe 2,500 shares in the Farmers' and Mechanics' Bank.

Before the war of 1812 money was scarcely ever seen in ILLINOIS, the skins of animals supplying its place. The money which was brought in after the war turned the heads of the people so that by the whole country was in a rage for speculation. At that period "the country was flooded with bank notes, good, bad, and indifferent. Many counterfeit notes were in circulation.

The custom was to make contracts in "trade at trade rates," which was a system of barter, and displaced money just as it

162

had done in the colonies. Factory goods from New England and Kentucky reached that region about 1818, and the domestic textile industry ceased. Until 1833 there was no legal limit to the rate of interest. The common rate by contract was about 50 per cent. A law of the Territory, January 11, 1816, imposed very heavy penalties on counterfeiting, a peculiar feature being that the law applied whether the bank whose notes were counterfeited was in existence or not. December 28, 1816, the Bank of Illinois at Shawneetown was incorporated, with a capital of $300,000, of which the State might take one-third; to last until 1837. It was never to suspend under a penalty of 12 per cent. It is said of it in its earlier period that it was "so well managed that neither the government nor anyone else lost by it. The Bank of Kaskaskia was incorporated by the Legislative Council of the Territory January 9, 1818. Its capital was $300,000. It was to begin when $50,000 were subscribed and $10,000 paid in, and to last until 1838. On the same day the Bank of Edwardsville was incorporated with a capital of $300,000, of which one-third might be taken by the State. It was to begin when $10,000 were paid in. Upon subscription, $5 were to be paid in in specie or "bank bills which will command the same." It was to last until 1838. In the charters which were framed on the model of that of the Bank of the United States, the provision that the debts, exclusive of deposits, should never exceed a certain amount, presents a great number of variations. Apparently it was often not understood. In this charter the clause reads that the debts "shall not exceed twice the amount of their capital stock actually paid over, and above the moneys then actually deposited in the bank for safe keeping." It was never to suspend under a 12 per cent. penalty.

On the same day the city and Bank of Cairo were also incorporated. The owners of the point of land at the junction of the rivers are named, and their opinion is recorded that "no position in the whole extent of these western States is better calculated as respects commercial advantages, and local supplies, for a great and important city;" but the inundations are a drawback and dykes are needed. The proprietors desire to devote one-third of the proceeds of land sales to dykes, etc., and two-thirds to banking. They are incorporated by this act, as the president, directors, and company of the Bank of Cairo, for thirty years. Streets and lots are to be laid out and the price of the latter is limited to $150 each. Of this sum, one-third is set apart for a fund for the improvement of the city, and the other two-thirds goes into the capital of the bank, half of it belonging to the purchaser and half to the company. The bank is to be organized when 500 lots are sold, payment being due in three installments within six months. The bank is to be at Kaskaskia and the lots are to be distributed "by lottery." The debts over the specie paid into the bank are never to exceed twice the paid up capital. The capital of the bank is never to exceed $500,000, and it is never to suspend under a penalty of 12 per cent.

A Bank of the State of Illinois was incorporated March 22, 1819, but the charter was immediately repealed and no action was taken under it.

The public lands were sold at this time at $2 per acre, $80 to be paid on a quarter section at the time of purchase, with a credit of five years for the remainder. It was expected that the rapid settlement of the country would enable sales to be made at an advance before the expiration of the credit. The system therefore stimulated speculation, and everybody in the Territory was jobbing in land. From 1814 to 1818 we have the testimony of a man who was engaged in it that the most profitable business was the commerce in land. The country was rapidly improving; immigration was flowing in; "bank paper was circulating in great abundance." In the next two years the tide of immigration declined and an act of Congress of April 24, 1820, abolished credit for land after July 1st. Before any purchaser could enter land, he must produce to the register of the land office a receipt from the receiver of public moneys of the district for the amount of the purchase money. At that time $22 millions were due the Treasurer of the United States for land bought on credit. The transactions in the land office, during the speculation, stimulated the issues of the banks, and the government was parting with the lands in return for a credit in these banks which was almost entirely unavailable. We find the president of the Shawneetown Bank writing to Ninian Edwards, May 25, 1819, that the receiver at Kaskaskia takes his notes one day and refuses them the next. The Bank of Missouri is as bad or worse. It lately took $12,000 in specie from his bank. The public deposits give the Bank of Missouri great strength, which it abuses. He expresses sympathy with the Bank of Edwardsville. These banks being all engaged in the same operations, and all equally frail, never dared press upon each other; but whenever the Treasury, or a deposit bank, or the Bank of the United States, drew upon them for their debt to the United States, the whole combination must fall like a card house.

CHAPTER VII.

The Crisis on the Atlantic Coast

The Bank of the United States, in its internal administration, was found to be approaching a crisis in July, 1818. On the 20th, the directors ordered a reduction of discounts at Philadelphia, Baltimore, Richmond, and Norfolk, to the aggregate amount of $5 millions. Amongst the reasons given, the delinquency of the State banks in paying their balances is one of the foremost. October 30th, a report was made to the directors that these reductions had been only partially carried out.

The Bank resolved to insist upon further reductions, to get specie from abroad, silver being then at ten per cent. premium, and rapidly exported, and to draw $550,000 in specie from the West. The local currencies being now very unequal again and the Bank itself falling into distress, the task of equalizing the currencies was given up. August 28th, it was resolved to take no branch notes save at the branch which issued them; but the use of branch drafts was extended, with the same effect. They led to the device of drawing and re-drawing between the branches what were called "race horse bills," which combined the qualities of accommodation paper and endless renewals. They tended to draw the capital of the Bank away from the sounder and more conservative branches to the weaker and more reckless ones.

The directors ordered, October 20th, that all discounts on stock above par should be reduced, as to that excess, 25 per cent. every sixty days, and that in the meantime collaterals should be demanded for the excess. Nevertheless, on the 6th November, another vote was passed in the interests of stock jobbing, which allowed the president and cashier to accept the note and hypothecation of the buyer in place of those of the seller. During November and December, the discounts were greatly reduced.

It appears that there was a scheme on foot for an irredeemable government issue. Niles became convinced that there was such a scheme, and in the following April he said: "To speak plainly, let who be offended that may, let any power be exerted against us that can, we express an entire conviction of the belief that certain great proprietors of the stock of the Bank of the United States, with other speculators having a powerful influence on money affairs, aided perhaps by certain officers of government, are enrolled for a common exertion to bring about a suspension of specie payment by the establishment of a paper medium." Such a national currency of paper he called "the consummation of evils." December 7th, a meeting was held in Philadelphia, Matthew Carey in the chair, which appointed a committee to draft a memorial to prohibit the exportation of specie. It fell through and nothing was done, but a resolution to that effect was introduced in the Senate.

January 13, 1818, the Bank petitioned for an amendment to the charter to relieve the president and cashier from the labor of signing the notes. This was not granted because, as the session went on, more and more dissatisfaction was felt with the action of the Bank, and the growing disorder of the currency. The Senate passed a resolution, April 15th, that the Secretary of the Treasury should inquire and report at the next session in what manner the installments had been paid. Numerous other propositions for investigating the Bank were made, but they came to nothing. The one just mentioned produced little result, for the Secretary replied, in December, by simply enclosing a letter from Jones, the president of the Bank, which contained little information.

Spencer of New York introduced a resolution, in the House of Representatives, November 25, 1818, for a Committee to investigate the Bank and learn whether it had violated its charter. Such a Committee was appointed, and at once entered on an energetic investigation. It reported, January 16th, giving a history and criticism of the Bank, and laying before Congress a mass of documents and statistics which embodied the results of the investigation as to the facts. The Committee found that the charter had been violated in four points: 1.—The Bank, having sold $2 millions of public stocks in England in order to buy specie, and the Secretary of the Treasury desiring to redeem the stocks, the Bank had bought in the market and delivered to him that amount at a loss of $54,264, rather than disturb the arrangement in England. 2.—The installments had not been paid as the charter provided that they should be. 3.— Dividends had been paid to stockholders who had not paid the installments on their shares. This was forbidden by the charter. 4.—Persons had been allowed to cast over thirty votes each by the device of proxies. The Committee proposed no legislation except an act requiring that any person who offered over thirty votes at an election in the Bank should make oath that he was not the owner of the shares. Such an act was passed March 3, 1819.

Spencer proposed resolutions to withdraw the public deposits from the Bank, to refuse to receive its notes at the Treasury, and to order the Attorney-general to cause a *scire facias* to be issued for the revocation of the charter, unless the Bank should, before July 1st, accept twelve important amendments of it. Various other propositions of greater severity and more peremptory action against the Bank were proposed, but they all failed to pass. The opponents of the Bank claimed that over forty members of Congress were stockholders, and that a far greater number were interested on the side of the Bank.

At a stockholders' meeting in November, a committee recommended that the branches should be diminished in number, as the advantage of the Bank might require. In the following spring, J. Q. Adams expressed the opinion that the government was the party most interested in the continuance of the Bank and that the interest of the stockholders would be to surrender the charter.

On the receipt, in Philadelphia, of the report of Spencer's committee, William Jones, the president of the Bank, "fled in affright from the institution." Langdon Cheves of South Carolina was elected president March 6, 1819. In September, 1822, he laid before the stockholders at their triennial meeting an exposition of the state of the Bank as he found it, and a history of the steps by which he restored it. "It was not" he says, "until the moment I was about to commence my journey to Philadelphia, that I was apprised by a friend, who had been a member of the preceding Board, that he feared that, in a few months the Bank would be obliged to stop payment." "In Philadelphia it was generally expected." Curtailments were at once ordered everywhere except at New

York and Boston, where there was no room for them, but the branches at those places were obliged to reduce their business, being overwhelmed by the issues of the South and West which were not restrained. "The debt due in Kentucky and Ohio, instead of being reduced, was within this period [winter of 1818-9] actually increased upwards of half a million of dollars."

At the parent bank "all the funded debt which was salable had been disposed of and the proceeds exhausted. The specie in the vaults at the close of the day on the 1st of April, 1819, was only $126,745, and the Bank owed to the city banks, deducting balances due to it, an aggregate balance of $79,125. It is true there were in the mint $267,978, and *in transitu* from Kentucky and Ohio overland $250,000, but the Treasury dividends were payable on that day to the amount of nearly $500,000 and there remained at the close of the day more than one-half of the sum subject to draft, and the greater part, even of the sum which had been drawn during the day remained a charge upon the Bank in the shape of temporary deposits which were almost immediately withdrawn. Accordingly, on the 12th of the same month the Bank had in its vaults but $71,522, and owed to the city banks a balance of $196,418, exceeding the specie in its vaults $124,895. It must be again remarked that it had yet the sum before mentioned in the mint as well as the sum *in transitu* from Ohio and Kentucky. This last sum, $250,000, arrived very seasonably on the next day or a day or two after. The Bank in this situation, the office at New York was little better and the office at Boston a great deal worse. At the same time the Bank owed to Baring Brothers & Co. and to Thomas Wilson & Co. nearly $900,000 which it was bound to pay immediately, and which was equivalent to a charge upon its vaults to that amount. It had, including the notes of the offices, a circulation of $6 millions to meet." "In the office at Baltimore, of which James A. Buchanan was president and J. W. McCulloch was cashier, there were nearly three millions of dollars discounted or appropriated without any authority, and without the knowledge of the Board of the office, or that of the parent Bank. S. Smith and Buchanan, of which firm J. A. Buchanan was a member, James W. McCulloch, and George Williams (the latter a member of the parent Board by the appointment of the government) had obtained of the parent Bank discounts in the regular and accustomed manner to the amount of $1,957,700 on a pledge of 18,290 shares of stock of the Bank. These men, without the knowledge of either Board, and contrary to the resolve and orders of the parent Bank, took out of the office at Baltimore under the pretense of securing it by pledging the surplus value of the stock already pledged at the parent Bank for its par value and more, and other like surpluses over which the Bank had no control, the sum of $1,540,000. ... When this stupendous fraud was discovered, attempts were immediately made to obtain security, and it was nominally obtained to the amount of $900,000. It was probably really worth $500,000. ... The losses sustained at the office in Baltimore alone, the great mass of which grew out of this fraud, and others connected with it, have been estimated at the immense sum of $1,671,221. The aggregate of the losses of the institution growing out of the operations which preceded the 6th of March, 1819, exceed considerably $3.5 millions. The dividends during the same time amount to $4,410,000. Of this sum, $1,348,558 were received as the interest on the public

171

debt held by the Bank, which leaves as the entire profits on all the operations of banking the sum of $3,061,441, which is less by at least half a million of dollars than the losses sustained on the same business."

Of the measures taken by himself he says: "The southern and western offices were immediately directed not to issue their notes and the Bank ceased to purchase and collect exchange on the South and West. ... A correspondence with the Secretary of the Treasury was commenced entreating his forbearance and his aid." This correspondence was personal, and does not seem to have been published except in the appendix to Cheves's report of 1822. He made known to the Secretary the position of the Bank, and asked that notice should be given in advance of Treasury drafts, and also information of probable disbursements at designated places. He also asked for the use of a ship of war to bring specie from the West Indies, and for advance information of intention to pay the Louisiana debt. The Bank had three grievances: 1.—The receipt of notes for duties issued by other branches than the one at the place of receipt. 2.—The obligation to pay Treasury drafts on demand at any place. 3.—That debentures must be paid in coin while duties were received in notes. His counsel had advised him that the Treasury was obliged by law to receive any notes of the Bank at any place. Crawford assented to all his requests, and expressed the opinion that there must be either a great bank contraction or suspension, and that the Bank would be obliged to retire nearly all its circulation. Cheves thought that the Bank had too many branches and that its greatest difficulty was that it had not competent officers.

In April the directors passed a resolution to inform the Secretary that the Bank could not engage to meet the Treasury drafts without notice at other points than those at which the revenue was received or the notes were payable.

By continuing the curtailments, restraining the southern and western branches, collecting bank balances, demanding time for the transfer of government funds, paying debentures in the same currency in which duties were paid, and obtaining a loan in Europe of $2.5 millions, Cheves claimed to have "lifted the Bank, in the short space of seventy days, from the extreme prostration which has been described, to a state of safety and even some degree of power." The Dividend Committee, in 1822, found that the aggregate of the losses was $3,743,899.

The steps which Cheves took to draw the Bank back from the verge of bankruptcy precipitated a panic out of doors. They were resisted and criticised by the opponents of the paper money system as much as by others. Niles strongly denounced the contraction. "A policy directly opposite to that of the original makers of the Bank was speedily adopted and was still persevered in. It now issues none of its own notes. Present pecuniary profit is sacrificed to concentrate a power to command it hereafter; to regulate the transactions of individuals; to govern the money matters of the nation; to elect Presidents of the United States and enact laws for the government of the people." "What is the secret motive of the present proceedings of the Bank of the United States is not yet clear to us. It is possible it may grow out of its necessities from the losses and difficulties which it has encountered; but this is certain, that instead of equalizing the exchange, it has disordered it most severely, and that the present state of things cannot be permitted to endure if we can help it. The people cannot bear such a rapid retirement of the representatives of money as the proceedings of the Bank of the United States command."

In these passages we see already by what a direct transition the misfortunes and misbehavior of the Bank, at this period, entailed upon it that political suspicion and hostility which were the moving forces in the Bank war of Jackson's time. The two chief expectations of the public from the Bank,—the equalization of the exchanges, and the prompt performance of fiscal services for the government,—had proved so onerous to the Bank that it had given up the attempt to satisfy them. The bitter disappointment and dissatisfaction of the public in respect to these matters are also expressed in the passages just quoted. The concessions which Crawford had made in April to the petitions of Cheves became known in August. A particular refusal by the branch at Chillicothe to honor a draft of Governor Cass of Michigan for $10,000, which he needed in order to fulfill the stipulations of an Indian treaty, occasioned especial bad feeling. All the old fashioned, Jeffersonian republicans, who had suppressed their prejudices and convictions in obedience to expediency, now turned fiercely against the Bank. What had they obtained for their violation of "principle"? The germ of the great Jackson anti-Bank party was planted here. "It is now talked of as rank nonsense to expect that this institution should give us a currency of equal value in all parts of the republic; but who will be bold enough to say that, without an expectation and a promise of doing this, the Bank would have been chartered? It was *this* and *this only* which dragged the act through Congress, over prostrate consciences, if I may be allowed the expression, and the Constitution of the United States."

The whole local bank interest seized upon this dissatisfaction and fanned it zealously. Also the would-be popular leaders came forward with their quack remedies. "The political empirics," said Adams, "are already as busy as spiders in weaving their tangles for Congress and the national Executive." The banks seized eagerly upon the chance to turn attention from their own misdoings by complaints of the tyranny of the great Bank. One outcome of this feeling and these efforts was that several States tried to tax the Bank of the United States out of existence. February 11, 1818, Maryland laid a stamp tax on notes of any bank doing business in the State and not by or with the authority of the same. The tax was ten cents on a $5 note and varying amounts on other denominations. It might be commuted for $15,000. The Bank of the United States paid no heed to this law. In the case at law which resulted, the tax was held to be unconstitutional by the Supreme Court of the United States. It was held that the Bank was constitutionally endowed with a right to establish branches in any State. These branches were not taxable by the State, but real estate owned by the Bank, or the proprietary interest of citizens of the State in it, might be taxed like other property; Congress has power to charter a national bank as one means of carrying on the fiscal operations of the national government; the States cannot by taxation impede Congress in the exercise of any of its constitutional powers; if the end is legitimate and within the scope of the Constitution, any means may be employed which are appropriate and not prohibited. It remained uncertain whether the operations of discount and deposit were included

175

under the affirmation of this decision. In Osborn *vs.* the Bank of the United States, this point was discussed, and it was held that, although it was only as an aid to the national fiscus that a national bank was constitutional, yet it might be a true bank, adopted and used for this purpose, and hence endowed with the power of banking, and protected in the same. Kentucky and Ohio levied taxes on the branches in those States and Tennessee established a tax as a barrier to keep a branch out. In joint resolutions of the Georgia Legislature, December 18, 1819, it was affirmed that the law of the State taxing banks applied to the Bank of the United States, but the Treasurer was directed to suspend the execution of the law as to that Bank for the present.

In the spring of 1819 the exchanges rapidly grew worse, and so continued through the summer. The quotations at Baltimore in August were, in the local currency: Specie at a small premium; Boston, one or two discount; Massachusetts country banks, one to eight discount according to their repute in the city; Rhode Island and Connecticut, two to six discount; New Jersey, "specie paying," one or two discount; Philadelphia, par to a quarter premium; country notes, from one to sixty discount; "specie paying," one to five discount; Delaware, "specie paying," one discount; the rest eight to fifty; Maryland country notes, "specie paying," three to six discount; others, twelve to forty; District of Columbia, one discount; old banks of Virginia, one and a half to two discount; Bank of the Valley, two and a half to three; unchartered, seven and a half to twenty-five; North Carolina, twenty to twenty-five discount, nominal; South Carolina, eight to ten discount; Georgia, seven to eight discount; old banks of Tennessee and Kentucky, fifteen discount, nominal;

new ones, twenty to twenty-five; Ohio, the best, ten discount, generally fifteen to twenty, many forty to fifty; the rest of the Mississippi Valley, fifteen to sixty discount.

Adams' notes in his Diary, June 10, 1819, a conversation with Crawford about the "operations of the Bank and the gigantic frauds practicing upon the people by means of these institutions. The banks are breaking all over the country; some in a sneaking, and some in an impudent manner; some with sophisticating evasion and others with the front of highwaymen. ... Crawford has labors and perils enough before him in the management of the finances for the three succeeding years." This prediction was soon amply fulfilled. The Secretary of the Treasury was drawn into most serious difficulty by attempting to exercise those powers of supervision of banks and arbitration between banks which have been noticed above. In order to help the banks of the District of Columbia to resume, he distributed public deposits amongst them. Elsewhere from one end of the country to the other, he acted on the same policy, endeavoring to coax or help or reward and perhaps punish. He had bitter experience of the return which such action would obtain. Generally speaking the banks took everything they could possibly extort from him by any arguments or motives which they could bring to bear upon him, and they yielded nothing to him because he had no power of coercion, and they paid no heed to his remonstrances, pleading, or reasoning. The inducements which were offered to the western banks to resume specie payments and transfer public money to the place where it must be expended, "were believed to be both justifiable and sufficient to insure success, and the result has proved that nothing was necessary to the most complete success but the want of integrity in those who had the direction of some of those institutions." In 1823 an attempt was made to ruin him politically, by charging him with having acted corruptly in this matter. Although it did not succeed, it left behind an impression which undoubtedly hurt him politically. For our purpose this incident is chiefly important because it led to the production of a vast amount of correspondence which reveals the operations of the banks in 1819, and also because it furnishes some more links in the series of precedents by which the usage was established of arbitration by the Secretary between banks. Crawford, justifying himself for what he had done, referred back to action by Gallatin, in 1813. Gallatin was a strong name, but the precedent proves to have been an act by William Jones, acting Secretary of the Treasury; in the name of Gallatin, it is true. May 27, 1813, Jones wrote to Girard, referring to measures taken by Gallatin, in respect to the public deposits in Girard's bank, to shield Girard against the attacks of the incorporated banks: "It is a particular province and it has been the practice of the Department of the Treasury of the United States to direct the moneyed operations of the public to the preservation of credit, by maintaining the equilibrium between the moneyed institutions of the country; and as it has protected your institution by the arrangement alluded to, so it will guard those institutions against any undue pressure which the public funds in your vaults may enable you to direct against them. I am informed that you have made some very heavy and unnecessary drafts of specie from several banks, particularly from the Pennsylvania and Farmers' and Mechanics' Banks, with indications of a disposition to interfere, which has excited considerable apprehension. I

178

therefore deem it necessary to inform you that a continuance of that system will induce the prompt application of a specific remedy." February 13, 1817, Crawford wrote to the president of the Mechanics' Bank of New York: "The Secretary of the Treasury will always be disposed to support the credit of the State banks and will invariably direct transfers from the deposits of the public money in aid of their legitimate exertions to maintain their credit; but as the proposition of the Bank of the United States excludes the idea of pressure on its part, no measure of that nature appears to be necessary at this time." It is evident that the precedent was marching on very steadily. In the hands of Jones it had been formulated into a principle.

After speaking of the distress in England, April 10, 1819, Niles goes on to describe the condition of things here: "From all parts of our country we hear of a severe pressure on men of business, a general stagnation of trade, a large reduction in the price of staple articles. Real property is rapidly depreciating in its nominal value, and its rents or profits are exceedingly diminishing. Many highly respectable tradesmen have become bankrupt, and it is agreed that many others must go." He goes on to say that confidence is destroyed and that three per cent. per month is the rate for good commercial paper. May 22nd : "There is no remedy, but the reaction is hard to be borne. The plain fact is that wherever there is one bank that attempts to pay its debts, there must be great distress; but in those places where there are two or more, God help the people! The curse of borrowing, of suffering 'paper to do our business,' is falling heavily upon us." "With nearly $500 in notes of different sizes, and of many old and respectable banks, in his pocketbook, the writer of this article was compelled, on Saturday last, to borrow market money." "Misery abounds and the neighborhood of every bank is a neighborhood of bankrupts, positive or anticipated." Smith & Buchanan failed in June, "with a crash which staggered the whole city of Baltimore and will extend no one knows how far. ... The affairs of the house appear to have been desperate for many years, but they were Tyrian merchant princes and princely expedients have they taken to save themselves from sinking." They had controlled Baltimore, socially, politically, and commercially.

Matthew Carey stated that of thirty-seven merchants who signed a policy of insurance at Philadelphia in 1799, twenty-seven had become bankrupt in 1822. If the writers of the time were at all correct in their opinion that prices responded promptly to the inflation and contraction of the currency, how was it possible for anyone to do business?

Of course all this was attended by great suffering amongst the wages class. August 7th Niles says: "It is estimated that there are 20,000 persons daily seeking work in Philadelphia; in New York, 10,000 able-bodied men are said to be wandering the streets looking for it; and if we add to them the women who desire something to do, the amount cannot be less than 20,000." October 23d, he said that there were 7,288 persons idle in Baltimore. In the report of a Committee on Manufactures of the city of Philadelphia, quoted by him on that date, it is stated that trades which employed 9,672 persons in 1816, employed only 2,137 in 1819. "It is a singular fact, which conclusively shows the pressure of the times, that our master mechanics, even of the most necessary callings, such as shoemakers, hatters, and tailors, are not doing more than one-half or two-thirds of the business which they did three or four years ago." Many artisans returned to Europe. As late as August 3, 1822, Niles said, "almost everybody is wondering how other people live" in Baltimore. Evidence of the fall in prices is equally plentiful. In July, 1820, it was stated that houses which rented for $1,200 before the crisis, then rented for $450; fuel had fallen from $12 to $5.50; flour, from $10 to $4.50; beef, from twenty-five cents to eight cents.

At this point we must recall the fact that the return of peace in Europe, after twenty-five years of war, had had great effect on commerce and industry. The English hoped, upon the return of peace, to recover all their old markets. They made very large shipments to this country. Here, also, the peace had been fatal to a great many manufacturing industries which had grown up under seven or eight years of embargo, non-intercourse, and war. The tariff of 1816, which was intended to save them, did so only to a limited extent. These new elements of trouble and confusion were complicated with those already mentioned. It was the large imports which furnished the revenue which enabled the Secretary of the Treasury to pay off a part of the public stocks in the capital of the Bank. The Bank had sold $2 millions of these stocks in England, and was compelled to buy so much in order to put it at his disposal, which was a technical violation of the charter. Crawford stated that the reason for not letting the Bank buy public stocks, or sell them, beyond a small limit, was to prevent it from being able to control the credit of the government.

Niles had commenced a general onslaught on the "rag system" in his "Register" in the spring of 1818, and he seems to have had no little influence upon public opinion, in connection with banks and the great Bank. Banks were being multiplied on every hand and those which existed were growing worse and worse. We have here the explanation of the fierce denunciations of banks in which many men who lived through that period indulged, and of the suspicion and prejudice against them, which they never overcame. Niles's expressions about banks are almost fanatical. He talks of them as one would talk of gambling hells. It is impossible to understand this without observing what the institutions were which he knew under the name of "banks," and how they were treating the public. He states that four banks in Maryland, whose notes were at from six per cent. to ten per cent. discount, had eight hundred foreclosure suits on the docket. He mentions going to a broker's office to exchange some notes issued at a distance, and meeting a man who was trying to buy bank notes, and grumbling that they were not cheaper. This grumbler was the president of the bank whose notes he was trying to buy. He thus describes in a supposition the actual customs of banking at the time: "Let us suppose, and after what we know of banks, we may suppose anything! a majority of the board at Philadelphia, only thirteen men, resolve to get rich, or if rich, to get richer. They agree among themselves that the Bank *shall* lend to each of them, the *moderate* sum of $200,000, as a permanent accommodation for twelve months. Well, the amount being passed to their credit, they issue a peremptory order to the officers of the Bank, and its offices, that they shall not issue any more of their own notes. Within two months, money becomes scarce to those accustomed to a sufficiency of it—for all the prudent State banks are justly alarmed and know not what to do, except to get in their debts as rapidly as they can; and in two

182

months more every species of property has a diminished nominal value compared with what it was, of thirty-three and one-third per cent., and lawyers and sheriffs are 'over head and ears' in business. The *gentlemen* then buy whatever they *choose* to speculate in, and getting all things *snug*, they discount freely, and seem almost to throw their bank notes about in the street. The State banks, anxious to retrieve lost time and make a good dividend, do the same thing, and money becomes instantly plenty. Property speedily assumes a price beyond what it had before its fall; the house or piece of land, which sold, 'a little month ago' for $1,000, is valued at $1,500, and the *gentlemen* speculators then sell; offering to purchasers assistance from the Bank, if needful to make a good bargain for themselves."

Among the petitions presented to the Pennsylvania Legislature, in January, 1819, were several about banks. Amongst the rest, one "to annihilate the charters of all the banks in this Commonwealth; to make the property of the stockholders liable for the debts of the company, and to tax the Bank of the United States and branches."

The country bank notes of Pennsylvania were contracted as follows: 1816, $4.7 millions; 1817, $3.7 millions; 1818, $3 million; 1819, $1.3 millions. The consequence was that farms and houses were being rapidly transferred to the banks which had made loans upon them. The ground of exasperation was that the banks had loaned upon them nothing but bits of paper, multiplied until all prices had risen, so that now, in the revulsion, the transfer of the property appeared as the consequence of a mere financial thimble-rig. Indeed it was little else. The system was not even honest gambling. It was gambling in which one party had never put up any stakes.

The banks had adopted all sorts devices to avoid any risk of being obliged to redeem their issues, and had indeed employed in banking, devices which belong only to gambling. Then when the trouble came, they "suspended"— that is to say, they withdrew from the performance of their obligations while insisting on the payment of debts to them. The Vincennes Bank of Indiana issued notes payable nine months after date at Vevay. "Nine months" was printed at the top in small letters, so as not to be noticed. The report of a Committee on Currency to the New York Legislature, February 24, 1818, described some of the devices by which banks had evaded their responsibilities, as follows: "By adopting a variety of schemes to get their notes into circulation, such as placing a partial fund in a distant bank to redeem their paper, and after the fact becomes generally known that their paper is at par in that quarter, issuing an emission of notes signed with ink of a different shade, at the same time giving secret orders to said bank not to pay the notes thus signed, and subjecting the owners of them to loss and disappointment." "Others ... have issued a species of paper called 'facility notes,' purporting to be payable in either money, country produce, or anything else that has body or shape, and thereby rendering their name appropriate only by facilitating the ruin of those who are so unfortunate as to hold them." "A person this day paid us," says Niles, "a note which he received as having been issued in Philadelphia, and so it was; but unfortunately for him it was 'New Philadelphia' the 'New' printed very small and the 'Philadelphia' very large." One of the commonest abuses in the banks was that the directors were supposed to have a right to large loans. In cases where the banks had been organized in the way which has been above described, this was a matter of course. The men who formed the bank, and gave their stock notes for the stock, borrowed the circulation as soon as it was printed, and had the advantage of holding it in the first hand; hence Niles says, apropos of the City Bank of Baltimore, in which all the officials, except one clerk and the porter, had taken out loans amounting to $426,083, and where, if the loans to the directors were included, the whole group had borrowed $100,000 more than the whole capital: "This is the great principle of modern banking; a cheat, a bubble, a machine for the exclusive benefit of a few scheming men."

The bank which Niles was fond of using as a proverb was the Owl Creek Bank of Ohio, or, as he nicknamed it, the "Hoo Hoo Bank." This bank gave notice that, in order to counteract the injurious tendency of the United States branch banks in that State, it had thought proper to follow the example of other banks and suspend payment.

The Bank of the State of North Carolina tendered an oath to all persons who demanded specie of it that the notes had not been exchanged or bought up for the purpose of making the demand. The Bank of Darien, Georgia, forced everybody demanding specie to take an oath before a justice of the peace in the Bank, to each and every note, that it was his own, that he was not an agent for any other person, and this oath must be taken in the presence of at least five directors and the cashier. If they could not be found together, the demand could not be made. The sum of $1.37 1-2 on each note must also be paid on the spot by the person making the demand.

A volume might be filled with facts and incidents of this kind from this period. They account for language like the following about the abuse of banking: "We have had melancholy proof of this at the sacrifice of millions on millions of dollars, by the industrious poor, to pamper the pride and glut the inordinate appetites of *speculating scoundrels*. I use these words deliberately. Notwithstanding all the shavings, quirkings, twistings, and fraud, which the people generally are acquainted with, I feel authorized to say, that the history of *modern banking*, particularly in the middle and western sections of the United States, is as yet but very imperfectly known. The imagination of an honest man can hardly conceive the stupendous villainies that have been contrived, and which must, and will forever exist in every country where paper can be forced upon the people in lieu of money." And again: "It has always been my opinion that of all evils which can be inflicted upon a free State, banking establishments are the most alarming. They are the vultures that prey upon the constitution and rob the body politic of its life blood." "I have a letter from an honest man who was coaxed to his ruin by a bank. ... Driven to the wilds of the West, he laments the friends of his youth and loss of society, details the hardships that belong to a new settler, and enumerates many privations, but 'blesses God that he is out of the reach of a bank.'"

Let it not be supposed that the passages which have been quoted contain the rant of a crank or an agitator. Niles often dogmatized about things which he did not understand. He was opinionated and prejudiced, but of his absolute integrity of mind and heart there is no question. He uttered the moral indignation of an honest man. The writers of the time exhaust the adjectives of disgust in their attempts to describe the filth and raggedness of the notes. The banks reissued them and kept them in circulation because, if they were worn out, or

186

became illegible, or were lost, that meant that the public, which had borrowed them out of the bank, had to pay back to the bank true value for them. This state of things also gave the counterfeiter his chance, and the literature and the laws prove that counterfeiting was one of the most lucrative industries of the time. There were three kinds of paper afloat 1.—Notes of regularly incorporated banks, with more or less pretense to solvency. 2.—Notes of banks which had no other existence than an office, room with furniture, an engraved plate, and a bundle of paper. Their notes were kept out at as great a distance and for as long a time as possible; also in as great an amount. When they came home, the bank ceased to be. 3.—Counterfeits in enormous amount; although they differed from the second class only in borrowing a name which somebody else had invented, instead of inventing a new one.

The instances which have been mentioned are the more striking ones of abuse and outrage and are, perhaps, in so far, exaggerated. There were good banks, but such made little noise and have made little mark on the record. They also were exceptional. The most interesting record of one of them which we have found is the following. It is entitled "An Anonymous Communication containing the History of Some Bank from 1806 to 1837, which at first was Managed very Conservatively; No Renewals, No Accommodation Paper, etc." "It was ascertained soon after the Bank was fairly in operation that its ability to discount had no sort of connection with or dependence on the amount of its capital." It required punctual payment by other banks of their notes, and so maintained its circulation by new discounts, while they, as they gave extensions, could not circulate their notes except by giving them to agents who forced them into circulation by exchanges. "The possession of capital was of no use except to inspire confidence." This being once fully established, the capital was an inconvenience. It was a trouble to invest it. The stockholders could have done it better individually. Therefore, in July, 1816, half the capital was paid back to the stockholders in specie. Still it suffered from the annoyance of unemployed capital. "To employ it in discounting commercial paper, experience had shown was not sagacious, as the bank's credit, which cost nothing, already supplied all the demands of trade." It therefore lent $25,000 of its remaining capital on mortgage in 1821. The remaining capital was $100,000, of which one quarter was thus invested. Subsequently a large part of the remaining $75,000 was lent on mortgage.

The banks brought loans to every man's door. When a bank was established in a country town it became the current fashion to get a loan and undertake some enterprise. The need for a loan did not arise from a growth of affairs up to the point where a need of more capital was experienced. Not every man is fit to have credit. It is far from being a blessing to everyone. An education in the use of capital is needed before one is fit to use credit. This was illustrated by the colonial banks; it accounts for such diatribes as we have just read, and we shall see it illustrated later in the history of the great banks of the South and West.

CHAPTER VIII.

The Crisis in the Mississippi Valley

The crisis and reaction began in the West in the summer of 1818. The immediate agent was the Bank of the United States. We have noticed above, the orders which were sent to the western branches from Philadelphia, the effect of which was to transfer the capital from the East to the West. It may perhaps be just to say that but for the Bank of the United States the West would never have been drawn into the inflation. The great Bank, however, as we have seen, was in great distress in 1818, and was obliged to curtail its operations in order to save itself. On account of its responsibilities to the Treasury, it was necessarily the agent of the correction of the mistakes which had been made in the West. As an equalizer of the currency, as an agent for the transfer of the public funds, and as the agent to discipline the State banks, it was certain to become extremely unpopular. It appeared to all the local banks and debtors as a "monster." It hardly appears, however, that the first outburst of hostility against it was on account of any contraction, or disciplinary action which it exercised; but rather due to a jealousy of it as a foreign institution, present in some of the States, perhaps against their will; possessed of privileges; paying no taxes, and holding the attitude of a school-master. In Kentucky an act was passed, February 3, 1818, to tax each branch of the Bank $5,000 per annum, commutable at 50 cents on each $100 of capital in each branch, or 25 cents on each $100 of

189

loans and discounts, as they might stand on the 10th of March in each year. This act was considered entirely reasonable in amount and method.

The popular temper in those days went through oscillations of mania for banks and rage against banks. Within a year or two, two Legislatures would be elected which might represent the extremes of these two feelings. Governor Slaughter opened the session of the Kentucky Legislature of 1818-19 with a message in which he expressed fear of banks and of a moneyed aristocracy founded on them. He proposed to the Legislature that they should propose an amendment to the federal Constitution, providing that after a certain time no incorporated banks should exist in the United States. Resolutions were introduced in the Kentucky Legislature, January 4, 1819, that banks with private stockholders were "moneyed monopolies tending to make profit to those who do not labor out of the means of those who do, * * * tending to tax the many for the benefit of the few," and that the federal and State governments ought "to abolish all banks and moneyed monopolies and, if a paper medium is necessary, to substitute the impartial and disinterested medium of the credit of the Nation or of the States."

As the Bank had paid no attention to the tax law of the previous session, another act was passed, January 28, 1819, which showed a different temper. A tax of $60,000 per annum was laid on the Branches or offices of any bank doing business in Kentucky and not incorporated by that State, to be paid monthly, commencing March 4, 1820. The Sergeant of the Court of Appeals was authorized to break open and enter the Bank and distrain for the tax. If the Bank of the United

States would promise, within six months, to withdraw its branches, the tax would not be collected. This law of Kentucky was passed just at the time that the Supreme Court of the United States decided the case of McCulloch *vs.* Maryland. In December following, the case of the Commonwealth against Morrison came on before the Court of Appeals of Kentucky. Judge Rowan delivered a long opinion on the tax of the Bank of the United States. If the States cannot tax any such institution doing business within their borders, they are petty and insignificant. Banks are not necessary to collect the revenue. "Their location in a State is as if done by a foreign nation." The taxing power is concurrent; neither federal nor State government should interfere each with the other. If the government uses its funds for stock jobbing or traffic in a State, it is liable to taxation. Although the Court believes that the Bank is unconstitutional, yet it must bow to the decision of the Supreme Court of the United States. Such was the decision of the Court, but it is said that Rowan thought that they ought to stand out for a further struggle in the interest of State rights.

The Bank found it necessary to very much contract its business in Kentucky. Its circulation there, in 1819, was over $630,000. It was gradually reduced until in 1825 it was only $170,000; then it began to increase again, and in 1828, was $1.3 millions. This was the ground of the charge which was brought against it in the bank war, of having discontinued business during a period of seven or eight years. This conflict between the Bank of the United States and the local banks, with all the reasons for the same, are completely set forth in a letter by Crawford, in 1823. The Bank agreed to accept, in trust for the Treasurer of the United States, all notes of banks

191

selected by itself as depositories where it had no office, and of such others as it might agree to credit. This arrangement could not be maintained in 1818, when the crisis came on. The Bank could not receive notes of banks which would not redeem. The banks complained of its demands. The Bank refrained from issuing its own notes and refused to receive for the credit of the Treasurer of the United States anything but specie or its own notes. Thus the debtors for the public lands became liable to pay specie for all their debt. Crawford regarded this state of things as creating a political peril which the Executive was bound to avert, if possible, and this is his defense of his interference to favor banks with the use of the public money, that they might favor the debtors to the Treasury for public lands.

The Bank of England through this period and long afterwards, received country bank notes for revenue, but did not become responsible to the Exchequer for the amounts until the notes were converted into coin or Bank of England notes.

February 6th, 1819, the charter of the Bank of Kentucky was extended to 1841. No more branches were to be established except by a vote of two-thirds of the State directors and two-thirds of the stockholders' directors, with the assent of the Legislature. The stockholders were to appoint one visitor and the Legislature another, to inspect and examine the bank. The present stockholders may withdraw after December 3, 1821. After May, 1819, no bank was to issue any note for less than $1.

"In the early part of 1819, the price of all articles produced in the Western States fell so low as scarcely to defray the expense of transportation to the ports from whence they were usually exported to foreign markets. This condition of things, which had not been anticipated when the debt for the public lands was contracted, produced the most serious distress at the moment, and excited alarming apprehensions for the future."

CHAPTER IX.

The Liquidation on the Atlantic Coast

During the summer and fall of 1819, on the Atlantic Coast, the good and bad banks were being rapidly separated from each other, the former growing steadily stronger, and the latter rapidly falling or their notes becoming uncurrent. In July, the Committee on Banks of New Hampshire reported all the banks solvent, although one was thought to have made excessive issues, and the New Hampshire Bank, in which the State owned $25,000 stock, had made some bad debts. A legislative committee in Massachusetts reported all the banks solvent. From Connecticut it was reported that no bank had failed or suffered a run. In the Middle States laws to restrain banking were passed by nearly all the States. In New York there was a penalty of ten per cent. for non-redemption. Pennsylvania passed an act, March 29, 1819, providing that any one of "the forty" banks incorporated in 1814, which did not pay specie on and after August 1st, on demand, should forfeit its charter. The Governor in his next message said that this act had not been enforced against any one of them, but the Treasurer of the State gave notice, in February, 1820, that the charters of five specified banks were null and void. In Maryland a law was passed providing for a *scire facias* to annul the charter of any non-specie paying bank. Several of the New England and Middle States passed laws within a year or two, forbidding notes under $5. Thus the currency was steadily improved during 1820. As early as October 16,

1819, the Bank of the United States gave notice that it would receive, at any office, its notes for $5 issued at any office. It had saved itself and thrown the consequences of all its folly and misdoings on its customers (who were not indeed blameless), and on the public. The loans and discounts of the Bank, in July, 1817, were $26.2 millions. They steadily increased to $41.4 millions one year later. Then they declined to their minimum for the period, $28.0 millions, in January, 1822. The circulation was lowest in July, 1820; $3.5 millions.

The difficulties which the Bank of the United States experienced in equalizing the exchanges became especially manifest at Savannah and at Cincinnati. At the former city, the balances due to the branch by the local banks, chiefly on account of the accumulation of their notes in it by the payment of duties, were $100,000 or $200,000, during 1817, 1818, and 1819. Sometimes they were more than $400,000, and at the beginning of 1820 they exceeded $500,000. These balances they at length refused to pay, whereupon the Bank refused to accept their notes and account for them as cash to the credit of the United States. The Bank agreed to allow them $100,000 as a permanent deposit, the payment of which should not be demanded; but when payment of the excess was required, they refused it. The local banks, defending themselves, objected to daily cash settlements, which the Bank had required. A committee of the directors at Philadelphia said: "The practice of daily settlements prevails, it is believed, among four-fifths in number and in amount of capital of the banks of the principal cities of the United States." Other evidence does not support this assertion, and if it was true at the time, in the days of penance after the panic, the custom soon after fell into disuse. The committee of directors, however, recommended to relax this so far that the settlements be weekly. The Savannah branch was also forbidden to issue its own notes while the exchanges were adverse. The president of that branch reported that weekly settlements would probably be as little palatable as daily ones. He thought that monthly ones would be agreed to, but gave his own opinion that there was no need for settlements more frequently than semi-annually or annually. From this discussion it is very easy to see that, if there had been no Bank of the United States, the local banks could have followed an unrestrained policy of inflation, but that the drift of their notes into the Bank, which was the same as to say the Treasury of the United States, brought about a demand upon them which limited their issues. We learn from the same correspondence that the notes of Georgia and the Carolinas circulated far into the West and Northwest, were received for lands, and were sent into the eastern branches to be collected. Thus the collision between the national bank and the local banks was direct and violent. It was only by means of it that the local currencies could all be equalized by all being brought to par. It is clear that the first requisite of success in this duty was that the Bank of the United States should itself be as sound and as correct in its methods as any bank could possibly be, and that the thing which lamed it in its efforts to regulate others was the revelation by the Committee of 1819 of what its own misbehavior had been.

In July, 1821, the notes of the Planters' Bank of Georgia were thrown out by the branch of the Bank of the United States because it had suffered them to be protested. Out of this another quarrel grew. Cheves said that "the avowed object of the Planters' Bank is to prevent the office from receiving its notes, in order that it may be in no shape called upon to redeem them in legal money." The amount which the Bank now had locked up in Savannah was over $400,000.

The Bank and the local banks reached a concordat in January, 1821, the latter agreeing to pay interest on all over a maximum balance, but their notes still continued to accumulate in the Bank. In the followihg summer, the Planters' Bank broke the arrangement, and again entered into open hostility with the Bank. In a letter to Crawford, the president says: "Aided by such an immense capital, and having the additional weapon of the federal revenue, it is impossible to maintain intercourse with such an institution." "A feeling of dissatisfaction or irritation against the government never existed in the banks or in this community, until this mammoth came here to destroy our very substance." "You will perceive readily that our main object is to prevail on the Bank of the United States to refuse our paper and to deal on their own. While they decline issuing their own bills, and none comparatively of the public revenue is expended in this quarter, it is impossible for the State banks located in the same place with it to exist." To this Crawford replied that if the local notes were not received by the Bank, people who had duties to pay would demand specie of the banks, with the same result. "Experience has shown that so long as the notes of the Bank of the United States and its offices are everywhere received in payment to the government, they will circulate only where the principal part of the revenue is disbursed." He explained that the drain of specie from Georgia to the North and East was "in no degree ascribable to the Bank. It is the result of the operations of the government." He tried not to be drawn into the controversy, but put the

Planters' Bank entirely in the wrong. In a later letter the president of that Bank regretted that the discretion of the Treasury could not have been "exercised in behalf of the community that has suffered so much as this under the lash of the United States Bank." "Congress can hardly consent to see the southern States torn to pieces and rendered disaffected towards the federal government, which would seem to be the inevitable consequence of the present measures of the United States Bank, which it is enabled to pursue only by the means derived from the collection of the revenue."

During this controversy, the Georgians had made constant threats that they would invoke the interference of their own Legislature.

A Committee on Banks made a report to the Senate of Georgia, November 30, 1821, in which they say that Georgia has aimed to furnish herself with a currency by her own banks, and at the same time to get an investment for her State funds. She has been frustrated in this by the intrusion. of the Bank of the United States which long refused to issue notes. It got possession of the notes of the State banks and by demanding specie for them, drained away specie. The Committee advises against any collision, but recommends that no notes presented by anybody with a demand for specie shall be paid unless an oath is taken that the notes do not belong to the Bank of the United States and are not presented in its interest.

December 24, 1821, it was enacted that State bank notes presented by the Bank of the United States for specie should not be paid unless the agent would take oath that they were not collected for this purpose. If an officer of a State bank suspected that a person who demanded specie was an agent of the Bank of the United States, he might demand of him to take an oath before a magistrate that that Bank had no interest. If such person refused to take this oath, he might be refused redemption of the notes. Whenever the Bank of the United States demanded specie, it must send with the notes a schedule of their numbers, date, letter, amount, and page, dated the same day. The notes of the State banks in the Bank of the United States should not bear interest on account of any refusal to redeem them.

This law was repealed December 20, 1824.

In April, 1822, the branch at Savannah was taking no Georgia notes except on special deposit, "inasmuch as an act of the Legislature authorizes ' them to refuse specie payments to the Bank of the United States or offices thereof, and interest, if sued."

In South Carolina, at the session of 1819-20, "nothing but the great exertions of some able and distinguished men probably prevented a system of State paper money from being adopted." In the opinion of Cheves, the motive was to get a currency the redemption of which could not be enforced by the Bank of the United States.

A similar quarrel occurred at Cincinnati. In August, 1818, the Bank called on the banks of Cincinnati to pay 20 per cent. of their debt to it monthly, and to pay interest on it. The local banks replied, through a committee, in a tone of astonishment and indignation, saying that they were ready to meet all demands in the ordinary course of business, but "are not prepared to redeem, at a few months' notice, all the paper they have issued for years past." They have paid to the branch $1.4 millions in eighteen months, which has forced them to withdraw almost all their circulation. They are called upon to pay, either in specie, United States notes, or eastern funds, none of which can be had. "We consider the liquidation of an interest account at the expiration of every thirty days as a grievance unprecedented. An interest account, it is believed, is not usual between banks. In the western country it certainly is not." To this Jones replied: "He must be a sturdy debtor indeed who boldly withholds both principal and interest, and defends it as a matter of right."

The office at Cincinnati was discontinued in September, 1820. In 1822 the debt to the Bank in Ohio and Kentucky had been reduced not quite $1 million.

These cases show why it was that, during the years of liquidation, the Bank of the United States found it impossible to maintain any circulation in the western and southern countries. Its notes were gathered up and used as a remittance to the North and East. At the same time the local banks, whose notes had been paid into the Bank in the public revenue from lands, were unable to redeem them. The local banks thus became possessed of the capital of the Bank of the United States, and the latter was forced to pay out their notes in order to make any use of them, thereby neglecting its own circulation.

The dividends of the Bank of the United States were as follows: 1817, eight per cent.; 1818, five and one-half per cent.; 1819, nothing; 1820, nothing; 1821, four per cent.; 1822, five per cent.; 1823, five per cent. In the meantime, the United States was paying five per cent. quarterly on its stock notes, so that in 1824 it was calculated that $500,000 had been lost by the public Treasury through its shares in the Bank. The stock was at 122 1-2. Niles thought that the public shares should be sold. The average of the dividends from

1817 to 1831 was a little over five per cent., paid semi-annually; so that the public investment showed, until that time, neither gain or loss.

In a report on the currency, February 12, 1820, Secretary Crawford estimated that the circulation in 1815 was $1 millions and that it was greater in 1816. At the end of the year 1819, he estimated it at $45 millions. Nearly two-thirds of the circulation had been reduced to waste paper. The Secretary said: "As the currency is, at least in some parts of the Union, depreciated, it must in those parts suffer a further reduction before it becomes sound. The nation must continue to suffer until this is effected. After the currency shall be reduced to the amount which, when the present quantity of the precious metals is distributed among the various nations of the world in proportion to their respective exchangeable values, shall be assigned to the United States, when time shall have regulated the price of labor and of commodities, according to that amount, and when pre-existing arrangements shall have been adjusted, the sufferings from a depreciated, decreasing, and deficient currency will be terminated. Individual and public prosperity will gradually revive, and the productive energies of the nation resume their accustomed activity."

It took time for this liquidation and readjustment to be accomplished. Specie was imported in the winter of 1819-20, and in July of the latter year Niles said: "It is stated, and we think with probability, that there was never more specie in the United States than at this present time." It was largely imported from Mexico, through New Orleans, during the next years.

The international relations, however, had changed since 1816. The European nations, England especially, were struggling in 1819 to resume specie payments. Specie was moving from country to country in an unprecedented manner. Several of the great nations were contracting loans, partly in order to resume. The whole civilized world was in the midst of the financial storm through which the equilibrium of peace was restored, after the prolonged artificial disturbance of the Napoleonic wars. Prices were falling and business was stagnant the whole world over. The reaction therefore went on, as it always must under such circumstances, to a point below the real point of equilibrium. The nations had to bid against each other for the supply of the precious metals by lower and lower prices. The exchanges were in constant fluctuation and produced strange and complicated phenomena which lay outside the experience of people then living. Since 1797, England had had inconvertible bank paper which had been depreciated from one per cent. to 25 per cent.—for the greater part of the time, about eight per cent. or ten per cent. Since 1814 there had been a redundant and depreciated currency here. Thus there had been various combinations working on the sterling exchange on both sides; sometimes both currencies had been good; sometimes both bad; and sometimes the English had been good and the American bad, and *vice versa*. At the ratio of 15 1-4 to 1, the par of exchange would be $4.64 for £1 sterling, and as $4.44 4-9 was traditionally taken as 100, the par, under the fashion of quoting, was 104 1-2. Americans had been accustomed to see the exchange quoted between 90 and 100, which figures were especially calculated to produce confusion and error. In 1821 it averaged above 108; in 1822, 112. In 1822, it reached 114; it had been seen as low as 80. There was also a change going on in the relative value of gold and silver, on account of which, under the false rating of the American coinage at the time, gold was exported from this country. It was said that, between 1820 and 1822, the last gold coin was carried away. The ratio of the metals was for a time above 16 to 1. $10.60 or $10.70 in silver were given here for eagles to be exported to England in order to draw exchange against them. The consequence was a check to imports, an encouragement to exports, and a discouragement to the investment of capital here if the profits were to be paid here. The Bank of the United States found it necessary to recede from an offer it had made to pay dividends in London, on account of the loss on exchange. The amount of American stocks held in England at this time was estimated at $30 millions.

During the years of liquidation, the rate of interest was very low, and first rate securities were so high as to net only four or five per cent. In 1821, Spanish dollars were at par of the currency in all the chief cities of the coast, except Boston, where they were at one-quarter or one-half of one per cent. premium. In May, 1822, there was a flurry in the money market of the chief cities. United States Bank stock fell at New York from 110 to 98. The banks there and at Philadelphia and Baltimore stopped discounting, "and it appeared as if some frightful mischief was rapidly approaching." A great stringency in the money market of Boston, and numerous failures, was the report from that quarter. In June and July, there were said to have been more than eighty failures. The best explanation which was offered of these incidents was that they were due to weakness left behind by the crisis of 1819, in which Boston was not spared, although it had been outside of the earlier troubles between 1814 and 1817.

CHAPTER X.

Liquidation in the Mississippi Valley – Relief Measures

It might naturally be supposed that frontier society, consisting of a very sparse population with few and poor means of communication, would not easily be united on any opinion or policy. It is very true that such society had a very low social organization, and that the civil authority was powerless to enforce the most salutary measures which were irksome and unpopular, but the history of all our societies in their early stages has shown that they are far more susceptible to gusts of passion and storms of opinion than older societies. One chief explanation appears to be that life was so dull and tame that any excitement, and especially social contact, was eagerly sought. Men went twenty miles to the county town to see the Court come in. A camp meeting, a barbecue, a convention, sufficed to draw together all the people of a county. On these occasions passion, prejudice, argument, etc., inflamed the people, and the mysterious sympathy of a crowd seemed to act more intensely on people who were unused to it. The orators curried popularity and applause. The crowd was very capricious. It was not easy to tell in advance what would "take" and what would fall dead. The ambitious men sought only to perceive the currents of popular feeling. The consequence was that they always exaggerated the tendencies which had once started. They tried to distinguish themselves by their zeal and excess in the popular cause. Therefore everything tended to run the current of the moment to excess and abuse.

If these facts are noted they go far to explain the extravagances of the relief system, of paper money banking, of internal improvements, etc.

There is in every commercial community a general indebtedness. It is constantly being dissolved and renewed. It is quite a different thing when a simple agricultural community consists of householders, nearly every one of whom is under a load of long debt, by which he has pledged his future production and savings; even if the load is not, under favorable circumstances, excessive. Taking into account the vicissitudes of life:—natural calamities, disease, personal and family misfortune, there will be a percentage of such debtors who will fail to carry out successfully the enterprises which they incurred debt. This is so even in a new country, where the drafts on the future are in fact honored to a marvellous extent, even when they were rashly and unwarrantably drawn. In the case, however, in which the plans are excessive, extravagant, and ill-devised, and where the capital is carelessly and recklessly managed, the only consequence must be a wide sweep of financial disaster. Then, if the bankrupts are voters, and the institutions of civil government are those of a democratic republic, a general indebtedness comes to appear like the worst of political and social diseases. This disease has ravaged the United States again and again within two hundred years. It is no doubt attendant on a spirit of feverish enterprise, indomitable industry, and a sanguine temperament. It has impressed on our national life a character of endless vicissitude, and alternations of heats of prosperity and chills of disaster. How much more capital have we, how much more secure are fortunes, how much more really efficient is the productive power of the nation, than it would have been on a system of cash and patient accumulation with realizations?

"Money is scarce" when a great many people have given money for goods in the expectation of giving the goods for money again at a gain. Then the time comes when the people who have money will not part with it for goods at the prices ruling because they think them too high. They withdraw the money from circulation. This is the "contraction" which tells. There arises a complaint of "sluggish circulation of money," of "over-production," of the "cruelty of competition," and the "tyranny of the conjuncture." The attempt always suggests itself to remedy the trouble by "issuing money enough for the wants of trade." If this remedy could be made operative it would force the holders of money to part with it for goods at rates satisfactory to the holders of the latter. This device has never been made to work. To see the reason why, it suffices to ask one's self whether one would allow it to be put in effect against one's self. "In vain the net is spread in the sight of any bird." The people who have the advantage of the market must be slaves, imbeciles, or cowards to give it up and exchange places with those who are on the other side. As to outstanding contracts the case is different. There the "sovereign" steps in. Ethics and metaphysics are invoked. We hear of "distributive justice," and the legislator and judge go to work to administer it. Stay laws and legal tender laws are their chief engines. The only effect which results is a dissolution of the bonds of society and a reign of injustice, with a suspension of all the recuperative operations which would otherwise automatically begin.

KENTUCKY.—The Bubble having burst, the time had now come for "relief." Relief meant that some were left long of goods on a market which had dropped. They wanted something to raise prices again long enough for them to unload on somebody else.

The history of the relief laws of the western States runs back to the first settlement of Virginia. Through the eighteenth century the laws for execution on judgments oscillated between security to the creditor and leniency to the debtor. Whenever "times were hard," the collection laws were relaxed; when the exigency passed, they were restored. The preambles of the laws throw an interesting light on the experience of these two lines of policy. It came to be the standard of severity, amongst those who had grown up under the Virginia tradition, that a debtor whose personal property was taken in execution might replevin the goods for three months on giving bond with surety for the debt and costs. In Kentucky, land was made liable to execution although it had not been so in Virginia. When land was taken, an old Virginia institution was applied in a modified way. Appraisers were appointed and the land was valued. Originally this was a fair device where there was no proper market to make a price. It was adopted in all the States and Territories of the Mississippi Valley, except Louisiana and Michigan. In times of general indebtedness it became a means for the debtors to band together against the creditors. The laws provided, with various minor differences, that the land or property should not be sold unless it would bring at auction one-half or two-thirds or other fraction of the appraisal made by neighbors who were all likewise debtors. If it did not, it was restored to the debtor for a year or other period. The term of replevin was also sometimes extended. Later, this was connected with a provision that the debtor should have a replevin for a year or other set time unless the creditor would endorse on the writ that the officer might accept in payment some specified kind of currency; being always a depreciated kind. These laws always provided that, if the debtor did not avail himself of his relief, the property should be sold on a credit for a term which corresponded to the delay which he might have had under the law; the buyer to give a bond to pay at the term.

The collection laws of Kentucky were brought back, in the first years of the century, to the old standard above described, but at the beginning of the inflation period they began to be relaxed again. The laws staying execution, unless the creditor endorsed the writ, were extended from year to year; but in 1818 the required endorsement was only for notes of the Bank of the United States or of the Bank of Kentucky.

February 6, 1819, the endorsement law was further extended till February 5, 1820, but the endorsement was now to provide for notes of the Bank of Kentucky only. This Bank of Kentucky, whose notes the creditor must agree to take, had suspended in the middle of November, 1818, but was compelled by public opinion to resume within a week. It was, therefore, limping along during the year 1819.

Committees of the Bank of Kentucky, the Farmers' and Mechanics' Bank of Lexington, the Commercial Bank of Louisville, and the Louisville branch of the Bank of the United States held a meeting at Lexington, May 22, 1819, to consider the distressed state of the country and devise a plan of relief; but their real purpose was to "counteract the objects of those who are disposed to suspend specie payments and establish replevin laws."

In June of that year, the gross amount of debts due to the banks in Kentucky was estimated at $10 millions; $5 millions to the Bank of Kentucky, $3 millions to the branches of the Bank of the United States, and $2 millions to the independent banks. County meetings were held to get a suspension of specie payments, more paper money, and an extra session of the Legislature to pass relief laws.

At a county convention in Jefferson County the vote was three to one against approving a suspension of specie payments by the Bank of Kentucky.

In August, 1819, the independent banks refused to do anything but exchange little notes for big ones and *vice versa.* They nearly all failed before the end of the year.

During the year the Bank of Kentucky became heavily indebted to the Bank of the United States on account of the great advances which the former made to the independent banks. In November, the latter bank ordered the debt to be collected. The Bank of Kentucky suspended and compromised. Its notes were at fifteen per cent. discount. May 4th, 1820, the stockholders of the Bank of Kentucky voted to suspend specie payment. This suspension became permanent and the bank ceased to exist. "What did we tell the people of Kentucky when they littered their banks and were so anxious to introduce the offices of the Bank of the United States?"

The Legislature of 1819-20 showed itself to be a relief Legislature. December 16, 1819, a law was passed over the Governor's veto to suspend for sixty days sales on execution, whether on judgment or on bonds. January 10, 1820, the law of ten per cent. damages on foreign bills of exchange was repealed; a blow at the Bank of the United States. February

10th the independent bank law was repealed. The act has a very long preamble; it states that all men are equal; that there is no monopoly in the social compact; that all power is inherent in the people. These propositions are to lead the way up to the next one which is, that all laws granting privileges to the few are tyrannical and therefore repealable by the supreme authority. To say that charters are irrepealable is to say that abuse must be perpetual. All laws which harm the people are against the social compact, and "are subject on first principles to the condition of being repealed." A bank charter gives privileges to the few. "To the end, therefore, that the good people of this State be delivered in future from the baneful effect of the power and privileges granted by the law establishing independent banks in this commonwealth, which have been exercised in many cases in the plenitude of tyranny, oppression, and abuse, to the great injury of the good people of this State," that act is repealed from May 1st.

The forty banks which were overturned with these solemn and dogmatic enunciations had been founded, not by capitalists and monopolists, but by a beneficent Legislature, pursuing a policy of prosperity on behalf of "poor men."

It is plain that one of the chief reasons for the popular antipathy to banks was the notion that they made the rich richer and the poor poorer. This was the meaning of the endless declamation about aristocracy and equality in connection with banks. That banks of the kind which then existed in such immense numbers, organized by insolvents, destitute of capital, engaged in paper money mongering, had this effect is beyond question, except that, in the end, they almost invariably ruined also those who had at first won by them; being in this like all gambling devices, with which in fact they ought to be classed. The popular feeling did not, however, attach to this view of them. It was because they loaned only to the "rich" that they were alleged to have this effect, and the popular demand was for real democratic banks which would act "equally." Equality before the banks, however, could only mean that all men ought to have equal credit. When the doctrine of equality comes to be applied to commercial credit it receives its final and most pitiless refutation. The great Banks of the States were built upon this notion, and they made an experiment of it which was ample, unreserved, and conclusive. The effect of giving equal credit to all, at least who were freeholders, was to ruin everybody and at last the banks also.

February 11, 1820, another relief law was passed. The creditor might endorse that notes of the Bank of Kentucky would be received. In that case the debtor had a replevin of one year, or the property was sold at one year's credit for the bond of the purchaser, and on such bonds there was no replevin. If the creditor made no endorsement, the replevin was for two years. After judgment and before execution, the defendant might enter into recognizances with one or more good sureties to pay in one year with interest. If he did so, all proceedings were stayed for one year; then there was summary judgment, as on a replevin bond; but if there was no endorsement that Bank of Kentucky notes would be received, the recognizances ran for two years, not one. Where no recognizances were entered into, there was to be no execution until ten days after the rising of the Court. This act was to be enforced until March 1, 1821.

It is evident that in all these stay laws the effort was to get a postponement, such as was employed in the earliest development of bankruptcy proceedings. What is the sense of such an act of the sovereign power? It can only be that a solvent person, disappointed of his receipts, is momentarily unable to pay, but has bills receivable in excess of his bills payable; so that in a short time he can pay. To force him to liquidate on the spot would sacrifice his assets. Another case where such an act would be justifiable in a less degree would be where it is assumed that the debtor can and will win a surplus out of his business in another period of production. In this case, a delay would involve risk on two points,—his success in production, and his persistent frugality to save what he produces and devote it to the payment of his debts. In the stay laws now before us, the pretense was that they were justified under the second head; and it is very possible that there may have been individuals who fitted the theory, and who successfully emancipated themselves from debt under the system; but the debtors, as a class, were persons who had bought for a rise, to whom a delay could be of no use unless the inflated prices should return.

February 14th, it was enacted that no damages or interest on notes due to the Bank of the United States, or on any debts to it, should be awarded by any Court in excess of one per cent. per annum. For the future, any greater rate should be usurious and void. This act was to come into force March 15th, but if the Bank should pay $5,000 to the Auditor before April 1st, the act was no longer to be in force. On the same day, an act was passed to enable the independent banks to collect debts due to them in liquidation. Those which appointed commissioners in liquidation were not to be liable to suit for a year.

The forty banks had been founded in the period of inflation, as a means of developing industry and as a policy of prosperity. They had all been smashed in a reaction of legislative petulance. Next a big paper money bank was founded as another step in the system of relief to the debtors whom the prosperity policy had created.

November 29, 1820, the Bank of the Commonwealth of Kentucky was incorporated. It had no stockholders. The officers were elected annually by the Legislature. Their salaries were paid by the State, and they were incorporated. No one was to have a loan of more than $1,000, except the directors, who might have $2,000. It was to issue $2 millions in notes, which were to be apportioned between the counties in proportion to the taxable property in each, in 1820, and were granted in loans on mortgage securities. Loans were to be made in 1820 only to those who needed them, "for the purpose of paying his, her, or their just debts;" or to purchase the products of the country for exportation. Borrowers during 1821 were to take oath as to the purpose for which they wanted the loan. Here then was a novelty in banking, an institution which sought as borrowers, not solvent persons of high credit, but embarrassed and perhaps insolvent debtors. When complete, the bank had twelve branches; its capital was to consist of all money thereafter paid in for land warrants, or land west of the Tennessee river [this was a contingent revenue, which, inasmuch as the land speculation had passed by, proved very small]; the produce of the stock owned by the State in the Bank of Kentucky, after that bank should be wound up [the compulsion to take the notes of the independent banks had ruined this bank, and destroyed the value of its stock]; the unexpended balances in the Treasury at the end of the year [during the life of this bank there were none]. The profits of the bank were to go to the State. The notes were legal tender to and from the State. The Legislature appropriated $7,000 to buy books, paper, and plates for printing the notes. This is all the real capital the bank ever had. Stripped of all pretense, therefore, it was the State Treasury put into the hands of a commission, elected by the Legislature. This commission was said to be "incorporated," but they held no assets, and some acts of legislation look as if it required a vote of the Legislature to pay judgments obtained against them. It was asserted that the notes of the bank got into the hands of speculators, who held them in order to buy property when the crash should come. This was expected when the stay laws would expire.

In the Bank of the Commonwealth of Kentucky *vs.* Mayes, in the Circuit Court of Mercer County, Kentucky, in 1834, the Court said: "This bank is owned and governed by the State; it is established in the name and on behalf of the State; the State pays and defrays its entire expenses; all individuals are indicted from participating in it; its paper is circulated as money; it is receivable and redeemable by the State, and derives its circulation and negotiability from the credit of the State. If its notes are not bills of credit within the meaning of the Constitution, it will be difficult to characterize a bill of credit." From this decision we also learn that the lowest denomination of the notes of the bank was twelve and a-half cents.

This bank was a mere paper money machine. If by a "bank" we understand an institution having some permanency, and intended to continue an action and reaction through some prolonged period, for the satisfaction of

215

constant or recurring financial necessities, this institution would not properly be called a bank, nor yet even a loan office. The idea and intention were to inflate the currency and raise prices until the indebted persons could discharge their debts. Then the issues were to be recalled and burned, and the purpose would be accomplished. It was never proposed to make these issues legal tender, because that was understood to be hopeless under the federal Constitution, but the stay laws were to put the coercion on the creditor which was necessary to make the system work. Gouge quoted from somebody else a description of a similar period when "creditors were seen running away from their debtors and debtors pursuing them in triumph and paying them without mercy."

A supplementary act was passed, December 22, 1820, by which the issue of the Bank of the Commonwealth was extended to $3 millions and the limit of single loans to $2,000. Property mortgaged to it and sold under foreclosure might be redeemed in two years, at ten per cent. advance; notes under $1 might be issued; special officers were appointed to sign them. Debts to this bank were made preferred debts, to be paid first, by executors and administrators. This provision was held valid and enforced in a case in 1829.

In connection with the establishment of the Bank of the Commonwealth of Kentucky, the stay laws were advanced still another stage. If the creditor endorsed the writ that notes of the Bank of Kentucky or of the Bank of the Commonwealth might be received, the replevin was three months; if there was no endorsement, it was two years. This act was not to apply to executions on replevin bonds, but it was to apply to executions which were in the hands of the Sheriff when it was passed. On an original judgment, if the debtor did not avail himself of the replevin, a sale was made at two years' credit, the bond of the buyer being taken. In an execution on a replevin bond, if the above mentioned notes were not endorsed, the replevin was for one year, or there was a sale on one year's credit. Recognizances were to be employed as before. This act was to be enforced from March 1, 1821, when the existing law would expire.

December 26th, the charter of the Bank of Kentucky was extended to 1829, with some new limitations. The stock of the State was to be paid over to the Bank of the Commonwealth in three annual installments, beginning December 31, 1824. At the next session, all laws by which the State was to buy or pay for stock in the Bank of Kentucky were repealed. Imprisonment for debt was abolished, and equitable interests were made liable to execution.

The Bank of the United States applied to the Federal Court at Lexington, Kentucky, in 1822, to instruct the clerk to issue on application the writ of *ca. sa.*, the law of the State abolishing the writ notwithstanding.

The "Union" of Washington, Kentucky, said in March, 1822, that the circulating medium seemed about to cease to circulate. In the previous winter it had been understood that the Bank of the Commonwealth was not to put out any more paper, and that its issues would be regularly withdrawn, on the theory that its only intention was to secure for the debtors a delay of a year or two that they might be able to save the property which they had pledged. This expectation had caused the exchange to rise, although returns, on the exports had not begun to come in. The "relief" had been given to all

217

who were solvent. The Legislature, however, increased the issue. Those who had property would no longer sell it for the notes. If the notes were not restored to value, there would be no currency at all.

This complaint lasted through the year. In October the "Louisville Public Advertiser" argued that there was less money, in value, in circulation than ever before; as follows: "When the paper of the old Bank of Kentucky was nearly as good as specie, it had bills in circulation to the amount of two million and a-half, which was barely sufficient for the purposes of trade, and this bank now has in its vault as large an amount in the bills of the Bank of the Commonwealth as those of its own in circulation. The whole issue of the new bank amounts to $2.3 millions; but as, in the present rate of exchange and price of commodities, this amount only does the business of $1,150,000, the real circulating medium has been reduced nearly one-half."

In 1822 the Legislature used its power in the election of State directors of the old Bank of Kentucky to put in "relief" men who would make that bank accept Commonwealth notes. The effect was that the stock of the old bank at once fell to fifty and this was its death blow. In October, 1822, a specie dollar was worth $2.05 in Commonwealth notes.

The power of the Bank of Kentucky to discount notes and bills was repealed December 5, 1822, and it was ordered to wind up. Its notes were to be burned. The Bank of Kentucky and the Bank of the Commonwealth were to exchange notes with each other. The Auditor was to inform the president of the Bank of the Commonwealth of the amount of revenue in his hands from the lands, the sales of which had been appropriated to that bank; notes of the bank were to be burned, equal to this revenue, and also all notes paid in the cancellation of loans. In February, June and November, similar burnings were to take place, equal to the same income, but not to exceed $750,000 before the next meeting of the Legislature. In another act it was recited that the notes of the Bank of Kentucky and the Bank of the Commonwealth were so dirty and worn that lists could not be made of them, by letter and number, as required by law; therefore the president and directors were to make lists, showing the amount of each denomination burned and the aggregate of each class.

At the session of the Legislature in 1822-3, evidence of trouble with the Bank of the Commonwealth already appears. A resolution was passed November 26, 1822, ordering that the Bank of the Commonwealth should call up only one per cent. per month of its loans, instead of two per cent., which it was demanding, and a committee was appointed to examine the bank. Under the replevin law, the Judges instructed the jury to find "scaling verdicts," rating the judgment sum in specie according to the depreciation at the time of the contract. This sum could be collected after two years, unless the creditor endorsed the execution. If he did that, he obtained payment in three months in paper worth about fifty cents on the dollar,—that is, he obtained about one-fourth of his original claim.

One chief reason of the great interest attaching to the history of Kentucky at this period is the number of great and important elements which became combined in it. The Kentuckians had been the strongest anti-federalists. It was they who, in 1798, had been used by the great Virginians to enounce doctrines of State rights which the latter dared not utter themselves. Until Louisiana was bought Kentucky had been more than lukewarm to the Union. The Legislature, as early as 1796, had been at war with the judiciary; had tried judge breaking and legislating judges out of office. They had shown their respect for vested rights by revoking a pension to Judge Muter after securing his resignation by granting it. In the midst of the history with which we are now occupied, in 1821, the Supreme Court of the United States decided the case of Green *versus* Biddle, which touched the people Of Kentucky to the quick. The man in occupation of land was a voter, neighbor, friend, relative. By the carelessness of Virginia and of the settlers the titles were often disputed. The Legislature represented the occupiers. The public men sought the favor of the same. An occupier, if ousted, presented a real object of commiseration, for he had lost the labor of years. Still the law, right, and justice of the case might be all against him, and his troubles might be all his own fault.

The laws of Kentucky, for twenty-five years, aimed to enlarge the rights of the occupying claimant against the successful contestant.

In Green *versus* Biddle those laws were declared void because they were in violation of the compact with Virginia at the separation. All efforts were exhausted to get a reversal of this decision. In Bodley *versus* Gaither (1825), the Supreme Court of the State refused to be controlled by the decision in Green *versus* Biddle. Inasmuch as the Supreme Court of the United States, in Hawkins *versus* Barney's Lessee (1831), very materially modified the ruling in Green *versus* Biddle, the Kentucky State rights men could claim to have been the champions of justice, truth, and right. The connection between the stay laws and the banking system has already been shown.

The Kentuckians were alarmed at the course of the decisions of the Supreme Court of the United States. They anticipated the effect on their bank and relief system, and they went to meet the inferences hostile to their pet measures, which seemed to flow directly from the law as expounded. Thus a clash between the Legislature and the judiciary, and another between the federal and State authorities, lay in the relief system of Kentucky.

This subject, in all its length and breadth, was opened by R. M. Johnson in the Senate of the United States, January 14, 1822. The document is, like many others which were prepared in Kentucky at this time, and in connection with these measures, very ably written. It must have been prepared with great care in advance, so that its origin goes back to some time early in 1821, and soon after the decision in Green *versus* Biddle. On the points which now most immediately interest us he said: "I know of no clause in the federal Constitution that gives the power to the judiciary of declaring the laws and Constitution of a State repugnant to the Constitution of the United States and therefore null and void." "No State shall emit bills of credit. This prohibition has not yet produced collision, but it is fairly to be presumed from the principles established by other acts of adjudication that, if the measures of certain States relative to banks were brought before the Courts of the United States, they would be declared unconstitutional and void, nor would it be any matter of surprise should the supreme judiciary yet, by such a decision, obtain control over the policy of a whole community, relative to a circulating medium for any special

221

and necessary purposes, though it might not be pretended that such currency was made a legal tender. Kentucky has incorporated a bank for necessary purposes. The crisis of the country demanded it, and the people have sanctioned it with a unanimity almost unparalleled. If the constitutionality of this subject were brought before the federal judiciary, I have little doubt that the law would be declared null and void, and the State, by such a decision of persons neither interested in her policy nor responsible to her citizens, deprived of the power of relief in these times of overwhelming difficulty." No State shall pass any law impairing the obligation of contracts. "The Constitution recognizes a principle of morality founded on justice'and religion. ... Each State is the judge of its own honor and the keeper of its own conscience." "The fund upon which executions shall operate is a regulation of a political character and subject to the absolute control of the Legislature. That fund may be extended or contracted at the will of the State." In 1821 Kentucky abolished imprisonment for debt, but at the same session of the Legislature, extended the prison bounds to the limits of the county, "under a belief that the federal judiciary will declare this law abolishing imprisonment for debt unconstitutional, as impairing the obligation of contracts."

Stay laws, paper money, squatters' rights and State rights had now become intertwined, and acted and reacted on one another, constantly intensifying the popular exasperation against vested rights, creditors, the Bank of the United States, and the federal government.

In a great political debate, in the Senate of the State, in 1838, Wickliffe reviewed all this history in the face of the men who had had part in it. He denied that the Bank of the

United States had ruined Kentucky. He referred to the creation and repeal of the forty banks, and to the sacrifice of the Bank of Kentucky to try to bolster up those banks, and then its destruction. "It was this outrage against the rights of contract and the sacred honor of legislators that prostrated Kentucky, and not the Bank of the United States. These mad measures left the country nothing but the Bank of the United States to hang upon. She kept the even tenor of her way. ... No, sir, it was not the Bank of the United States but independent bank makers, property law makers, judge breakers, and paper money schemers that then ruled and ruined Kentucky."

In no case which we have found, did any Court of any grade, in any State, support the stay laws. The next step in this history, which we have to notice, is a collision between the people of the State of Kentucky represented in the Legislature, and their own judiciary.

Judge Clark decided the case of Williams *vs.* Blair, at the Bourbon Circuit Court, ordering the recognizance of the defendant to be quashed with costs against him, the endorsement act of 1820 being unconstitutional. May 28, 1822, a Committee of the House of Representatives was appointed "to inquire into the decision of [Judge Clark] and report thereon to this House." The preamble recited that the Judge had "given a decision in contravention of the laws of this Commonwealth called the endorsement and replevin laws, and therein has grossly transcended his judicial authority and disregarded the constitutional powers of the Legislature of this Commonwealth." Three days later the Judge was cited to appear and show cause why he should not be removed from office. May 27th he sent a written answer.

He gave a list of cases in which the Supreme Court of the State had ruled acts of the Legislature unconstitutional and argued the necessity and propriety of this power in the Judges, both under the federal and State Constitutions. The vote on the motion to address the Governor to remove the Judge was 59 to 35. "The National Intelligencer," from which the account is taken, says: "The key to the unusual excitement caused by this opinion is to be found in the fact which is stated in the 'Louisville Advertiser' that this opinion of Judge Clark was supposed to have an indirect bearing upon the charter of the Bank of the Commonwealth. A majority of the Senate is said to have been opposed to the proposed removal of the Judge."

Upon appeal, this case of Williams *vs*. Blair, and that of Lapsley *vs*. Brashears came up together and the decision of them formed a crisis in the great drama whose elements had been gathering for eight or ten years. The records of these cases were burned in the civil war, but the reports state the essential features of them. In the former case, Blair, Ingles, and Barr gave a note to Williams, November 12, 1819, which they did not pay at maturity. He obtained judgment, whereupon, under the stay law, they entered into a recognizance, in the clerk's office, to pay within two years. Williams moved to quash this recognizance, on the ground that the law was unconstitutional. He won as above stated. The decision, on appeal, was rendered by Judge Boyle, October 8, 1823, as follows: "A law passed after a contract is made, extending the term of replevin on a judgment rendered on such contract impairs the obligation of the contract, and violates the Constitution of the United States."

The case of Lapsley was argued on both sides by the leading public men of the two political parties, which were now forming in the State, upon the issue of the relief system; Harrison, Breckenridge, and Wickliffe for Lapsley; Haggin, Barry, and Rowan for Brashears.

The story of this latter case is worth telling at length, as an illustration of the relief system. Brashears was indebted to Lapsley on a contract. Lapsley got judgment for the debt, with interest from March, . Brashears was imprisoned for the debt and then allowed the liberty of the prison rules on a bond, with Barr as surety. He broke the rules. Lapsley brought suit against him and his surety on the bond, and got judgment, January, 1816. Soon after this Lapsley died. His administrator, also named Lapsley, got judgment to have execution in January, 1817. A *fieri facias* was issued April 23d. June 17th, the defendants and an additional surety executed a replevin bond to pay within twelve months, and the sheriff returned the writ endorsed to that effect. The bond was lodged with the clerk of the Court. August 15, 1818, a *fieri facias* was issued to the sergeant of the Court of Appeals on the replevin bond, but it was returned "stayed by injunction." September 25th, the injunction was dissolved. October 12, 1821, a new *fieri facias* was issued on the replevin bond. October 23, 1822, the three defendants, bringing in now another surety, as was necessary at every step, executed another replevin bond to pay in two years, under the endorsement law of 1820. The sheriff made return accordingly. In January, 1823, Lapsley moved to quash this replevin bond and the return. This motion was overruled; both sides appealed. October, 1823, the Court of Appeals held that the endorsement law was unconstitutional, and

225

remanded the case to the Circuit Court for reversal and disposition, in accordance with this decision. Here we lose sight of the case, after eight and a-half years of litigation, and are left to wonder whether Lapsley ever got his money.

It was because the defendant in this case was frustrated in the course of action which he was pursuing to escape an adjudicated debt that the relief orators were so alarmed about rights and justice, and so vehement in their denunciation of the judiciary and of "judge-made" law.

It is significant of the entanglement of this question with the other great political and social questions of the time that, in a petition for a new trial, although the whole matter was a case of debt in a State court, Bibb enlarged upon the danger that diminution of the power of the States would make a consolidated government, which, in so vast a territory as that of the United States, would be inconsistent with the existence of a free republic.

Instead of producing acquiescence and a settlement of pending controversies, this decision became the starting point of a political struggle which lasted for seven or eight years, and was marked by the bitterest and most malignant passion. Indeed a direct train of consequences may be traced far down into the history of the politics and constitutional law of the federal government. The proceedings of the Court were regarded, by about half of the people of Kentucky, as a usurpation by the Judges.

Governor Adair, in his message of that year, approved of the relief system and denounced tho courts for deciding the replevin laws unconstitutional After his term expired, he petitioned for redress on account of the payment of his salary in depreciated paper.

At the following session of the Legislature, the all absorbing topic was the decision of the Court in these cases. December 29, 1823, a long document was adopted, containing an argument against the right of the Courts to declare laws unconstitutional. It went deeply into the metaphysics of obligation, the old subtleties of distributive and commutative justice, the social compact, and the laws of nature; then followed an argument against the decision. Of the Bank of the United States it was said: "Its motto is, 'Pay me that thou owest me.'" "A rigid punctuality (but ill according with the agricultural habits and varying condition and resources of most of the States) is exacted by that institution." The decision means that the existing remedy is binding on the State and the debtor, but not on the creditor. Hence the Legislature protests against the doctrines of the decisions, "as ruinous in their practical effects to the good people of this Commonwealth, and subversive of their dearest and most invaluable political rights." The decisions are then declared erroneous. The Legislature will take no steps to interfere with the administration of justice; but Kentucky will not submit to judicial tyranny. A protest is then uttered against Green *vs.* Biddle and it is declared that a protest ought to be sent to Congress, and that such an organization of the Supreme Court ought to be secured, that no State law could be declared unconstitutional without a two-thirds majority of the Judges. A remonstrance and memorial to Congress of this character was later adopted. Thus we find, at this point, the stay laws, the banks and the squatters' rights all commingled.

In 1824, the Court of Appeals decided that a remedy which was applicable to a note for the payment of money could not be given for a note "payable in the money of this

State," which was held to mean the current paper money; but bank notes are not money.

January 5th, of that year, the Judges were ordered not to scale debts for contracts in notes of the Bank of Kentucky or the Bank of the Commonwealth, but judgment was to be given in the paper. If the plaintiff endorsed this paper on the execution, the replevin was to be only three months. The Court of Appeals, construing this law, held that it did not apply to any contract made before its passage, no matter when the action was begun, and that the Court could not take judicial notice of the value of the notes of the Bank of the Commonwealth on any particular date. It was also decided, in another case, that bank paper was not money, nor an ultimate measure of value, the point at issue being whether it could be sold without imputation of usury.

All the two year replevin laws were repealed January 7, 1824, to take effect from June 1st following. Replevin after that was to be for three months, and if no bond was given, the sale was to be on credit for three months. The date of the contract was to be on the judgment. Real estate in execution was to be valued by the county commissioners in gold and silver. On the same day, the Bank of the Commonwealth was ordered to continue its calls at one per cent. per month. All its notes and those of the Bank of Kentucky were to be called in from the branches and held subject to the order of the Legislature. Officers of the Bank of the Commonwealth were to be called on to pay their loans, like other debtors. Three years from this date were allowed for the independent banks to wind up, provided they would endorse on writs to collect their loans that they would receive Commonwealth notes. One point in the endorsement law of December 25, 1820, which provided that no fee bill should be put in execution within two years after it became due, unless endorsed to receive Bank of Kentucky and Commonwealth notes, remained in effect until February 22, 1834.

December 6, 1824, the Legislature appointed a Committee of Investigation to find out the character of the debts to the Bank of the Commonwealth, and report how many of them were bad. They also stated in their resolution that some directors of the Bank had not complied with the law to pay their debts to it.

At the State election of 1824, the struggle was to elect a Legislature, two-thirds of which would address the Governor for the removal of the Judges who had decided the relief laws unconstitutional. A majority was obtained, but not two-thirds.

Another course was therefore adopted. November 13, 1824, a select committee on the behavior of the Judges was raised, which made an elaborate report to the effect that the Legislature ought to be supreme, and ought not to be ruled by the judiciary. Resolutions were reported that the decision under review encroached on the field of the Legislature and the rights of the people. This led up to a law of December 24th, by which all the laws organizing the Court of Appeals were repealed, and a new court was organized.

The old court denied the constitutionality of the repeal and of the new court, and continued its existence; so that there were two courts. The new court ordered Achilles Sneed, clerk of the old court, to deliver the records to Francis P. Blair, clerk of the new court. Upon Sneed's refusal, he was fined and his papers were seized. A war of vituperative pamphlets ensued. It is said that Blair and Kendall were amongst the pamphleteers on the new court side. Kendall had described the relief system very justly in 1821. His biographer says that he never doubted the constitutionality of the relief measures, and so was driven to defend them. As a director of the Bank of the Commonwealth, he insisted on a conservative policy in that institution. There is a gap in his autobiography from 1823 to 1829, and it is unfortunately impossible to trace the influences which moulded his feelings and opinions. All the leading men on the new court side imbibed the intensest animosity against the Bank of the United States, Blair and Kendall perhaps more than any others.

When Kendall went to Washington, in 1829, he became responsible for a positive and circumstantial assertion that the Bank of the United States gave pecuniary aid to the old court party in the election of 1825; which statement became of the very first importance in the Bank war. When Kendall was called on for his proofs, he could only repeat the assertion from hearsay, but could not produce the responsible authors of it. Nevertheless, the story was often repeated, and the "Globe," in 1831, re-printed it in its original form.

The new court held the records during 1825 by military force, and civil war was avoided only by the moderation of the old court.

In November, 1825, Niles quotes a Kentucky paper that more people had left the State than had come to it for many years. It is plain that two classes of persons were driven away by the relief system,—those who were prevented by it from securing such fruits of their industry as they could accumulate, and those who despaired of ever freeing themselves from their embarrassments.

In the mean time the federal Supreme Court had gone on its way making decisions which established the authority of the federal Constitution and the federal judiciary and so integrated the whole national system. Of these decisions, one which was rendered in 1825, Bank of the United States *versus* Halstead, directly affected Kentucky. It was held that the federal courts could alter the forms of execution which were in use in the States in 1789, so as to subject to execution lands and other property not then subject, and that the law of Kentucky of 1821 did not apply to writs issued from the federal courts.

These decisions were all received with astonishment, contempt and abhorrence, not only by the radical, but also by the moderate State rights men of the time. There was a great deal of declamation in Kentucky in 1825 about rights, liberty, justice, and the sovereignty of the people; but as the "Lexington Reporter" said: What a mockery to talk of justice, freedom, and happiness when the Constitution was brought to the level of such legislative acts as had been adopted by the relief party.

The concurrent effect of the distress in the State, the sad position of the debtors, the political animosity which had been aroused, and the anxiety about great principles of constitutional liberty which had been caused by the judicial decisions which have been referred to, was, to make the political campaign between the old and new court parties in 1825 exceedingly intense. The old court party won a majority in the lower House. The Senate which held over was still of the new court party. A crisis had therefore been reached, but it could not be solved for the time being, because neither party was in a position to win a victory.

The message of Governor Desha of November 7th, 1825, reflects all the elements of excitement and warfare which were in the situation. "The most prominent objects," he says, "which will arrest your attention are the existing differences in our judiciary and the encroachments of the federal tribunals." Two branches of the Bank of the United States have been established in the State without due consideration of the interests of the people, who "justly alarmed for the fights of the State and the purity of their republican institutions" want these banks removed or taxed. "But the Judges of the federal Court, assuming to themselves the prerogative of restricting the taxing power of this State" forbade this tax, and the State judiciary, although they thought the Bank of the United States unconstitutional and the tax constitutional, have yielded to the Supreme Court of the United States. "Since this surrender of the acknowledged rights of the State by those who were made their special guardians, the branches of the United States Bank, exempt from the burdens imposed on the wealth of our own citizens, have proceeded to purchase up the real property of the country and fill it with tenantry." [It was never ascertained what facts he meant to refer to by this statement.] "These institutions for a series of years have carried on a systematic attack upon the legislative power of the State for the double purpose of curtailing the sphere of its exercise and rendering themselves wholly independent of its authority." He refers to the relief laws as "statutes whose principles have been sanctioned by all authorities, State and federal, from the date of the Constitution down to the establishment of these institutions" [the branches of the Bank of the United States]. They and their friends have attacked these laws. The State Court of Appeals has declared them unconstitutional, and the federal Supreme Court has decided that if they were constitutional, they were not binding on the federal court. "And the federal Judges for the Kentucky district have actually made their code, and put it into operation, by which our citizens are imprisoned in direct violation of our laws, and their property seized and sold in modes not provided in their statute book." This is "nothing short of despotism." The federal courts have made the Bank of the United States independent of State laws and tribunals. "The wrongs suffered by this State from the decision of the Supreme Court of the United States declaring our occupants' law to be unconstitutional have not been redressed." "It is my firm belief that in the insecurity now felt by numberless cultivators of our soil may be found the chief cause of that extensive emigration which is now thinning the population of some of the finest sections of our State." "The doctrine of our late Court of Appeals that an opinion of the Supreme Court of the United States on subjects involving the rights of the State is binding and conclusive upon the State authorities is believed to be not only erroneous but fatal to the sovereignty of the States." The Supreme Court is a part of the general government whose encroachments are complained of. The States can get no more justice, therefore, than an individual could, if judged by his oppressors. The new court of the State has banished "the doctrine of ready submission to the unconstitutional decrees of the Supreme Court." What Kentucky wants is another reformation of the federal judiciary, such as occurred at Jefferson's accession. The relief laws have been repealed "as to all contracts formed after the repeal, and their operation has almost ceased to be felt in our courts of justice; but the questions of legislative power and judicial right, which have sprung from some of those laws and outlived them, are of vital importance to the government as well of this State as of every other in the Union." Virginia had a law like the replevin law in 1789 and re-enacted it afterwards several times, even after Kentucky became an independent State. Kentucky has practiced on the same principle and the principle has never been wholly eradicated from her laws. The constitutionality of these laws "seems never to have been doubted until the interest of the United States Bank made it necessary that new and more rigid principles should be incorporated into our system of government." The decision of the State court "that the remedial law in existence when a contract is made, constitutes the obligation, and that no State Legislature can so change that law as to delay the remedy" has "wrested from the representatives of the people the power to suspend the operation of the laws in any case of contract even in time of insurrection, war, pestilence, or famine." He justifies the act legislating the old court out of office in order to "rid the country of these erroneous and dangerous principles," including the notion that the Judges could not be called to account. The old court has gone on, but without any breach of the peace; hence the Executive has not thought it his duty to molest them. Lately they have shown a disposition to force the execution of their orders. If they do this the writer will perform his painful duty. "Instead of quieting the country as was ardently desired, the act of the last session re-organizing the Court of Appeals, together with other causes made to operate, has filled it with new agitations." The people are dissatisfied with the re-organizing act. Neither the old nor the new court can unite upon themselves the confidence of both parties or exercise judicial power without doubt as to the validity of their acts. If the Legislature sees fit to provide for the appointment of an entirely new set of appellate judges, he will select them equally from both parties. The salaries should be reduced to $1,500, which by the appreciation of the currency would be equal to $2,000, a year before. The salaries of the officers of the Bank of Kentucky, the Bank of the Commonwealth, and the officers of the Transylvania University should be reduced. The stock of the Bank of Kentucky owned by the State and the profits of the Bank of the Commonwealth are a disposable fund which should be used for turnpike roads and other improvements. The appreciation of the currency has increased the burden of taxes. This should be remedied. The execution laws are in a state of chaos on the statute-book and require revision.

The offer of Desha to constitute a new court equally from the two existing ones, if all the Judges would resign, was due to the fact that the new court was losing ground. The bar of the State was not willing to risk the validity of its decisions.

At the session of 1825-6, the House voted to abolish the new court; but the Senate, by the casting vote of the Lieutenant-governor, refused to concur.

The bitterness of the parties to this old and new court contest is illustrated by the fact that a three days' argument, shared in by all the leading lawyers of the day, was held upon the application of a gentleman to be admitted to practice in the Woodford Circuit Court, he having been licensed as an attorney by the old court after that court had been legislated out of existence. The Judge did not dare to decide the question, but allowed him to practice out of courtesy.

After another hotly contested election, in 1826, the old court was in control of both Houses. December 30, 1826, a law was passed over the Governor's veto, "to remove the unconstitutional obstructions which have been thrown in the way of the Court of Appeals." In the preamble it is said: "The above recited acts have been decided by the good people of this Commonwealth at two successive elections, to be dangerous violations of the Constitution, and subversive of the long tried principles upon which experience has demonstrated that the security of life, liberty, and property depends." The two acts erecting the new court and fixing the salaries of the Judges in it were repealed, and all the acts which the new court act had repealed were revived. January 11, 1827, an act was passed to try to bridge over the new court time. The period from November 30, 1824, to April 1, 1827, was to be considered non in the Court of Appeals, and the clerk of the new court was to deliver to the clerk of the old court all papers "in any wise pertaining to the Court of Appeals." The second volume of T. B. Monroe's reports contains the decisions in seventy-seven cases, which have never been cited by the Supreme Court of the State, being the decisions of the new court.

In 1827, the currency of the States in the Mississippi Valley was very much improved. There remained, as was said, only $800,000 of Commonwealth paper out, and this was merchandise, not currency. The bank held notes of individuals to the amount of one and a-half millions and real estate worth $30,592. Hence there was due to it a balance from the public, after all its notes should be paid in, of $600,000. Its debtors had this to pay in specie or its equivalent, or else the Bank would get their property. No other instance is known in which debtors had to endure so great an appreciation between the time of borrowing and repaying as in the case of this paper money machine. No one has ever explained how any paper money machine could act otherwise unless there should be constant new issues, depreciating more and more until they reached zero. On its paper issue of notes nominally for $3 millions it had won $600,000 worth of property in five years. Who got this gain? It seems that there must have been personal interests at stake to account for the intensity of feeling which was enlisted in its defense, especially on the part of a clique of leading politicians.

No positive evidence has been found as to the course of prices in the State from 1820, but nothing indicates that the issues of the Bank of the Commonwealth raised prices in the interest of debtors. In general, the history of currency in this country shows that the doctrine that prices will respond promptly and proportionately to changes in the amount of the currency (or even, more strictly, of the money of account), cannot be accepted without important limitations.

In 1827, the old court Chief Justice, Boyle, resigned and Bibb, new court, took his place. In 1828 Owsley and Mills, old court, resigned and Governor Metcalf re-appointed them. The Senate, which was then in the hands of the relief party, refused to confirm them. They had been members of the Court which had declared the relief laws unconstitutional in 1823, and this action was an expression of the relentless animosity with which they were pursued by the relief party. Two other anti-relief men, Robertson and Underwood, were appointed and confirmed. Bibb then resigned; whereupon the other two Judges declared the new court acts null and void. In 1829, Robertson was made Chief Justice and Buckner, anti-relief, was appointed, making the Court complete again.

In 1828, the parties were still relief and anti-relief, but the ideas had changed somewhat. The banking and currency parts of the relief creed had sunk out of sight and the political elements remained. A relief man was a State rights man and strict constructionist who wanted to set limits to the supposed encroachments of the federal power, especially the judiciary.

If the amounts of Commonwealth notes reported burned, in Niles' Register, from time to time, during 1823, are added, the total is $2,171,000, although the amount to be burned in that year had been limited by the Legislature to $750,000. In November, 1823, it was reported that the Legislature had resolved to issue no more, and that one-sixth of the total issue had been burned. The total issue, up to October, 1825, was reported as $2,943,620, of which $1,436,239 were still out. Notes to the amount of $420,000 were reported as withdrawn, boxed, and sealed by order of the Legislature. The specie and specie funds of the bank were $16,000. The amount ordered burned by the Legislature, from year to year, by the resolutions which are to be found in the Session Laws from 1825 to 1834, is $1,775,414. The last order is that all which is taken in shall be burned. In 1828, on the other hand, the Legislature allowed $1,000 of the notes of this Bank to be taken from the Treasury by the Cumberland Hospital to pay for new buildings. The note in Briscoe's case was made in 1830, so that the Bank must have been doing business then. By an act of that year, January 29th, the president and directors were ordered to withdraw branches which did not pay, which had been mismanaged, and which the interests of the State required should be withdrawn. An agent was to go to such branches and do the business, including the renewal of notes half-yearly. If the renewal was neglected for sixty days, suit was to be brought. Semi-annual reports by the branches to the head office were to be required. All debts were to be called in, so as to be paid by June 1, 1834. No renewal was to be made without security, and no new loans were to be made under any pretense whatever. Salaries were to be paid in Commonwealth notes. All receivers for the Bank were to pay to it the same paper which they received, or other of equal value. In that year, several branches of the Bank of the Commonwealth were broken open and notes were stolen. January 15, 1831, the agents of the Bank of the Commonwealth were to take oath that they were complying with the requirement to pay to the bank the currency received by them.

In 1831, a new Commonwealth Bank was projected. A later generation of debtors did not see why the State should not repeat on their behalf what it had done for those of 1820.

In 1833, and again in 1837, the bank was required to credit the Treasurer with the amount which he owed to it, and in the last year it was enacted that "the said bank shall hereafter redeem all its notes in specie, as well when presented by the Treasury as other persons."

The counsel for the bank, in Briscoe's case, declared that there were not over $40,000 of its notes outstanding, and that perhaps that amount had been lost. In 1834, an official report showed $56,843 outstanding, and notes of the Bank of Kentucky to the amount of $31,081. The former were quoted at Philadelphia in 1830 at thirty-five discount; the latter at twenty-five discount. In 1835, the corresponding quotations were Commonwealth, sixteen discount; Bank of Kentucky, thirteen discount. The sales of land, at this time, had absorbed them to such an extent as to raise their value.

This means, as the net final result of this financial device, that the State had given to the debtors of 1820 its lands with which to pay their debts; or, more strictly, that it had tried to do so, and, in the attempt, had lost its lands to such persons as were in a position to take advantage of the opportunities offered them, during the fifteen years in which the process was going on, to win gain from it. It is not impossible that here and there a debtor who was extraordinarily shrewd and hard-headed may have availed himself of the relief system successfully, but the number of such must have been very small. In all the cases of relief attempted by big paper money machines the advantage was won by influential individuals who got the management of the undertaking into their hands and turned it to their own profit.

It may be said, almost without limitation, that all paper money issues and stay laws for the relief of debtors have had, as their sole result, to curse debtors with life-long poverty, misery, and debt; and further, that, in the history of this country, "relief" has been the word of the most direful omen to those-who-have-not that the dictionary contains.

A law of February 10, 1845, provided for an audit of the accounts of the president of the Bank of the Commonwealth, and he was called on to report the best means of realizing something from the unavailable debts to the bank.

The agent of the old Bank of Kentucky was directed, February 21, 1846, to hand over all the papers and books of that bank to the first Auditor, with $28,209.74 cash which he seems to have; or the Attorney-general is ordered to sue him. The first Auditor is to audit and settle the accounts, put the money in the Treasury, and draw on it for dividends to the stockholders. He is to carry on the liquidation, redeem the notes, and burn them. The president of the Bank of the Commonwealth is to hand over all papers and money to the first Auditor, who is to audit and settle. He is made president of both banks, and the Commissioners of the Sinking Fund are appointed directors for the purposes of liquidation.

Successive acts continuing the liquidation of the old Bank of Kentucky, the independent banks, and the Bank of the Commonwealth were passed every few years until the civil war. In 1855, commissioners were appointed to find out the facts about the liquidation of the first mentioned, since 1836, and to report its status at the time of the act. It was characteristic of all banks of this kind that their liquidation was interminable.

If the following table of the statistics of the bank note circulation of Kentucky is compared with the above history it will be found that the fluctuations in the composition and total amount of that circulation present phenomena in the history of currency more interesting and instructive than any other similar data which can be found. The case is unique for the study of currency. The table is taken from the document, 26 Cong. I Sess. V Exec. No. 172, p. 1354. The figures present millions and decimals thereof. Variations may be noticed between the figures here given and some which occur above and which are taken from other authorities. All statistics of that region and period must be taken with some latitude, which, however, does not affect the value of these figures for purposes of illustration:

YEAR.	Total.	Bank of Kentucky.	Branches of U. S. Bank.	Bank Commonwealth	New Bank of Kentucky.
1810 □.□.□.□	$0.124	☞			
1811 □.□.□.□	0.161				
1812 □.□.□.□	0.289				
1813 □.□.□.□	0.501				
1814 □.□.□.□	0.576				
1815 □.□.□.□	1.2				
1816 □.□.□.□	1.9				
1817 □.□.□.□	1.5				
1818 □.□.□.□	1.9	1.2	0.64		
1819 □.□.□.□	1.6	0.6	0.63		
1820 □.□.□.□	1.5	1.3	0.28		

TABLE.—Continued.

YEAR.	Total.	Bank of Kentucky.	Branches of U. S. Bank.	Bank Commonwealth.	New Bank of Kentucky.
1821 □.□.□.□	$3.8	1.2	0.20		
1822 □.□.□.□	3.5	0.9	0.19	2.4	
1823 □.□.□.□	2.2	0.48	0.18	2.3	
1824 □.□.□.□	2.3	0.40	0.18	1.7	
1825 □.□.□.□	1.5	0.11	0.17	1.3	
1826 □.□.□.□	1.3	0.083	0.25	0.9	
1827 □.□.□.□	1.3	0.058	0.67	0.6	
1828 □.□.□.□	1.7	0.041	1.3	0.3	
1829 □.□.□.□	2.8	0.038	2.4	0.3	
1830 □.□.□.□	3.2	0.033	2.8	0.3	
1831 □.□.□.□	3.7	0.032	3.5	0.2	

1832 □.□.□.□	4.3		4.1	0.13	
1833 □.□.□.□	3.8		3.7	0.10	
1834 □.□.□.□	3.3		2.9	0.05	0.3
1835 □.□.□.□	5.7		3.1		2.6
1836 □.□.□.□	4.1				4.1
1837 □.□.□.□	3.4				3.4

It seems best to introduce here a notice of the litigation which arose in connection with the Bank of the Commonwealth and bills of credit, although we shall be compelled, in so doing, to anticipate several years. The decision in Briscoe's case fell in the midst of important events which have not yet been narrated, and it is an especially important fact in regard to it that it was not rendered until several States had been committed to the great Bank of the State policy beyond what would appear from our history so far as it has yet advanced.

In the Bank of the Commonwealth of Kentucky *vs.* Wistar *et al.* (1829) the Supreme Court of the United States held that the bank must pay specie on demand in return for a deposit which had been made with it of its own notes, although these notes were, when deposited, worth only 50 cents on $1. It had been provided in the act establishing the bank that it should pay specie. The bank tried to plead the non-suability of a State, but it was held that if the State was the sole owner of the bank, and issued as a sovereign, it would be non-suable; then, however, the notes would be bills of credit. If the State issued as a banker, not a sovereign, then it was suable under the decision in the case of the Bank of the United States *vs.* the Planters' Bank of Georgia.

In Craig *vs.* Missouri (1830) the law of Missouri of 1821 establishing loan offices was declared unconstitutional with respect to the notes issued, which were bills of credit. It was held that "to emit bills of credit conveys to the mind the idea of issuing paper intended to circulate through the community for its ordinary purposes as money; which paper is redeemable at a future day." "If the prohibition means anything, if the words are not empty sounds, it must

245

comprehend the emission of any paper medium by a State government for the purposes of common circulation." Bills of credit and legal tender laws were declared to be the objects of two separate and independent prohibitions.

The case, however, through which the Bank of the Commonwealth of Kentucky obtained national importance and effected the whole law of banking in this country was that of Briscoe *vs.* the Bank of the Commonwealth of Kentucky. Briscoe and others gave a note in 1830 which they did not pay at maturity. In the State Circuit Court Briscoe pleaded "no consideration," on the ground that, the note was given for a loan of notes of the Bank of the Commonwealth, which were "bills of credit" within the prohibition of the Constitution and therefore of no value. The State Court found for the bank. The Supreme Court of the State had held, in 1822, that,—no consideration because bills of credit,—was not a good defense on a suit. The State Court of Appeals affirmed the decision in Briscoe's case. The case was carried to the Supreme Court of the United States on a writ of error. Two of the seven judges were absent in 1834. Of the five who heard the argument in Briscoe's case, three thought that the notes of the Bank of the Commonwealth were bills of credit under the decision in Craig *vs.* Missouri; but there was not a majority of the whole Court who concurred in this opinion. The rule of the Court was not to pronounce a State law invalid for unconstitutionality unless a majority of the whole Court should concur; hence no decision was rendered.

The Circuit Court of Mercer County, Kentucky, decided, in 1834, under the decision in Craig *vs.* Missouri, that the notes of the Bank of the Commonwealth were bills of credit.

Judge Johnson died in 1834. Duvall resigned in January, 1835. Wayne took his seat January 14th, 1835. Hence there was one vacancy in 1835 and Briscoe's case went over. Marshall died July 6th, 1835. In 1836 there were only five Judges on the bench of the Court. Taney was confirmed March 15th, 1836, as Chief Justice, and P. P. Barbour was confirmed the same day. This made the Court complete again. Five of the seven Judges were now Jackson's appointees.

Briscoe's case was decided in January, 1837. The decision was by McLean, who had dissented in Craig *vs.* Missouri. It was held that a bill of credit "is a paper issued by the sovereign power containing a pledge of its faith and designed to circulate as money." "The act incorporating the Bank of the Commonwealth was a constitutional exercise of power, by the State of Kentucky, and the notes issued by the bank are not bills of credit, within the meaning of the Constitution of the United States." It is said to be very difficult to define bills of credit, as the term is used in the Constitution. "In the early history of banks, it seems that their notes were generally denominated 'bills of credit.'" A bill of credit "which includes all classes of bills of credit emitted by the colonies and States, is a paper issued by the sovereign power, containing a pledge of its faith, and designed to circulate as money." It would be unconstitutional for a State to make any bank notes legal tender. "A State cannot emit bills of credit, or, in other words, it cannot issue that description of paper to answer the purposes of money, which was denominated before the adoption of the Constitution bills of credit; but a State may grant acts of incorporation for the attainment of those objects which are essential to the interests of society. This power is

247

incident to sovereignty, and there is no limitation on its exercise by the States, in respect to the incorporation of banks, in the Constitution." Reference is made to the Bank of North America and the Bank of Massachusetts, as existing when the Constitution was adopted, and it is inferred that bills of credit "do not include ordinary bank notes." Then "it follows that the power to incorporate banks to issue these notes may be exercised by a State." A State could not incorporate a company to coin, because it is forbidden to do so itself; nor could it incorporate a company to issue bills of credit. "To constitute a bill of credit within the Constitution, it must be issued by a State, on the faith of the State, and designed to circulate as money. It must be a paper which circulates on the credit of the State, and so received and used in the ordinary business of life. The individual or committee who issue it must have power to bind the State. They must act as agents, and of course not incur any personal responsibility, nor impart, as individuals, any credit to the paper. These are the leading characteristics of a bill of credit, which a State cannot emit. The notes issued by the Bank of the Commonwealth of Kentucky have not these characteristics."

Story rendered a very strong and vehement dissenting opinion. In it he gave a summary history and analysis of "bills of credit," as they existed before the Revolution, and as they were understood by the Constitution-makers, and he showed what a great variety of them there had been in the use of the colonists from whom the expression was inherited. These notes of the Kentucky bank were, he said, fully under the description. "The history of such a currency constituted the darkest pages in the American annals, and had been written in the ruin of thousands who had staked their property upon the public faith,—always freely given, but too often grossly violated." "It is the substance we are to look to. The question is whether it is issued, and is negotiable, and is designed to circulate as currency. If that is its intent, manifested either on the face of the bill, or on the face of the act, and it is in reality the paper issue of a State, it is within the prohibition of the Constitution." He explicitly referred to the former hearing of the case and said that Marshall had been in the majority against the constitutionality of the issues.

In a philippic against Guthrie, in the Senate of Kentucky, in 1838, Wickliffe charged him with belonging to a party who once issued $3,000,000 in bills of credit without a dollar to redeem them with. "And it is equally true that a portion of his party raised a pony purse and promised great lawyers $50,000 to have their acts declared unconstitutional and void by the Supreme Court, that they might be thereby released from paying their debts to this Commonwealth's bank."

The decision in this case was a distinct victory for Kentucky relief banking and politics. It opened the door wide for abuses of banking by the States. If the degree of responsibility and independent authority which the directors of the Bank of the Commonwealth of Kentucky possessed (which was really nil), and the amount of credit which they gave to the notes, aside from the credit of the State, was sufficient to put those notes outside the prohibition of the Constitution, then no State could find any difficulty in making a device for escaping the constitutional prohibition of bills of credit. Wildcat banking was granted standing ground under the Constitution, and the boast that the constitutional convention had closed and barred the door against the paper money with which the colonies had been cursed, was without foundation.

We have seen, however, that this institution was only a caricature of a bank in any point of view. The great Banks of the States were financially unsound and mistaken, but this is the only one which deserved to be characterized as a shameless fraud. It was devised only to wipe out debts. Its pretenses were all transparently false. The Court was obliged to hold aloof from a real examination of it and to accept all its false pretenses with remote and artificial respect, lest a close and faithful investigation should reveal its rottenness in such a light that it would have been impossible to let it stand. A whole series of decisions has been built upon this case and it has contributed to fasten on the country the federal legal tender law. It would be worth the trouble, on proper occasion, to trace through the cases derived from it, and decided upon it, with reference to the mischievous consequences which have flowed from it.

It is very true that the definition of bills of credit is extremely difficult. No analytical definition has ever been made, which is satisfactory. In fact the Court in this decision labored inconclusively with the analysis, and satisfied itself with an historical definition. Its statement amounts to saying that whatever the Constitution-makers meant by bills of credit is unconstitutional. Now it is entirely beyond question that the antipathy of the Constitution-makers did not attach to the fact that those bills were issued by the State, but to their nature and operation as currency. Their antipathy was equally great against Continental bills of credit, issued by the Confederation, for the same reason; and the notes of the Bank of North America and of the Bank of Massachusetts did not come under this hostile intention because they were regarded as credit instruments of a different character. The term bill of credit, according to its history, was generic and not specific. It meant any current evidence of an obligation. The Colonies and Congress had issued them under a great variety of forms and of varying tenor, until they carried no language which expressed any legal character at all. "This bill shall be current for one shilling." "One dollar, by resolution of Congress."

Even the obligation of the issuer was only assumed and understood. If a member of the Constitutional convention had been asked why he wanted to forbid them, he would have answered that it was because experience had shown that they displaced specie; became the money of account; were in fact forced on everybody's acceptance, as the only medium of exchange; were liable to political control; in short, that they usurped the functions of money and belied every one of those functions so that there was no money. The people lacked all the utilities of money and suffered instead from a political and commercial curse. He would have said that if bills of credit bore interest, they would not circulate. Hence the prohibition did not touch State bonds, and that, if they were cash specie obligations for value promptly enforceable at law, all their evil features would disappear. He would have said that bank notes were of the latter character. The history of the following fifty years showed that the Constitution-makers placed too much confidence in this latter distinction. Unless the cash specie obligation, promptly enforceable at law, was an established actuality in the fullest sense of the words, the bank notes reproduced all the evils of the colonial bills of credit. The discriminations, therefore, presented by Briscoe's case were not really difficult. The distinction between a

251

legitimate bank note and one which. had degenerated into the form of a colonial bill of credit was not difficult, and it would have been an immeasurable benefit to the country to have had that distinction then defined and established. A State which was creating. institutions which were issuing notes of the former kind would have been within the Constitution; one which was creating banks whose notes were of the latter kind would have been outside of it.

In a report on the "Exchequer," at the session of 1841-2, Caleb Cushing said: "It seems to be a strange anomaly of the fundamental law; or if not anomaly, then oversight, to provide that a State shall not issue bills of credit by the instrumentality of a natural person called its 'Treasurer,' but may, by means of a legal person called its 'bank;' in other words, that it cannot, and yet that it can, be the derivative source of the issue of bills of credit. Nor does it vary the principle to enact that the bank shall consist in part or in whole of incorporated private stock."

In his annual report for 1861, Secretary Chase said that emissions of bank notes by State banks "certainly fall within the spirit if not within the letter of the constitutional prohibition of the emission of bills of credit by the States."

Our history has shown that there were, at the time of this discussion, a number of large Banks of the States, in regard to which the State feeling was very strong; and also that the passions which had been enlisted on behalf of the Bank of the Commonwealth, in Kentucky, were intense. It will appear below that the State interest in these institutions before 1837 had been very much extended. In the party politics of the time it was very important to make a decision which should be popular in Kentucky (Clay's State), and also in the other

States which were interested in Banks of the State. It seems safe to say that political considerations entered largely into the decision; but it is also true that the educational effect which the current banking system exerted on the minds of the people was discernible on the Bench. As the Court was now strongly Jacksonian, it was a remarkable anomaly that they should have declared the Bank of the Commonwealth of Kentucky constitutional, when their party was assailing the Bank of the United States, on the ground that it was unconstitutional.

The law, so far as the Constitution of the United States prescribed it, was now decided to be that States alone, in the strictest sense, may not issue bills of credit. The United States may; banks, municipalities, associations, and individuals may.

We may now turn our attention to the measures of liquidation and relief adopted by the other States of the Mississippi Valley at this time.

TENNESSEE, fearing the oppression which Kentucky was suffering from the Bank of the United States, laid a tax of $50,000, in 1817, on any one who should engage in banking in the State without the authority of the same. In the following year a petition was addressed to the Bank of the United States by citizens of Nashville, asking it to establish a branch in spite of the law. The reply was that the Bank had ample occupation for all its capital, and that it could more conveniently test the right of a State to tax it elsewhere.

The banks of this State stopped payment in 1819. Although there was no office of the Bank of the United States in the State, the banks made use of the current excuse for suspension and attributed it to emissaries of the Bank. No doubt it had transactions there. Senator White said that the people of that State had never been accustomed to the punctuality which the great Bank enforced. Thirty years later it was said of them: "Although the planters are the safest and most infallibly solvent class of customers, it is impossible to induce them to observe punctuality."

An extra session of the Legislature was called in June, 1820, on account of the distress. The Governor recommended a property law, saying that his observation of that of 1809, had led him to believe that such a law, although to be used carefully, might be very beneficial.

In compliance with these recommendations, the Bank of the State of Tennessee (No. II.) was incorporated July 26, 1820, "for the purpose of relieving the distresses of the community and improving the revenue of the State." It was to be established "for and in behalf of the State of Ten- nessee." Its seat was to be at Nashville, with a branch at Knoxville to which four-tenths of the capital was appropriated. The president and directors were to be elected by joint ballot of the Legislature from session to session. It was to last until 1843, to issue notes from $1 to $100. Its capital was to be $1 million "in bills payable to order or bearer, all of which shall be emitted on the credit and security of the borrowers, and the whole be warranted by the State," on the income from sales of land "and the ordinary revenue of the State, not otherwise appropriated." It was to be a depository of public money. Loans were to be secured by bills and notes with two or more sureties, or by mortgage, and not to be made for more than one year. No loan might be renewed unless interest was paid in advance, and not more than one-tenth of any loan might be called in when it was due, without sixty days' notice. In case of default, judgment and execution were to follow. The bank was not to owe over $1 million before the next session. Within twenty days after it was ready to start, an agent to make the loans was to be appointed in each county. The notes were receivable for all dues to the State, to colleges, and academies, on account of the public lands, and on account of such lands as had been appropriated to the educational institutions mentioned. In the midst of this act it is provided that no executions shall take place within two years after judgment, unless the writ is endorsed that the notes of this bank will be received as well as the other notes mentioned in previous laws. The loans were to be allotted to the counties in proportion to the State tax of 1819. All sums paid in were to be re-loaned in the same county. The Treasurer of East Tennessee was to issue six per cent. stock at the request of the president of this bank, "on the faith and credit of the funds vested in said bank by this act" up to the maximum amount of $87,500. The Treasurer of West Tennessee was to do the same up to the amount of $162,500. The bank was to pay the interest on these bonds and sell them from time to time at par. Here was a provision which provided for touching some capital at last. No loan was to be over $500; the Legislature was to make rules for the bank. The Nashville Bank or the previous Bank of the State might consolidate with this. A supplementary act, three days later, pledged to the bank the revenue from the State lands to make up its capital. As there had been some difficulty to find anyone to take the offices, it was provided that, if no suitable persons in Knoxville would accept the positions, the bank might be set up elsewhere in East Tennessee. The Treasurer of West Tennessee was to furnish money to buy the plates, etc. The bank was to commence by issuing $500,000. The notes were not to be in excess of twice the paid in capital. The power of the Legislature to make rules for the bank was repealed. This act, like the others creating the big Banks of the States, contained obvious incongruities. The old Bank of the State of Tennessee would have nothing to do with this new one.

This act was passed in the Senate, 13 to 7; in the House, 20 to 19. There was very strong opposition to it. General Jackson, Colonel Ward, and others of Davidson County, presented a remonstrance against it. The memorialists object to the bank bill as unconstitutional and inexpedient. They object to the two years' delay, quoting the bill of rights that "right and justice shall be administered without sale, denial, or delay;" also to the provision which makes the "loan office notes a direct tender in discharge of debts due to colleges and academies from our citizens south of Holston and French Broad." As to the "policy of passing the bill under consideration, the undersigned believe that no one can hesitate to pronounce it ruinous of both public and private interests who will give it a careful and impartial investigation." They do not think the distress so severe as to justify this kind of interposition on the part of the Legislature. Paper notes cannot relieve the distress, because they have no solid basis. "It has heretofore been admitted by every judicious political economist who has devoted his attention to the subject that the large emissions of paper from the banks by which the country was inundated have been the most prominent causes of those distresses of which we at present complain. They greatly increased the facilities of borrowing money, gave property a fictitious value, and introduced amongst us every species of extravagance and folly." "It would appear to the undersigned that the poison which generated the disease is here attempted to be administered for its removal." They also made a special objection to any arrangement by which citizens of the State would become debtors to the State and referred to the debts already due from purchasers of State lands as an illustration and warning. "The undersigned feel no small share of surprise that so much sympathy should be indulged for the debtor and none for the creditor. Although there may be some extreme cases that solicit relief, yet it is suggested as the best policy to keep the courts of justice open and accessible to every citizen, and permit those who are involved to extricate themselves by additional industry and economy." They end by citing the oath taken by members of the Legislature and declare that this measure is a violation of that oath.

This memorial was laid upon the table in the Senate 11 to 5, and two members claimed the right to spread upon the record their reasons for voting to lay it on the table. They cite the passage about the oaths of the members as a ground for declaring that the memorial "is extremely exceptionable and indecorous in its terms and language." They add that "one of the distinguished characters who appears to have been actively zealous in producing the above memorial, but a few days since, at the seat of government, and in the presence of some members of the Legislature, in the most indecorous manner stated that any member who voted for it would perjure himself, ahd that if the law did pass, twelve honest jurymen upon oath would convict those who voted for the measure of perjury."

Although the adjuration to the Legislature to heed their oath is very pointed, and would not probably be put into a similar paper nowadays, there is nothing in the paper which is indecorous in substance or manner.

October 24th, the grand jury of Davidson County begged leave to present their opinion in condemnation of the action of the two old banks in opposing the new Bank of the State, which has a strong capital and all safeguards. "Those banks ought to recollect that they exist by legislative aid and permission. They are barely tolerated by the people whose breath can annihilate them in an instant. They surely forget on what a precipice they stand."

In May, 1821, the Supreme Court of the State had occasion to pass upon the stay law. The clerk of the Supreme Court of the second circuit had been requested to issue an execution on a judgment rendered in the Supreme Court, without the endorsement required by the act of 1819. He refused to do so. The Court was moved to order him to grant the execution, disregarding the endorsement law as unconstitutional. The Court said: "Suspension of execution, as directed by these acts of the Legislature now under consideration, is forbidden by the prohibition of tender laws as a direct consequence of the prohibition; also by the interdiction to pass laws impairing the obligation of contracts (suspension of execution being an impairing of such obligation); and furthermore by the declaration that justice and right shall be done without delay in all cases, the process of execution being one sense of the term 'right' which is not to be delayed. We are therefore bound to say that these acts are repugnant to the Constitution and void so far as relates to the suspension of execution, and that execution ought to issue immediately without any such endorsement as the act requires."

Judge Haywood, who read the decision, went on to urge at length that injunctions should issue against creditors who demanded payment in specie for debts contracted in paper. Judge Emmerson, who joined with him in the decision, as above, dissented on this point on grounds not stated. Final decision on this point (which was, as the Judge declared, not before the Court) was reserved until the third judge, Whyte, could decide it. It seems that the presiding Judge must have brought it in only as some consolation to those who supported the endorsement system. There seems to have been peaceful acquiescence in this decision in Tennessee and the relief system there came to an end.

The Bank of the State of Tennessee was far more moderate in its issues than the Bank of the Commonwealth of Kentucky, and the evils which were occasioned by it were by no means so serious.

In 1821-2, legislation is aimed against the banks. The act of November 13, 1821, forbade any bank to sell its specie stock; the penalty for the president was $1,000 fine and imprisonment not exceeding five years. The banks were ordered to resume on the first Monday in April, 1824, or forfeit their charters, except the Bank of the State of Tennessee. They were ordered to settle accounts with each other every three months. November 15th, a law was passed to give the holders of notes for less than $100 an execution against the bank, with a process for discovering its property and garnishment against the debtors of the bank. On the same day the Bank of the State was authorized to issue $50,000 in notes under $1, to be distributed amongst the counties in the ratio in which the large notes were distributed. November 8, 1823, the same bank was authorized to issue $25,000 in notes for 50 cents and less. The smallest denomination mentioned is six and a quarter cents. November 27th the resumption law was repealed, and the banks were ordered to pay in specie one-quarter of each note presented between April, 1824, and January, 1825; one-third, between January, 1825, and October, 1825; one-half between that date and July, 1826; and after that, the whole. If the State Bank at Knoxville or the Nashville Bank do not pay specie, they shall be liable to six per cent. damages for delay, unless they agree to the conditions of this act about resumption.

October 23, 1823, a new stay law was passed. Executions were to be endorsed according to the existing law. If the creditor did not do this, three valuers were to be selected from the neighboring householders. If the property did not sell for three-quarters of the valuation, it was to be returned to the defendant. The plaintiff might then sue out another execution. The plaintiff may take slaves at three-quarters of their value, or they are to be returned to the defendant; so of land. This law is not to apply to specific contracts for specie or eastern funds, nor to cases where a bank is the defendant, nor to contracts made after April 1, 1823. It is not known that this law ever was tested, but the relief system in Tennessee is said to have declined even before this time, as above stated.

The following year we find the Bank of the State in full operation; new agencies are appointed in the new counties. December 3, 1825, it was enacted that upon application of any person, with security, to the agent of his county, it shall be the duty of the agent to lend from $10 to $500 from any money he has. When a note is reduced to $50 by payments, it shall not be lawful for the agent to demand the remainder in one payment, but in fractions, as before. In that year the

Governor congratulated the State on the prospect of resumption. The premium on silver had fallen in a year from 25 to 4 or 5. "The earnest prayer of all should be that we may never again experience the evils of depreciated bank paper." He was confident that the managers of the banks were striving to resume. In 1826, the Nashville Bank did resume, but $260,000 were drawn from it in seventy days and it failed again, leaving only the Bank of the State. December 11th a law was passed in regard to the Nashville Bank which is so carelessly drawn that it is scarcely intelligible. The sense appears to be that, in order to prevent a depreciation of its notes, they are made receivable for State and college lands, if the college trustees agree, and the Bank of the State is to take them for one-half its loans called in. The notes of the Nashville Bank, however, fell at once to fifty per cent. discount, and so remained until 1833, when they were quoted at ten per cent.

The law which had barred out the Bank of the United States was repealed in 1826, and a branch was established at Nashville.

In 1827, the avails of the Bank of the State were constituted a school fund. A peculiar feature of the history of Tennessee was the excessive degree to which the educational organization of the State was entangled with its banking, which also involved an entanglement with its "improvements."

Gov. Carroll, in his message for 1829, said that the Bank of the State ought to be wound up. Within a year it had taken three hundred judgments against debtors, and the Knoxville branch had taken a hundred more. He added that a statement made by the Bank showed that its debtors were paying, in interest, commissions, and charges, from twelve per cent. to twenty-five per cent. for every dollar which they had borrowed of it. It was employing sixty-two agents, at great risk, and cost the State $14,000 per annum. "Our experience furnishes but too much proof of the bad policy of the State's permitting its citizens to become its debtors."

In that year the Bank of the United States had the business of the Valley almost to itself. Judge Catton of Nashville published an address in which he pronounced the crisis a dangerous one on account of the great debt of the people to the Bank of the United States, and the excessive usury everywhere prevailing, namely, from five to ten per cent. per month. He especially warned the people against endorsing for each other.

The cashier of the Bank of the State of Tennessee at Nashville was found short in his accounts in February, 1830, to the amount of seventy or eighty thousand dollars. He refused to give up the books because the deficiency was due to overdrafts by persons whom he would not expose. The charter was amended so that the Legislature should elect the cashier. The total overdrafts by "distinguished persons" were two or three hundred thousand dollars. Lest they should be exposed the matter was hushed up and the cashier was allowed to go.

The Legislature, however, demanded of the president and directors of the Bank of the State, December 20, 1831, that they should report the defalcation of the cashier and the names of the persons who had made the overdrafts, with the amount, and whether they had settled.

In 1831, the State was draining the life out of the Bank of the State No. II., by exactions for internal improvements, etc.

The president and directors were ordered to find out how much money there was in the agencies, and also to find out the county apportionment of the total of it, according to the census of 1830, and to apportion it. The School Commissioners of each county were incorporated in order that they might take and hold it. The county loan agencies were to be discontinued, May 1, 1832.

Senator White said, in 1838, that this bank had been converted into a specie-paying bank, but that its capital and profits had all been lost, and that the State was trying to recover what it could from the wreck.

OHIO.—February 5, 1819, an act was passed to discipline the banks which did not redeem their notes. Six per cent. damages might be recovered, the evidence being the notes in one's possession. In an execution against a bank, the Sheriff might enter it and seize specie, notes, or books; and if these did not suffice, he might garnishee the debtors of the bank, beginning with the directors or cashier. Bank notes payable on a future day were made unlawful; notes under $1 were forbidden. An act of February 8th made it a misdemeanor to take a bank note at less than its face, the penalty being a fine of not over $500. Anyone who should pay away a bank note at a discount might recover the discount in an action at law, and the defendant was to have no stay of execution. It is stated that the grand jurors of the City Court of Cincinnati decided that this act was unconstitutional, and refused to notice violations of it. It was repealed January 24, 1820. Of twenty-five banks in the State, in 1819, only six or seven were redeeming their notes. They were classified, November, 1819, as seven good, four decent, four middling, and four good for nothing. The Farmers' and Mechanics' Bank of

Cincinnati was believed to have been greatly indebted to the United States before it received a share of the public deposit. It was allowed a permanent deposit of $100,000. "Are we to lose the whole for the benefit of the rag barons? but no cost can be too great if modern banking is destroyed by it."

A more stringent and comprehensive law to enforce payment by the banks was passed February 18, 1820. The plaintiff against a bank might declare for money had and received, if over $100, and put the bank notes in evidence if payment had been demanded. He could recover with six per cent. interest, and have an execution as by the previous law. A Sheriff executing a judgment in favor of a bank was to take its notes. When payment was demanded of a bank on its notes, and not given, the cashier was to endorse upon it "payment demanded" with the date; then it bore interest at six per cent. until paid in money of the United States. The cashier must keep a book of record of such refusals, and the person who demanded payment might demand an opportunity to see this book, to verify the entry of his own demand, and might sign an attestation of it. If the cashier refused to do these things, the penalty was ten per cent. on the notes refused. A year later it was enacted, February 2, 1821, that in a suit against a bank, on its notes, real estate might be levied on; either the fee or the equitable interest. After the sheriff has exhausted the goods and chattels, he may levy on lands held in trust for the bank, in which case he may appoint three disinterested persons to find out and report the amount due on the trust deed, putting the parties on oath. If the trustee refuses to deed to the buyer, under the execution, the Court shall award the property with 25 per cent. damages on its value, against the trustee.

264

These laws undoubtedly testify to their own inadequacy and failure.

In the Cincinnati City Court, in 1820, the Mayor charged the jury that the Bank of the United States had no power to discount notes, because that power was nowhere in the charter conferred in so many words. The jury found for the defendant accordingly, the Bank being plaintiff.

The war between the State of Ohio and the Bank of the United States began February 8, 1819, when it was enacted: "Whereas the president and directors of the Bank of the United States have established two offices of discount and deposit in this State, at which they transact banking business, by loaning money and issuing bills in violation of the laws of this State; and whereas divers companies and associations of individuals within this State, unauthorized by law, continue in like manner to do business as bankers, and banks, by loaning money and issuing bills, and by trading in notes and bills; and whereas it is just and necessary that such unlawful banking, while continued, should be subject to the payment of a tax for the support of government;"— if, after the 1st of September, any of these associations continue, they shall be taxed; the United States Bank, $50,000 per annum for each office, and every other company $10,000. On the 15th day of September, in each year, the Auditor is to charge these taxes against the companies, and to make out his warrant to the agent whom he shall choose and appoint to demand payment. In case of default, the agent is to levy on the goods of the Bank or its credit. He is to seize the specie or notes, searching the Bank for them. The officers may be put to oath to disclose where the funds are, and they may be summoned to court and examined, a refusal to answer constituting contempt. Debtors to the banks must pay the State. The agent is to pay the sum collected to the Auditor and he to the Treasurer. The agent is to have, as his remuneration, two per cent. of the specie or notes; five per cent. of goods taken in execution; and if further proceedings are required, ten per cent.

At the September term of the federal Circuit Court, an injunction was obtained forbidding the Auditor to collect the tax under this law. His legal advisors were of the opinion that there were various irregularities in the injunction and in the service of it.

September 17th, John L. Harper, appointed agent of the Auditor, Ralph Osborne, and bearing his warrant, accompanied by two others, entered the office of the branch at Chillicothe, jumped over the counter, took possession of the vault, and demanded whether the cashier was prepared to pay the tax. Upon a negative reply, Harper took from the vault $120,425. Five days later he left on the counter the amount in excess $100,000. The Governor, upon hearing of this, did all in his power to have the money restored, and offered to give security for it; but could accomplish nothing. "I view," said he, "the transaction in the most odious light, and from my very soul I detest it. ... I am ashamed it has happened in Ohio."

The bank suspended operations for a few days.

An injunction was served on Harper while on his way to Columbus, and on Osborne before Harper arrived. The money was deposited with Currie, the State Treasurer.

Harper and Orr, one of his assistants, were arrested by the deputy marshal for a trespass with violence, in taking the tax, and bail was required of each of them to double the amount of the money they had taken. They were put in prison, where they lay, an application for *habeas corpus* having failed, until the following January, when they were released by the federal Circuit Court on the ground that the arrest was irregular.

In the meantime, November 22d, the United States District Judge granted an injunction against any disposition whatever being made of the money. Upon the meeting of the Legislature, Osborne made a report of the proceedings. He was under a *subpoena* to appear in January to answer in a petition for a return of the money, and an injunction.

January 5, 1820, application was made in the federal Circuit Court for an attachment against Osborne and Harper for contempt, in disobeying the injunction of the previous September; but after argument, the Court held the case, on account of the important constitutional questions involved, under advisement until the following September.

In September, a bill was prayed for to enjoin Currie, Sullivan, his successor in office, the Auditor, and his agents, from paying away the money or acting further under the law. This was granted. Currie in his answer stated that he received $98,000 from Harper (the latter having retained his fee); that he had held it separate and unused, and had delivered it to his successor. Sullivan, in his answer, stated that a committee of the House of Representatives had, in January, 1820, seized the moneys in the Treasury. The Court decreed that the identical notes and coins which had been taken from the Bank must be restored to it, and that interest on the specie part, $19,830, must be paid. A perpetual injunction was granted against the collection of any tax in future under the act of Ohio. By an arrangement between counsel, the attachment for contempt was dismissed at the cost of the defendants, and the action of trespass was continued, to be dismissed, at the defendant's cost, if the Supreme Court affirmed the decree.

Sullivan refused to obey the decree, and was imprisoned for contempt. On the third day of his imprisonment, the Court granted a writ of sequestration against all his property. The commissioners under it took from him the key of the Treasury, from which they took the $98,000 and brought it into Court, where it was delivered to the agents of the Bank. The defendants appealed, but it was agreed that the appeal should operate on the $2,000 yet wanting.

We now meet with utterances of the high State rights doctrine from Ohio. A committee of the Legislature made a long report, about January 1, 1821. They proposed acts of compromise with the Bank, and also of outlawry against it. A resolution which they proposed affirming the doctrine of the resolutions of '98 was passed, 58 to 7; a protest against the action of the Court, 58 to 7; declaring a determination to tax any corporation doing business in Ohio under the authority of the United States, unanimously; protest against the doctrine that the Supreme Court of the United States can decide on the political rights of States, in cases between individuals, 64 to 1; ordering the committee to bring in the bills proposed, 57 to 8. These resolutions were transmitted to the States. Massachusetts answered that the action of Ohio, if allowed, would defeat the purposes of the law by which the Bank was established.

January 29, 1821, an act was passed "to withdraw from the Bank of the United States the protection and aid of the laws of this State in certain cases." No sheriff or jailer, after September 1, 1821, is to take any debtor into custody on suit of the Bank of the United States; nor any person committed for offenses against its property, rights, etc. No officer of justice is to take proof of a deed or other instrument to which the Bank of the United States is a party, and no recorder is to receive or record such deeds. No notary is to protest a note payable to that Bank. The penalty on a sheriff or jailer for violating this act is $200 fine; a judge or other magistrate, if he does what is here forbidden, will be guilty of a misdemeanor, and shall be fined not over $500. A disobedient notary shall be removed.

At this point the Legislature seemed disposed to recede; for it was enacted, February 2, 1821, that the State was willing to forego the tax if the Bank would pay four per cent. on the Ohio business profits, and withdraw its suits against the State officers. If it agrees to this, or will withdraw from the State, the Governor is to certify the Auditor, who is to return $90,000, after which the tax shall be $2,500 per annum, or the above percentage of the dividends on the Ohio business. Anyone who impedes the Auditor in the discharge of duty laid upon him by law is to be imprisoned not over six months, and fined not over $500.

The Supreme Court of the United States affirmed the decision in Osborne's case, March 19, 1824, except that interest should not be paid on the coin part of the money taken.

The law outlawing the Bank of the United States was repealed, January 18, 1826.

The State finances were in a most prosperous state at this time, or would have been so if its cash on hand had had value. The Treasurer reported, 1820, that the balance in the Treasury was $155,147, including $98,000 taken from the Bank of the United States, but the rest was nearly all in

269

uncurrent notes of the banks in the State. He gives a list of them in which appear nearly all the banks of 1816.

In his report for 1821, he reported that he had obtained judgments against a number of the banks of the State, and was trying to find their property. In 1822, at least eight of them were bankrupt. A law of February 5, 1825, provided that all the banks under the law of February 23, 1816, should be re-invested with the shares which had been set off to the State, if they would pay the State two per cent. on their dividends from their organization until this time, and four per cent. on their dividends for the future, and concede to the State the right to tax them. During the next years these banks were in liquidation. An act of March 3, 1824, provided that the Treasurer might compound and settle all claims of the State against seven or eight of them. In 1831, twenty were reported broken, including our old acquaintances the Banks of New Philadelphia and Owl Creek.

INDIANA.—January 8, 1818, interest at six per cent. was imposed on bank notes not paid on demand in specie. Any officer of the bank was to endorse the demand and refusal or be fined the amount of the note, and witnesses might be called in on whose testimony a justice of the peace should endorse.

The Vincennes Bank, acting as a bank of the State, became an object of suspicion and examination in 1821. A joint resolution provided for an investigation, to find out whether the mother bank had issued notes, payable by its branches, without their knowledge. At the following session, in December, the State Treasurer was directed to make a formal demand on that bank and its branches, for payment of their notes in the treasury. If payment was refused, he was to tender to the mother bank at Vincennes the said notes, in payment of the loans of the bank to the State. A week later, a joint resolution was adopted that a *quo warranto* should be brought against the bank for a violation of its charter and the laws, and that if judgment was obtained against the bank, the Governor should appoint three receivers to wind it up. In this suit the bank was found guilty on four points, each of which would work forfeiture. Its debts were more than the legal limit; it had made fraudulent over-issues which it could not redeem; it had made large profits while suspended; deposits left for safe-keeping had been embezzled.

The tide now seems to turn against the relief system. January 3, 1822, it was enacted that there should be no execution on replevin bonds. If seven year rents, on being offered for sale, do not bring enough to pay the debt, the land is to be sold. Replevin bonds are to date from the judgment and not from the sale on execution. The jury of freeholders is to consist of five. This last provision was declared unconstitutional. January 11th, the old territorial law was revived, which established a limited stay, varying from thirty days, on a debt of $6, up to one hundred and eighty days on a debt of over $100, and property taken on execution was to be sold for what it would bring.

In a report of the State Treasurer, January 13, 1825, there is returned amongst the liabilities of the State a sum due to the "United States, assignee of the Vincennes Bank," and payments on this account occur in the reports of the following years. This is, no doubt, a debt for a federal deposit in that bank, for which the State found itself liable. There were then $20,000 of treasury notes outstanding. From the forfeiture of the Vincennes Bank, in 1823, until 1834, there was no bank in Indiana. There is no evidence that the State found itself any the worse for the lack. In 1829, we find a law making further provision for the liquidation of the Farmers' and Mechanics' Bank. As a specimen of loose legislation, it may be noted that the act continues "all the privileges and franchises heretofore granted." In 1834, the time was extended, but it was forbidden to do anything but liquidate. All its notes were redeemed.

ILLINOIS.—January 16, 1821, all executions were suspended until November 20th, and property which had been levied on was restored to the debtor.

At the same time, the Bank of the State of Illinois was chartered against the veto of the Council of Revision, in which the vote was 3 to 5. It was established at Vandalia, for ten years, with $500,000 capital, all owned by the State, and was to have four branches and no more. The president and directors of the principal bank were to be elected by the Legislature. The first issue of notes was to be for $300,000, from ones to twenties, bearing two per cent. interest, receivable by the bank or the State; to be allotted to the districts in which the branches were established in proportion to population. The presidents and directors of the branches were to lend the notes out over the district in proportion to population, on mortgage for loans over $100, on personal security for loans under $100, at six per cent., the loans being renewable yearly, and to be "considered as standing accommodations," the notes for the loans being made payable twelve months from date. The notes of the borrowers ran to the president and directors of the bank "for the use of the people of said State." The lands and revenues of the State were pledged for the debts of the bank and the Legislature pledged the State to pay all the currency issued by the bank within ten years, in gold or silver. No execution was to issue on any replevin bond or judgment, until November 1, 1821. On all causes of action, before the following May, replevin was to be granted for three years, unless the plaintiff would endorse that the notes of this bank would be received. The loans of the bank were to be repaid on installments within ten years, and one-tenth of the notes were to be withdrawn annually and not re-issued. The State funds were to be deposited in the bank; the school money receivable from the United States was to be paid over to it, with all specie or land-office money, and notes for double the amount of these funds might be issued and allotted in loans as above. This last provision seems to be a kind of addendum,—no doubt tacked to the bill in its course through the Legislature. It was repealed February 18, 1823. This State squandered and misappropriated its school money for ten years. February 12th, a supplement to the act for the Bank of the State enacted that there should be sixty days replevin even when there was an endorsement. On contracts after May 1st, for State Bank money, the same stay was provided, and in the same way, as that already provided for other contracts; but if the contracts were for gold or silver, the stay should be thirty days for a debt of $10, and a longer time for larger debts, up to one hundred and fifty days for a debt over $40.

The bank went into operation in 1821. All who could get endorsers borrowed a hundred dollars. The people cut the bills into two pieces so as to make halves of a dollar. For about four years there was no other money but that of the Bank of the State. Few pretended to pay their debts to the bank. More than half of the borrowers considered their debts as clear gain and never intended to pay them. Many debtors refused to pay on the ground that the notes were bills of credit.

The Supreme Court of the State decided, in 1826, that a debtor to the bank could not raise the question of its constitutionality; that is, could not dispute his own liability on the ground that the notes were bills of credit. This decision prevailed as long as the Bank existed, but was overthrown in 1833, when the notes of this bank were decided to be bills of credit. It was decided, in 1829, that a debt to this bank was a debt to the State which the State could forgive.

From 1821, auditors' warrants were made receivable for bank debts. They had been issued at one-third of their face value, and were so quoted, while the State was liable for the full face value. There was a peculiar provision that each member of the Legislature was to receive such a sum, by way of remuneration, not exceeding $7 a day, as he should designate, by writing the same on a piece of paper, that he was willing to receive.

At the same time that the Bank of the State was chartered, all unauthorized paper currency was forbidden, under a penalty of $10,000. If it was issued by a corporation, the charter was to be forfeited and the members were made individually liable for this fine.

February 17, 1823, the execution and stay laws were codified, with slight modifications. Thirty days were allowed for the redemption of personal property sold on execution, fifteen per cent. advance on the price being given. On the following day, another law on the same interminable subject forbade any execution to issue on a judgment by a justice of the peace, until thirty days after it was rendered. At every

274

meeting of the Legislature, a new attempt was made to modify these laws so as to deprive the creditor of his rights and remedies. The only plea which has ever been made on behalf of these laws is that under them the debtors and creditors were led to make compromises and settlements with each other, and that, in the existing state of things, probably this was the most just and reasonable course that could be adopted.

December 16, 1824, commissioners were appointed to make an examination of the branch of the Bank of the State at Shawneetown. The president and directors of it were to pay over all moneys to the cashier of the head bank. This indicates some malfeasance in that branch.

The cashier of the Bank of the State was ordered, January 10, 1825, to burn all the notes in it, including those unsigned and unissued. This marked a revulsion against the institution. All notes which should be paid in afterwards were to be stamped "reissued," and to bear no interest. The cashiers of the branches were to pay over, at the half yearly audit, to the head bank all the money on hand. The bank was to receive no more individual deposits, and was to receive auditors' warrants in payment of bank loans.

January 28, 1826, it was ordered that State paper should not be paid out of the treasury at more than fifty per cent. discount, and the Bank of the State was to determine every three months the valuation at which that paper should be paid out during the following three months. No debt to the Bank of the State was to be scaled by the Court. If any debt had been scaled and endorsed, under the act of January 18, 1825, the sheriff was to collect, In specie or State paper, or bank notes. The wording is extremely confused and unintelligible, but it seems to mean that he shall take paper enough at the scale of depreciation to equal specie.

In speeches which he made in the State campaign of 1826, Ninian Edwards declared that the State was paying out notes of the Bank of the State at 33 cents on $1, but had to receive them for taxes, etc., at their face, and that the non-resident taxpayers bought them up at that rate, although it appears that they had, by so doing, raised their value; for he said that they would cost them 50 cents on $1 at the time of speaking. In five years, about $100,000 of the bank notes had been withdrawn, but auditors' warrants had been issued in place of them and had depreciated to about the same extent. The debtors to the Bank of the State were buying them at from 30 to 50 cents on $1 and were paying their debts to that bank with them. The loans, therefore, if all paid in, would fail to cancel the notes of the bank, for which the State was liable in specie, dollar for dollar.

Edwards was elected Governor, and brought about an investigation of the Bank of the State whose officers he charged with mismanagement and corruption. The committee's report showed mismanagement, but such was the influence of a bank conducted by public officers that this committee was packed to make a report against the charges. Ford makes far better criticisms on the Bank of the State system than any other contemporaneous writer. He noticed the cardinal fact, in respect to these institutions and to public improvements also, that the communities in which they were undertaken could not furnish competent men for their management. Scarcely a word is to be found to show that the legislators had any idea that the management of a great bank would require any special ability, skill, or training. They set up a bank, with $1 million or $2 millions capital, assuming that it was going to run itself and produce great profits, never troubling themselves at all about the question who was competent to manage it, to attain these results. The Legislatures always furnished from amongst their own members a large number of candidates for the offices in the bank. These men had no training whatever, except what they had obtained from some participation in politics. The case was fortunate when the worst that could be laid to them was incompetency. They had crowds of hungry adherents; there were rivals who were eager for rotation in the bank. They were forced to favoritism towards a clique of supporters, and they could not be independent against the leading politicians of the State. In many cases, also, it is beyond question that they sought the positions, and used them in a shameless manner, for their private interests. It never proved possible to call them to account or to hold them to responsibility.

The deposits in the Bank of the State were ordered to be paid back February 13, 1827. The debtors to the Bank of the State might renew their notes, and no execution was to issue against one of them for three months. Here begin the enactments, half of indulgence, half of coercion, showing the uncollectibility of the bank loans. The debtors were allowed, January 23, 1829, to pay in three annual installments, giving three notes. If they did not accept this arrangement, and give security, before September 1st, the bank was to sell the previous security and take three notes for the purchase money at one, two, and three years, with security, "which bond shall have the force of a replevin bond." A record was to be kept of the kind of money received in these transactions. Any debtor who paid by July 1, 1830, was to be released from interest, and those who paid before September 1, 1829, were to get ten per cent. discount. Year after year, either the bank or the bank debtors besought the Legislature for relief.

In 1829, Gov. Edwards tried to draw the three per cent. fund due from the United States. The Treasury Department would not pay it because it was not satisfied that the State was using the money as the law prescribed. Edwards wrote a letter substantially to the effect that it was none of the Secretary's business what the State did with it. It was used in buying up the State debt as an investment. The Commissioners of the Fund bought State bank notes which were cancelled, and the Auditor of public accounts gave them a certificate of the indebtedness, so that the State simply borrowed the school fund and used it in paying old debts, under a promise that it would some time establish and support schools by taxes. The big State paper money machine led the people to despoil their own children of the bounty of the federal government. Edward's letter is a splendid specimen of the State rights literature of the period.

At every turn therefore, we find proofs that "the paper of this bank was floating through the atmosphere of Illinois for ten years, as a poisoning and pestilential vapor, that withered and blighted the country for that length of time. The paper never was at par, and sunk at times as low as twenty-five cents on the dollar."

In the course often years the bank must have lost more than $150,000 by receiving depreciated currency; $150,000 more by paying it out; and $100,000 of the loans which were never repaid by the borrowers, and which the State had to make good.

The cashier of the bank was in default, in 1831, and could not close his accounts. Commissioners were appointed to examine and make a settlement.

The State was bound, according to the terms of the incorporation of the Bank of the State, to redeem all the notes of that bank in specie in 1831. All parties had shirked preparation for this obligation until the last moment. January 27, 1831, the Governor was authorized to borrow $100,000, with which to redeem the outstanding notes of the bank, this loan to be payable after 1850 in specie or notes of the Bank of the United States. This was the "Wiggins Loan." February 15th, it was provided that the notes of this bank might be funded in six per cent. bonds, redeemable at the pleasure of the State. Any specie in the treasury was to be applied to the redemption of the notes, and they were to be burned.

The last enactment in reference to the debtors to the bank was February 14, 1835. They might have three years to pay their debts. All the interest and twenty-five per cent. of the principal was remitted. Thus those who had been the most remiss were the most rewarded, and anyone who had paid earlier saw that he had made a mistake.

The MISSOURI Loan Office, which became famous through the case of Craig *vs.* Missouri, was established at a special session of the Legislature, June 27, 1821, as a relief measure. The State was divided into five districts, and a loan office was established in each under the supervision of commissioners elected by the General Assembly. The Auditor and Treasurer were to issue certificates for $200,000, in denominations from 50 cents to $10, of the following tenor: "This certificate shall be receivable at the treasury or any of the loan offices of the State of Missouri, in discharge of taxes or debts to the State, for the sum of —— dollars, with interest for the same, at the rate of two per cent. from this date." The loans in each district were to be proportioned to the population, and to be secured by mortgage or personal security; the mortgages not to exceed one-half the value; the loan to be for not more than one year; the interest to be six per cent. in advance; the repayment not to be required more rapidly than ten per cent. every six months; no loan on personal security to exceed $200, nor any other to exceed $1,000; one-tenth of the notes were to be withdrawn annually by the Auditor and Treasurer. The Governor was to negotiate a loan of specie for any amount up to the amount of the notes issued, and if the Legislature should approve the contract, such loan was to be a fund for the redemption of the certificates. An appropriation of $2,000 was made for expenses. The salt springs and lands attached thereto were to be leased, and the lessees were to stipulate that they would take these certificates for salt at the rate set by law. The State revenue from the salt springs, and all the State property and credit, were pledged, with the faith of the State, to redeem the certificates.

A comparison of this institution with the great Banks of the States, above described, will show what, if any, difference there was between them. If the Loan Office had been called a bank, and the commissioners directors, and if it had been said of the latter that they were "incorporated," no difference would have been discernible.

There was understood to be a strong implication that this Loan Office was to issue no more than the sum mentioned in the act; but within a few months another $100,000 were issued. The depreciation increased thereupon from 33 1-3 per cent. to 50 per cent.

The law was declared unconstitutional in the St. Louis Circuit Court, in February, 1822, in Missouri *vs.* Lane, the issue being pronounced to be bills of credit. The Judge in his decision gives us some glimpses of the situation. "Kentucky had got the start of us in the paper money system, and her citizens, finding there was nothing else to be had at home for their products, brought them here and sold them to us at reduced prices. The advantage of this to the consumer was overlooked, and we determined to adopt the paper system, to exclude the commerce of Kentucky. This purpose has been accomplished. The price of produce has been so reduced that that of Kentucky comes here no longer." "We are told of the 'pestilent effects of paper money on the industry and morals of the people.'" On this subject, let us look to the listlessness, the broken-hearted indifference to exertion, which, under the pressure of great pecuniary distress (the strongest incentive to exertion, where every ray of hope is not excluded) pervades the hardy population of this fertile country. Let us look for its effect on morals to the criminal docket of this court, at this term. Offenses, the offspring of wantonness, of folly, of desperation, of a cultivated contempt for the rights and feelings of others, and disregard for the opinion of the world, and disrespect for what men have been accustomed to hold respectable,—and in short of a total depravation of the moral sense and dissolution of moral obligation, encumber our proceedings and disgrace our records."

In connection with the Loan Office, a new and wider stay law was also enacted December 28, 1821. Each county court might appoint three valuers. The plaintiff might endorse that he would take property at two-thirds of the valuation. When the Sheriff makes a levy, the valuers are to value the property. After twenty days it is to be put up for sale. If no bid amounts to two-thirds of the valuation, the Sheriff is to deliver the property to the creditor at that limit. If the creditor makes no endorsement, the debtor is to have a stay for two years and six months, giving bond, with sureties, approved by the Sheriff. This law is not to apply to debts for lead ore delivered. Instead of giving a bond with sureties, the debtor may give land at two-thirds of the appraisal, as security, the judgment being then construed as a mortgage. At the expiration of this stay, if the debt is not paid, there is to be a peremptory sale. The act applies to foreclosures on mortgage. If the Sheriff violates this act in his proceedings, he is to be fined $20, and the sale is to be void. On January 11th following, the further provision was made that the plaintiff might endorse Loan Office certificates.

This act was also at once declared unconstitutional in the Circuit Court of St. Louis county, in the case of Glasscock *vs.* Steen, with a citation of Crittenden *vs.* Jones and Townsend *vs.* Townsend. The Supreme Court of the State confirmed this decision, and the people acquiesced. The stay law was repealed November 27, 1822.

The Bank of Missouri failed in the summer of 1821. Its capital was $210,000, of which the directors had paid $108,795 by stock notes. They had borrowed $79,569 on mortgage security, $60,075 on personal security, and they were liable for $37,310 as endorsers, so that they owed it more than $75,000 in excess of its capital. The notes in circulation amounted to $84,301. The bank also held United States deposits to the amount of $152,407.

The State expenses were provided for, January 2, 1822, by $50,000 Loan Office certificates. In the same month, two supplementary acts were passed to perfect the Loan Office system. December 29, 1821, $50,000 in Loan Office certificates were loaned to Neziah Bliss, to encourage him to establish iron works. January 11, 1822, $10,000 in Loan Office certificates were granted, under certain conditions, to some persons who promised to set up a grist mill, and $40,000 in certificates were reserved for similar encouragements to other industrial enterprises.

This was entering on a wide field of possibilities; but the next Legislature assembled with quite different ideas. One of its first acts, November 27, 1822, was to enact that no more Loan Office certificates should be paid out or loaned, and the grant to Bliss was revoked. December 18th, the whole system was arrested as far as possible. Loans were to be called in at the rate of ten per cent. every six months. The certificates were not to be receivable for the fees of State officers. Next followed the struggle to bring about a liquidation of the contract between the State and its debtors, as in all the other cases of this kind. We find a law for this purpose in 1829 and another in 1831. In the latter it is provided that the debtors shall be released at 50 cents on the dollar.

MISSISSIPPI.—A joint resolution was passed against the admission of a branch of the Bank of the United States, February 12, 1828, on the ground that any such bank ought to be taxable, like the property of Mississippians. This act was repealed December 13, 1830, and the Bank was invited to establish a branch in the State. One was established at Natchez.

283

ALABAMA.—At the session of 1820-21, we find the State struggling with the suspended banks. In a tax law of December 20, 1820, a tax of fifty cents per share was laid on bank stock, but it was to be doubled on any bank which was not paying specie on July 1, 1821. A year later it was enacted that after February 15, 1822, no note should be receivable by the State for dues or penalties, unless the bank which issued it was regularly redeeming its notes with specie. Any note-holder might get judgment against the bank for a note not paid on demand, and if any bank should not be redeeming its notes in July, 1822, the Governor was to inform the prosecuting officer of the county in which it was situated, directing him to try a *quo warranto* to forfeit the charter. In a tax law passed at the same time, the Governor was directed to inform the tax collectors of a suspension by any bank, in or out of the State; the notes of such bank were not to be received. The penalty tax was also re-enacted. November 29, 1821, the Governor was directed to pay the debt of the State to the Huntsville Bank in its own notes then in the State treasury.

A year later a *quo warranto* having been entered against the Planters' and Merchants' Bank, the suit was suspended, until March 1, 1823, on condition that the bank would pledge itself to resume during 1823. If it should suspend at any time after January 1, 1824, the Governor was to issue a proclamation that its charter was void. December 3, 1823, however, we find another act ordering this bank to resume August 1st of the next year, or forfeit its charter. If it assents to this, the *quo warranto* is to be further suspended; if not, it is to be prosecuted.

At the end of 1823, the distress of the people in the northern counties was very great. They had only Huntsville money. The collectors of those counties were therefore directed to take this currency for taxes if the bank would pledge itself to redeem the same in November, in the notes of specie paying banks. The collectors were to take oath that they had not obtained this currency by exchange. At the same time the Treasurer was directed to present the notes of the Huntsville Bank in the treasury to that bank and demand payment. If it refused, he was to sue it. The Governor declared its charter annulled, in February, 1825. The indulgence to the Planters' and Merchants' Bank proved vain and it also failed.

A charter for a Bank of the State of Alabama was enacted, December 2, 1820; $2 millions capital, half by the State. It never went into operation, presumably because the private capital could not be subscribed. December 20, 1823, another act for a Bank of the State was passed, with this preamble: "Whereas it is deemed highly important to provide for the safe and profitable investment of such public funds as may now or hereafter be in the possession of the State, and to secure to the community the benefit, as far as may be, of an extended and undepreciating currency." This bank differed from the one projected in 1820 in that it was purely a State concern and had no private stockholders. It had no specified amount of capital. The faith and credit of the State were pledged to make good deficiencies and losses, and the various funds and permanent revenues, either belonging to the State, or under its care, were put into it; so that it was to "bank" upon them for its own interest, instead of investing them. The proceeds of the school lands from the federal Government were to go into its capital, and the State was to guarantee to the State University its funds, paid into the bank, not exceeding $100,000. The federal three per cent. fund was also placed in it, the dividends on which were appropriated to roads and canals; also the lands assigned by the United States for the seat of government, and the revenues from leases of salt springs; furthermore all escheats and other perquisites of the State. Six per cent. State stock was to be issued in aid of the capital of the bank, and all the public funds, not pledged to the capital of the bank, were pledged for these bonds. No single loan was to exceed $2,000, and the debts were never to exceed twice the capital. The Legislature was to elect annually a president and twelve directors. It was to last until 1845, make annual statements, be inspected by the Comptroller as often as he saw fit, and report to him monthly upon his demand. The lowest denomination of its notes was $1, and they were receivable by the State. A peremptory process of collection in thirty days was provided for it. Its loans were to be apportioned between the counties in proportion to their representation in the General Assembly.

In April, 1824, the notes of northern and eastern Banks were at 26 to 28 premium in Alabama, and the notes of Kentucky banks at 30 discount. In November, the president of the Bank of the State brought to Mobile $100,000 in specie, obtained by the sale of the six per cent. stock at New York, and an Alabama newspaper said that the bank would go into operation with upwards of $200,000 capital on hand, "the prayers and predictions of the Shylocks, the shavers, the skinflints, and screw-drivers to the contrary, notwithstanding;" from which we infer that the capitalists of the State had disapproved of the enterprise and predicted its failure. December 24th, the Bank of the State was authorized to issue post notes, payable to order, in specie, having not over one hundred and twenty days to run. January 2, 1826, it was provided by law that the Legislature should, at each session, appoint a committee to investigate and examine the bank under an injunction of secrecy. January 12th, the bank was ordered to be removed to Tuscaloosa. January 13th, the injunction of secrecy on the report of the Committee of Investigation was removed, and the report was ordered published. A statement of the affairs of the bank, perhaps taken from this report, was as follows: capital, $253,646; circulation, $273,507; deposits, $164,735; loans, $448,859; specie, $141,330.

In the autumn of 1826, a rumor became current that the Bank of the United States was about to establish a branch in the State. Governor Murfee wrote to Biddle, stating that Alabama had established a bank system of her own, with which she was very well satisfied, and asked a postponement of the plan to establish a branch until the Legislature of the State could express its views on that matter. Biddle answered that a branch at Mobile was required for the purposes of the federal Treasury; that the Bank would be of great benefit to Alabama, and that it never did any harm to solvent banks, although firmly resolved to perform its great duty of maintaining a sound currency.

The Mobile and Tombeckbee Banks were resisting the attempt of the State to tax them, as all banks maintained, at this time, that they could not be taxed if the power had not been reserved in their charters. The State was suing them, but offered to release them from all penalties if they would pay the arrears, interest, and costs, and $500 to the State solicitor for prosecuting the suits.

A special subject of difficulty in Alabama arose from the question who should fix the salaries of the officers of the Bank of the State. In the charter, the president and directors were to do so; but a law of January 9, 1827, assumed this power to the Assembly. Frequent acts were passed in the next fifteen years, dealing with this subject. The directors were free from jury and militia duty.

In the case of Alabama, also, no sooner has the Bank of the State been in operation a few years, than we meet with legislation to enforce the recovery of its loans (January 15, 1828), and also to correct improper acts of the directors of the bank, and to maintain due discipline over it. January 14, 1828, the directors of the Bank of the State were ordered not to buy any real estate, except to secure debts due the bank. No single loan was to exceed $5,000, and two endorsers were required on each note, each of whom would be good for the whole. The legislative committee on the bank was authorized to send for persons and papers. At this time, also, the Governor, Comptroller, and Treasurer, with the president of the bank, as a Board, were authorized to issue certificates of stock of the State at six per cent., for twenty years, to the amount of $100,000, and sell them if they could get par for them, in order to increase the capital of the bank. As the Tombeckbee Bank failed in 1827, there were now no banks in the State, except the Mobile Bank and the Bank of the State.

In 1828 there was no local bank in operation in Kentucky, Indiana, Illinois, or Missouri, and only one each in Tennessee and Mississippi. The United States Bank was doing an extensive business.

CHAPTER XI.

The National Bank and the Local Banks Co-ordinated into a New System

§1.—Local Banks on the Atlantic Coast from the Liquidation of 1819-1822 until the Bank Expansion Produced by the Bank War.

The panic of 1819, with the wide-spread bankruptcy of the banks having passed away, the isolated cases of bank failure, which nearly always involved fraud or folly in some great degree, attracted very great attention. In 1823, the Bank of the Northern Liberties of Philadelphia failed. The overdrafts were nearly equal to its capital. The Bank of Hudson failed, the loans to its officers being $143,794, of which $100,000 was uncollectible. The State Bank at Trenton failed in 1825, having $92,400 capital, and $339,238 debts. It refused its own notes as an offset to a judgment, but after some litigation was forced to allow it.

MASSACHUSETTS.—The Suffolk Bank was chartered in 1818. It was "required to appropriate one-tenth of its whole funds to loan to citizens of the Commonwealth, residing out of Boston, engaged in agriculture or manufactures, in sums not less than one hundred or over five hundred dollars, with interest annually, these loans to be secured by mortgage." "The State was at liberty to subscribe for an increase of stock equal to one-half of the paid up capital; to appoint a *pro rata* proportion of directors; and to borrow at any one time any sum not exceeding ten per cent. of the capital of the bank, payable at any time short of five years, at five per cent. interest; and its total liability to the bank was limited to 20 per cent. of the capital."

A committee of this bank to take into consideration the subject of country notes reported, February 24, 1819, "That it is expedient to receive at the Suffolk Bank the several kinds of foreign money which are now received at the New England Bank, and at the same rates. That if any bank will deposit with the Suffolk Bank $5,000 as a permanent deposit, with such further sums as shall be sufficient from time to time to redeem its bills taken by this bank, such bank shall have the privilege of receiving its own bills at the same discount at which they are purchased." "That should any bank refuse to make the deposit required, the bills of such banks shall be sent home for payment at such times and in such manner as the directors may hereafter order and direct."

The Bangor Bank failed in 1822, having a large circulation at Boston. "Some say that there has been first-rate swindling in this affair, which is likely enough. It is estimated that before the failure of this bank, the people of New England had suffered a loss of more than $1.3 millions by the failure of country banks."

The difficulties with the country notes continued, although they had been reduced in amount during the years 1820-24. "The money thus exchanged was partly received back by the issuing banks, at the same discount at which it was sold here by persons who had received it at par, they making the whole profit of the discount, and was put again into circulation by them at par; part was purchased at the discount for the purpose of paying shopkeepers, tradesmen and marketers, by rich men and others who received their income in Boston money, and who thus made an ignoble profit by making their payments in a currency baser than they would consent to receive; and part was occasionally carried home to the issuing banks for redemption, by brokers who were compensated for the trouble and expense by the premium paid in the exchange."

"After the New York banks had adopted (1824) the measure of receiving country bills, and among others those of the Connecticut banks, at par, Connecticut money became a convenient and profitable remittance from this city [Boston] to New York, and in consequence came into demand at a discount of a half per cent., while other current bills remained here at one per cent. This state of things threatened to withdraw the Connecticut bills from their forced circulation here, and to leave their place to be occupied by those of this State [Massachusetts], New Hampshire and Maine. To avoid this misfortune, and to aid in regulating more to its own advantage the circulation of this city, one of the banks of Connecticut actually made a deposit of $50,000 in one of the banks of this city, for the term of one year, without interest, to induce that bank to undertake the measure of receiving all current money at a half per cent. discount. In consequence of this measure of the Connecticut bank, and of some competition which it produced, the discount was soon after reduced to a quarter per cent."

On the first Suffolk Bank scheme, the associated banks contributed $300,000 in their notes in proportion to their capital. This was a fund for taking up the foreign notes received by all, redeeming them in those notes in the proportion of the subscription, and sending them home. The specie replaced the fund. This business was commenced May 24, 1824. "The country banks naturally were very much excited and loud in their opposition. They felt that the result must be the curtailment of their circulation, and the necessity of keeping a larger specie reserve. In derision they called the associated banks the 'Holy Alliance,' and some dignified the Suffolk Bank with the title of the 'Six Tailed Bashaw,' but they soon became convinced that a promise to pay, printed on the face of a bank note, meant a promise to pay in specie on demand." To the complaints the Suffolk Bank replied that they thought it "unnecessary to make any remark upon the right which one corporation has to demand of another the payment of its just debts," which was a very pertinent reply, since the complaints were a noteworthy revelation of the strange perversion of mind which reigned in the banks, in respect to the difference of obligation of debts to the bank and from the bank.

Within two years, the business grew very rapidly and took a somewhat different shape.

"The general arrangement made with the New England banks, which opened an account with the Suffolk Bank for the redemption of their bills, was as follows: Each bank placed a permanent deposit with the Suffolk Bank of $2,000 and upward, free of interest, the amount depending upon the capital and business of the bank. This sum was the minimum for banks with a capital of $100,000 and under. In consideration of such deposit the Suffolk Bank redeemed all the bills of that bank which might come to it from any source, charging the redeemed bills to the issuing bank once a week, or whenever they amounted to a certain fixed sum; *provided* the bank kept a sufficient amount of funds to its credit, independent of the permanent deposit, to redeem all of its bills which might come into the possession of the Suffolk Bank; the latter bank charging it interest whenever the amount redeemed should exceed the funds to its credit; and if at any time the excess should be greater than the permanent deposit, the Suffolk Bank reserved the right of sending home the bills for specie redemption. As soon as the bills of any bank were charged to it, they were packed up as a special deposit, and held at the risk and subject to the order of the bank issuing them. In payment the Suffolk Bank received from any of the New England banks, with which it had opened an account, the bills of any New England bank in good standing *at par*, placing them to the credit of the bank sending them on the day following their receipt."

In 1826, there was great stringency of the money market in New England; the rate of discount at Boston being from one and one-half per cent. to two per cent. a month. This was charged by some to the Suffolk Bank system. Specie was moving about quite actively on account of the necessary steps to set that system in operation.

In 1826, a regulation was adopted of passing money received at the banks to the credit of the depositor only at the expiration of ten days from the date of deposit. "It is now only the regular depositors at the eight allied banks who have the privilege of exchanging country bills for Boston at par. Even the Savings Bank receives only Boston money in deposit, and all payments to the seven other Boston banks, and to the United States Bank, are required to be made in Boston or United States money."

The oppression of the allied banks of Boston was so keenly felt that a convention was called of stockholders of country banks, at Boston, January 16, 1826, to take measures to crush the Boston alliance by means of a more formidable one. This convention recommended its constituents to withdraw their deposits from the Suffolk and to arrange for redemption amongst themselves so as to lessen their circulation in Boston.

Under the old system, those banks had gained the most which were farthest from Boston, because it was harder to send their notes home, while those country banks which were near at hand and whose notes could easily be returned, gained the least. The effect of the Suffolk system was to put the latter comparatively in a much better position. Their support probably insured the success of the system.

It is evident that the great gains of the Suffolk system, when it was in full operation, came from the fact that it exploited the ignorance of the country bankers, who were over-issuing on accommodation paper, falling in debt to the Suffolk Bank, fearing its power and hating it. It did not really keep them sound, but let them go wrong only to a certain point, holding them by a cord and making them pay for the indulgence. Appleton said, in 1831, that the gain to the Boston banks by the Suffolk system was largely lost by the increase of banks in the country, yet near to Boston, which had gained the most by it. As time went on, the system was extended until it embraced nearly all New England, and held the notes of that region very nearly uniform. There was, however, always friction in it between the city and country banks.

RHODE ISLAND.— In 1826, it was stated that nearly one-third of the capital of the Rhode Island banks was loaned to directors and other stockholders. This accounted for the small proportion of notes in circulation. There were forty-three banks in the State, which was more than one for every two thousand souls.

CONNECTICUT.—In 1825, some New York speculators took up the charter of the Derby Bank, which had wound up and gone out of existence, and put about $80,000 of notes bearing its name in circulation. It then failed. The failure, however, which has remained the most famous in southern New England was that of the Eagle Bank at New Haven. It had loans outstanding of $2 millions, of which $1.7 millions were bad, being in the hands of a single firm. The liabilities were $1.5 millions, nearly all for circulation, and the assets were only $300,000 on a liberal valuation. The notes were quoted at 50 cents on $1. The president was arrested and imprisoned, but he compromised and was released. There was a clause in the charter of this bank, of the kind mentioned above, that various ecclesiastical and educational societies might at any time subscribe shares at par, with their funds, which shares should not be transferable, but should be withdrawable on six months' notice. In the first case of trouble, of course, the question arose whether these were deposits or shares in the capital, involving the question whether the owners were debtors or creditors in bankruptcy. In the case of the United Society against the Eagle Bank, it was held that the society could not, after the insolvency of the bank, withdraw its shares or recover the amount as a debt of the bank. Its position was that of a stockholder. The case of the Bishop's Fund *vs.* the Eagle Bank, involved the same point. The Eagle Bank had also $80,000 or $90,000 deposited by the New Haven Savings Bank, "all money which it had received," at four per cent. interest. An attempt to break down the special assignment in favor of the Savings Bank failed.

NEW YORK.—The scandals which had occurred in the State of New York in connection with legislative charters for banks led the Constitutional Convention of 1821 to put a provision in the Constitution that a two-thirds vote of both Houses should be required to incorporate a bank. This provision proved entirely useless for its purpose. It only made it necessary to take more comprehensive and elaborate measures when attempting to secure charters, and strengthened the monopoly of note issue in the hands of the existing banks.

In 1824 the charter of the Chemical Bank of New York was connected with great political and legislative corruption. It was also mixed up with the election of that year. The lobbyists of the bank were indicted for using improper means to affect legislation. Forty-seven charters were applied for in New York in 1824. Niles said, "It is to be feared that we are getting mad again." There were seventeen banks and forty insurance companies already.

There was great prosperity at New York. Three thousand new buildings were being erected. In the spring of 1825 the exchange with England showed that our currency was as good as theirs and our mint was reported well supplied with bullion silver and foreign coin. There was abundance of capital, the stock of the Morris Canal and Banking Company was subscribed at Philadelphia twenty times over, and that of the Blackstone Canal at Providence three times over.

In 1825, the banks of New York City agreed no longer to accept on deposit the notes of country banks which did not keep a deposit and an account with them. The "Evening Post" said that the city banks had, within twelve months, been at the expense of sending home $25 millions of country bank notes for redemption; they had suffered losses by the Eagle Bank of New Haven, from not having persisted in sending its notes home.

In January, 1826, the applications for charters in New York City included twenty-seven banks with a capital of $22,500,000, thirty-one other companies with a capital of $14,300,000, thirty-six country banks with a capital of $13,200,000, thirty-nine other companies with a capital of $5,400,000, and fourteen additional companies with a capital of $5,500,000. A year later there was a legislative investigation of alleged bribery and lobbying.

In order to escape the stringency of the New York law, several banks were also set up in New Jersey opposite New York, in order to do business there. In 1825-6, a number of these failed on account of more or less reckless or, as was alleged, dishonest banking. The two banks on Nantucket failed. They were one of Jacob Barker's jobs. It was another scheme for playing off banks at a distance against each other.

In January, 1826, occurred the failure, at New York, of the Marble Manufacturing Company, which had been founded by one Malapar, a French oyster-house keeper. He ran away, but we hear that he was admitted to the poor-house in 1834. In July there was a grand bank explosion at New York with trials for conspiracy. A large number of the companies which had been started in the preceding years were proved to be swindles. Two of the accused were sentenced to imprisonment for two years and two others for one year, but a year later the Supreme Court quashed the indictments for irregularity. The New Hope Delaware Bridge Company is a good specimen of one class of companies which were in fashion at the time. It had a charter for building a bridge across the Delaware river, with perpetual banking privileges, dating from 1812. The company failed in 1821 and their property was put in the hands of a receiver in 1824. In 1825 they issued new notes and failed again in 1826. We hear of them again, however, as making large issues of notes which were worth six to twelve cents on the dollar.

A law of December 3, 1827, enacted that the charter of every corporation that should thereafter be granted by the Legislature should be subject to alteration, suspension, and repeal.

Two pamphlets on banking were published at this time, which are worth noticing on account of the influence they had on public opinion and probably on legislation. McVickar maintained that banks were not necessary to support credit or supply currency. Credit supports banks, not *vice versa*. Law cannot regulate credit. The present system of banks is "in too many of its features, a dark and disgraceful picture." Contraction is a policy by which banks save themselves and ruin the community after leading it into error. The great fault of the banks is that they are not founded on real capital. He proposed a system of free banking, the capital to be invested in stocks, etc.; the fundamental idea of the free banking law of 1838. In "A Peep into the Banks," the anonymous author criticized adversely a project which was then proposed for a Bank of the State. "The time was," he says, "when to get a bank, it was thought necessary to have money to put in it; now men get a bank charter for the contrary reason,—because they have no money and want some. Fools and knaves in their individual transactions obtain little or no credit, but when congregated by a legislative act, have too frequently been invested in the eyes of humble but honest and industrious mechanics with a dignity and importance that have been alike ruinous to the possessor and beholder."

By an act of April 2, 1829, in accordance with a recommendation of Governor Van Buren, the safety fund system of banking was established in New York. There were forty banks whose charters were about to expire. In a work on "Banks and Banking in the State of New York" by A. C. Flagg, the system is said to have been imitated from a combination of the Hong merchants in China for mutual support. Hammond says that it was invented by Joshua Foreman. The notes were not to exceed twice the capital paid in, and loans were not to exceed two and a-half times the capital. Each bank was to put in the hands of the Treasurer of the State annually one-half of one per cent. of its capital stock until it had paid three per cent. of its capital. The fund thus constituted was to be used to pay the circulation and other debts of any one of the included banks if it should become insolvent, and if the fund was thus diminished, it was to be restored by *pro rata* payments as before. After the three per cent. fund was constituted, the accumulations were distributed amongst the contributing banks, unless the insolvency of some of them drew the fund down below its normal amount. The banks were thus to be compelled to watch each other.

Experience quickly developed two great faults in this system; the responsibility of the safety fund for all the debts of the bank, and the rating of the contribution to the fund on the capital and not on the circulation. Isaac Bronson touched the weak point of it, saying: "But it is not perceived how the

Commissioners of the safety fund are to have any influence in preventing all the banks in the State from suspending payment at once." All the banks, he thought, would continue to issue paper, as in the past, if the exchanges should continue favorable, and if there were no restraints by a national bank. This was exactly what happened. Gallatin, in his Essay of 1841, made the following criticism: "The annual tax of onehalf per cent., imposed under the name of 'a safety fund,' is unjust towards the banks which are well administered, and injurious to the community at large. To make a bank responsible for the misconduct of another, sometimes very distant, and over which it has no control, is a premium given to neglect of duty and to mismanagement, at the expense of the banks which have performed their duty and been cautiously administered. That provision gives a false credit to some institutions, which, not enjoying perfect confidence, would not otherwise be enabled to keep in circulation the same amount of notes; and it therefore has a tendency unnecessarily to increase the amount of paper money. The fund would be inadequate in case of any great failure; and it provides at best only against ultimate loss, and not at all against the danger of a general suspension."

The New York City banks opposed the scheme because it would reduce them to the level of the country banks, and they refused at first to come into the system, but afterwards did so. The number of banks with which it started in was thirty-one. Contributions were first made to the fund in 1831. There were three Bank Commissioners to supervise the system and report on it annually to the Legislature. The Governor appointed one Commissioner with the consent of the Senate.

The banks in the southern part of the State named the second and the other banks the third.

The first number of the New York "Sun," September 3, 1833, is a sheet of four pages, eleven by nine inches in size. One column, that is onetwelfth of the whole paper, is taken up with a list of banks in and near New York City, with a statement of their standing. On the whole the showing is not very bad, but we may see what interest such information had for all the people of that time and how important it must have been for merchants and others to study this column.

In PENNSYLVANIA the act of March 2, 1817, prohibited under a penalty the issue of any notes or tickets for less than $5 except by banks duly authorized, and also prohibited any bank to issue such notes after the 1st of October following, thus withdrawing a privilege which had been granted December 28, 1814. Small notes, however, came in from Delaware, New Jersey, and New York. The attempt to forbid these notes was frustrated from a fear that if they were excluded the people would have no money.

On account of the lack of small notes the Bank of North America was allowed, in 1819, to issue 1's and 2's "on the best paper." Niles timidly proposed that some Maryland bank should be allowed to do the same. A month later he complained of the flood of small notes.

In the early part of this century, as we have already seen, all the operations of banking were carried on with great secrecy. "A Friendly Monitor" writing in 1819, said that he had found great difficulty in obtaining information about the Bank of the United States. "If I ask a director, the seal of his finger is significantly impressed on his lips. There is a species of masonry in banking which to a certain extent is highly proper and necessary. It implies a mutual pledge among the directors that nothing shall be divulged which may be prejudicial to the interests of the bank." The banks of Pennsylvania made no regular returns to the Legislature until after 1817. Then annual accounts were published, but for many years before 1833 the Banks of Pennsylvania and North America had made no return.

The forty banks which had been chartered in 1814 sought a renewal in 1823, but in vain. They were, however, all re-chartered in the following year. By a law of Pennsylvania, in 1823, every note of the Camden Bank in New Jersey was made liable to forfeiture in Pennsylvania, the one who tendered it to pay the costs.

On account of the scarcity of money there were loud demands for a national currency.

One of the most elaborate statutes of this period to try to prevent the suspension of specie payments by the banks was enacted in this State in 1824. If payment in specie was refused the noteholder was to have six per cent. interest for three months, when he must make a new demand. If refused he was to have interest for another three months and so on. The cashier or president was bound to endorse the date of refusal on the note, or he became liable to the holder for the sum of $25. "Upon the refusal to pay, after three months from the first refusal, it shall be lawful for the holder to make application to any Judge of any Court to allow him or her to make proof of said refusal, on oath or affirmation, by one or more disinterested witnesses, whose duty it shall be to give at least ten days' notice to the president or cashier of such bank, in order that an opportunity may be afforded for rebutting the same. If the facts be substantiated, it shall be the duty of the

303

said Judge to reduce the same to writing and transmit it to the Governor, who shall issue proclamation declaring the charter forfeited. After the tenth day of the proclamation the charter shall be absolutely null and void." "In case of suspension it shall not be lawful for such bank to issue its own notes, except to claimants of deposit moneys, or make any new loan, until said bank shall pay, in gold or silver, its obligations. If such note be issued, the directors shall be liable, each in his individual capacity to pay the amount thereof."

At length, April 12, 1828, small notes were prohibited by law in Pennsylvania, and the prohibition appears to have been more effectual than it generally was in other places. After some struggle, the small notes of the neighboring States were excluded and silver came into use.

The new Constitution of DELAWARE, 1831, required a two-thirds vote for the passage or renewal of any act of incorporation, with a reserved power of revocation by the Legislature; and such acts could only run for twenty years.

MARYLAND.—The banks of Baltimore adopted a resolution, September 7, 1820, to withdraw all notes under $5 and to allow no small notes to circulate. As a condition of a renewal of their charters, in 1822, they agreed to build a piece of the Cumberland road, about ten miles long, the only part which was lacking between Baltimore and Wheeling.

An earnest effort was made in Maryland, at the session of 1829-30, to establish a Bank of the State; but it was defeated in the House, 46 to 23.

NORTH CAROLINA.—After the stress of the war passed away, the difficulties of the State finance ceased. In 1820, there was a surplus in the treasury which the Treasurer was directed to invest in bank stock. In 1823, a further issue of treasury notes was ordered to the amount of $100,000, in denominations of five to seventy-five cents, receivable for dues to the State. It appears that they were not needed for State expenses, so it was provided that they should be issued in exchange for specie or bank notes, which was to be expended for bank stock; so that the State manufactured and sold a State paper issue, in order to buy bank stock. In 1824, the Treasurer was directed to invest his balances in bank stock until otherwise ordered, or until a bank should be established on funds of the State. In the following years dividends on bank stock appear in the revenue of the State. In 1828, the Treasurer bought stock in the Bank of the State at 90 and in the Cape Fear and Newbern Banks at 80. He reported in that year that $106,469 in treasury notes had been burned, out of the $262,000 which had been issued in 1814, 1816, and 1823, as above. He said that those still out were very ragged and dirty. In the same year commissioners were appointed to vote on the State shares in the banks. They were instructed by law "not to give their consent to any proposition or regulation for the too rapid reduction of the debts to said banks, or to the too sudden winding up of the affairs thereof;" also to inquire and report on what terms the existing banks would merge in another bank to be made. During the first part of 1828, North Carolina notes were at from five to twelve and one-half discount at Philadelphia. The South and Southwest were flooded with them. This state of things appears to have led to a special investigation by a legislative committee at the session of 1828-9. Raguet says that the banks of North Carolina had long refused specie payments. "A law was proposed but not enacted which has induced them to call in their issues, the commencement of which has produced such an alarm throughout the State that the grand jury in several counties have recommended a special call of the Legislature in order to prevent a measure which they have the folly to believe will ruin the whole people."

The Committee of 1828-9 declared that the banks made usurious contracts, lending depreciated paper to be repaid with specie funds, and that they purchased their own notes at a depreciation. The Bank of the State put out its own notes in the purchase of cotton, and at one time they adopted a rule that anyone who demanded specie must take an oath that he was not a broker. It is in evidence that the Bank of the State has made false statements to the Legislature of the amount of specie on hand. It counted under that head stock of the United States Bank, which it had bought in violation of its charter. The amount of actual specie now in the Bank of the State is certainly not $1,000. This bank is now considering whether it will not wind up. It holds the notes of the people for more than $5,000,000. They proposed that the Attorney-general should be instructed to institute a judicial inquiry into the conduct of the banks, but it does not appear to have been done.

The Bank of the State declared two and a-half per cent. dividend; the Bank of Cape Fear four per cent., and the Bank of Newbern four per cent. for the year 1828. At the session of 1829-30, the State Treasurer was directed to call for returns from all the banks, as to the debts of directors and stockholders, and the amount of stock notes then due. The statement of the Bank of Newbern, in January, 1829, showed cash liabilities $961,041; cash assets $115,768. The bills receivable were $1,427,216. In a note, it is stated that this

306

report is as correct as can be made, on account of the confused state of the books. The accounts of the late cashier were under investigation. The defalcations of all persons in positions of trust during this entire period constitute a social feature. Some States carried along, as an appendix to their session laws, a list of persons through whose hands public money had passed, and who had failed to return it. The accountability which is a test and guarantee of all financial affairs grew up very slowly, and, in the early part of the century, was extremely weak. The lack of it went far to account for the calamities of banks. The great banks in the southern and southwestern States furnished lamentable proofs of the effects of a want of it.

Acts were passed to enable the Bank of the State, the Bank of Newbern, and the Bank of Cape Fear to wind up "gradually, and to fix a uniform rate of collection."

The new Bank of the State of North Carolina redeemed the issues of the Bank of the State, with which we have been acquainted up to this time, and of the Bank of Newbern. The affairs of the old Bank of the State were closed in 1837, a dividend of six per cent. being awarded. The dividends on the State stock, in the Bank of the State and the Bank of Newbern, were employed in retiring the treasury notes, which were burned; but in 1836, $50,887.75 of them, of the issues of 1814, 1816, and 1823, were reported still outstanding.

SOUTH CAROLINA.—The charters of the State Bank and the Bank of the State of South Carolina were extended December 2, 1822, for twelve years, each to pay a bonus to the State of $20,000. The Dorchester Free School was authorized to pay all its funds into the Bank of the State; the profits on the same to be paid by the bank to the commissioners of Dorchester. The Bank of Hamburg was chartered in 1822 to last until 1837, and the Bank of Cheraw in 1824, to last until 1836.

There appears to have been some difficulty in the Bank of the State, in 1824, when a committee was appointed to investigate it and report whether there had been any mismanagement. Perhaps as a consequence of this, private stockholders were allowed to be admitted by a law of December 20, 1826. Commissioners were to be appointed to value the existing assets, which the State should make equal to $1.2 millions; individuals might subscribe $1.6 millions, paying $20,000 bonus on each million. The charter was to be extended until 1848, but after 1840 the State might withdraw its capital. The next year another law was passed for the same purpose; but either the plan failed or the opponents, who wanted the bank to remain a purely State institution, prevailed; for the act was repealed December 19, 1828.

One Billis, having altered a note of the Bank of the State, pleaded on his trial that it was a bill of credit. The Supreme Court of the State decided to the contrary, laying stress on the fact that the bank had a real capital on the credit of which the notes were drawn. A debt to this bank was held not to be a debt to the State having such priority as a debt to the State would have.

GEORGIA.—The Committee on Banks reported in 1824 that all the banks were sound. The same report was repeated a year later by a committee which had been examining them during the recess, but they added that there were not banks enough, for which reason the notes of out-of-State banks circulated. December 20, the Marine and Fire Insurance Company of Savannah was incorporated with banking privileges, and, December 24, the Bank of Macon, with $300,000 capital on which the State had an option of $50,000; to last until 1850.

By Joint Resolution of May 31, 1825, it was ordered that the Treasurer should take Darien notes in all payments to the State, They were then at fifteen or twenty per cent. discount.

A law of December 22, 1826, provided that if any bank or broker should collect the notes of any bank and present them for redemption, not more than four per cent. interest should be paid on them. If anyone who demanded specie was suspected of being the agent of any bank, he might be put to oath, and if he acknowledged that he was such, he could obtain only four per cent. per annum on the amount he held. Individuals, except brokers or their agents, were to have the same rights as hitherto. The charter of the Bank of Augusta was extended December 22, 1826, until 1850, and the capital might be increased to $600,000. The charter of the Marine and Fire Insurance Company was amended December 24, 1827, so that if its notes were presented for redemption by any bank, it might redeem them with the notes of that bank; and that its branches might be compelled to take only each its own notes. December 26th, the Merchants' and Planters' Bank of Augusta was chartered; capital, $300,000; $20,000 at the option of the State. This charter contained a new provision similar to that which was common in Connecticut, that any religious, charitable, or literary institution incorporated by the State might deposit not more than $50,000 and have scrip for it at par of the stock, entitling it to dividends on the same terms as the stockholders. If it was desired to sell this stock, it must first be offered to the bank at the price paid for it. This bank was to last until 1858.

The Committee on Finance reported, December 22, 1826, that the cash balance in the treasury of the State was $792,122. Of this $590,301 was in notes of the Bank of Darien. November 21, 1827, the same Committee recommended the acceptance of an offer by the Bank of Darien, to pay in notes such as were receivable at the treasury, $75000 each half year until its notes in the treasury were redeemed. The amount, December 11th, had been reduced about $100,000; the remainder was sealed up in six packages of varying amount, and left with the Treasurer. In 1826, the notes of the State Bank of Georgia were quoted at Philadelphia at four discount; at the end of the year they were a little worse than the other Georgia notes.

The Central Bank of Georgia was another attempt to construct a great Bank of the State, as an improvement on the existing bank which bore that title. It was incorporated December 22, 1828, and founded on the funds of the State. The surplus in the treasury, the shares owned by the State in the Planters' Bank, Bank of Augusta, of the State, and of Darien, with all the credits and unliquidated claims of the State were put in the capital. The directors were to collect all these, but were to give extensions to the debtors of the State such as were customary on accommodation paper. The revenue from taxes and dividends was to go into the bank; the Governor to appoint three directors, each of whom was to give $100,000 bonds, and the cashier the same; to discount notes of two or more endorsers; debts not to exceed the capital; to last until 1840; all accommodation notes to be renewed every six months, six per cent. interest being paid in advance. The directors "shall loan as much money upon accommodation paper as the interest and safety of said bank will permit," and not call for more than 20 per cent. per annum on these loans unless the exigencies of the bank require it. The directors were to prepare notes as soon as they should be appointed, and to draw on the Governor for the expense; they were to "distribute their loans as equally as practicable among the citizens of this State, having due regard to the population of the different counties;" maximum loan to be $2,500; never to issue more than the aggregate it possessed of the notes of other chartered banks of the State and United States Bank notes and specie; to take no note for collection; to be suable. There was no provision for redemption of the notes. By an amendment to this charter, December 19, 1829, it was provided that debtors to the State for land might have their notes discounted in this bank, and upon filing with the Surveyorgeneral a certificate of the cashier "that his said debt has been fully settled by note or notes," such debtor may demand of the. Governor such a title as he would have obtained on full compliance with the original contract. In the Central Bank of Georgia *vs.* Little, it was decided that a debt to this bank was not on general principles such a debt to the public as would have priority of payment from a decedent's estate, but the Legislature could give priority to debts to the bank and it had done so by the charter. As to the bank, the State had divested itself of its sovereign character. "Bills of credit … are such as are drawn or issued by the State upon the general credit thereof, without the appropriation of any specific fund for the payment or ultimate redemption of such bills."

It appears that the notes of the Darien Bank lying in the treasury were amongst the assets which were delivered to the Central Bank. The contract with the Darien Bank that it should pay $75,000 every six months was re-affirmed, and the Central Bank was forbidden to demand more, December 22, 1829. A Legislative committee had reported, at the beginning of this session, in November, that the Darien Bank was sound again; that its notes were at par, having recovered from great depreciation; and that it had emitted new notes, which it was fully within its power to redeem. All the other banks were also reported to be in fine condition. A report was also made on the Bank of the State of Georgia, which dealt chiefly in complimentary commonplaces, as indeed all the other reports about banks at this session did; but the following passage occurred in it: "The Bank of the United States, wielding an immense capital, with powers more dangerous and imposing than ever were intended to be granted by the State, has and will, during its corporate existence, have a blighting influence on the State institutions, which will be felt as that influence is used by those who direct its operation and regulate its intercourse with the State institutions." This appears to show that the friction of 1820 had left an enduring inflammation behind.

A heavy fine was laid on the issue of notes under $1, November 25, 1830. All previous penalties which had been laid were remitted if the issuers would make tax returns and pay taxes on their capital.

In March, 1828, there were said to be excessive exports of specie. "Gold has disappeared." The banks were in distress, but dray-loads of specie were coming into Baltimore, or rather passing through, for three hundred thousand dollars' worth of it is said to have been sent on, and Niles reckoned up seven hundred and fifty thousand dollars, "which New York has gathered to herself within a few days, the whole of which is probably on its way to England." He tried to connect all this with the tariff, especially as it affected wool, but he had recorded, just before, the fact that there was a loss on all the dollars brought from Valparaiso and that it would have been profitable rather to bring wool and sell it at cost, if there had been no duty. He always used the importation or exportation of specie as an indicator of prosperity or the reverse. He was now compelled to change his argument, which he did by saying that the exportation of specie proved that there was no reciprocity in trade. The Americans worked for specie only to send it to England. The Baltimore Bank would take only notes. which were depositable in New York and Philadelphia. There was a great stringency in money and fall in prices. The auctions were said to be crowded with goods from England. With exchange at 111 and discount rates high, United States Bank stock advanced, being used probably as a remittance. In October of 1830 specie was flowing into the United States in abundance. It was being exported from England both to the United States and to the Continent. In January, 1830, the influx of specie had become an incumbrance. The banks did not have room in which to keep it. Niles says that this is the good result which he had promised, yet he states that the Baltimore banks would not pay the cost of bringing silver from Philadelphia to get it. Capital was plentiful. He puts the specie in the banks of the United States at thirty million dollars, besides ten million dollars in circulation. In April he says that great sums have been sent to the United States for investment, through the Bank of the United States, on account of apprehensions in

Europe. In October we find him complaining once more that money is very scarce among all who depend on bank accommodation, and that six or seven millions of dollars have lately departed for England. Prices are falling under forced sales. In 1831 the Bank of England exported specie and curtailed its circulation. In February, 1832, there are complaints of a great stringency of money and exportations of specie with bankruptcies because banking assistance is refused. There is a great contraction of the currency. In the same month McDuffie, in a report to the House, said that there was "not nearly enough money afloat to meet the general demand for it."

In the decade from 1820 to 1830, the banks of the Atlantic coast settled down to a system of circulation banking. Out of the troubles of the second decade, some rules and maxims for this kind of banking had been developed, and some men had been trained by experience to its methods. In fact, the system of banking which Hamilton had introduced might be regarded as now operating according to his theory of it, and the Bank of the United States was now acting as a regulator, according to the theory. Gouge, who had studied this system in its operation more thoroughly and with more intelligence than anybody else, maintained that it was a system of alternate expansions and contractions. The years of expansion and "good times" were 1821, 1824, 1827, 1830-31. The years of crisis and "hard times" were 1822, 1825, 1828-9, 1832.

That the system should have tended to these heats and chills seems a necessary consequence of its character. There was no limit to the bank note issue, except the utmost which each bank could keep afloat. The Specie reserve was made as small as the banker dared to risk. This specie became the vital nerve of the entire economic system of the country. The jealousy with which it was watched over seemed sometimes ridiculous and sometimes tragic. When things seemed prosperous and the exchanges were favorable, the banker put out his circulation. When one did it, the others did it, and the consequence was a general inflation. Presently the issue became excessive. The exchanges turned and a little specie was shipped. Thereupon, the vital nerve being touched, a shock went through the entire system. Discounts were refused; loans could only be obtained through brokers at extravagant rates; the circulation was contracted very suddenly; the commercial system was arrested; then industry stopped; production was reduced; wages were lowered; and finally the farmers, so far as they were debtors, were reached. This severe remedy operated a cure, and all were ready to begin again. This course was not accomplished, of course, in its complete round every few months. The minor fluctuations touched only the first mentioned part of the industrial organization. The greater ones produced little crises. The banks, generally speaking, sowed the storm and left others to reap the whirlwind. Considering the fact that the bank circulation was very strictly localized, it is possible that the expansions and contractions may have had that prompt effect upon prices which Gouge, Raguet, and others attributed to them. Amongst the evil influences which intensified the effects of these methods, the usury law must be put amongst the very first. Nine-tenths of the evil practices of the banks were due to attempts to evade that law in obtaining rates which were legitimately theirs by the operation of the market. If they had been allowed to operate on their discount rate, they would have had less motive to operate on the amount of their circulation.

§ *2.—The Bank of the United States from Biddle's Accession until the Bank War.*

Nicholas Biddle was appointed a government director of the Bank in 1819, and was elected a stockholders' director in 1820. After some contest, he was elected president of the Bank November 25, 1822. The struggle was between two parties in the Bank,—a conservative party, which was satisfied with Cheves's administration, and another which wanted a more enterprising policy. The latter party thought it bad policy to make such a free exposition of the affairs of the Bank as Cheves made in his report of 1822 which was laid before the triennial meeting of the stockholders.

The Bank held 37,954 shares of its own stock; forfeited collateral. Cheves considered this a useful reduction of a capital which was quite too large. The strictures passed by him in this report on the operations of Smith, Williams, and Buchanan called out a protest from Williams which was sarcastic and angry; but he did not even take up a single one of the allegations of fact. A committee of the directors resolved that Cheves had "fully and satisfactorily proved the facts detailed in his statement of the past and present condition of the Bank."

Biddle took charge of the Bank in January, 1823, when he was only thirty-seven years old. He was of a sanguine and poetical temperament, and it is only fair to him to emphasize the fact that he was surrounded and urged on by a party

316

which applauded bold financiering; at least as long as they could win under his leadership. Nathan Appleton, in the retrospect of Biddle's career, said that it was the opinion of those who watched him "that he was a bold navigator; that he kept his ship under a press of sail, relying upon his skill in taking in canvas in case of a squall; of which he has occasionally given us evidence himself."

When Biddle took charge, the circulation was $4.3 millions; the specie, $4.4 millions; the public deposits, $2.7 millions; credit of public officers, $1.5 millions; private deposits, $3.3 millions; loans, $30.7 millions; public stocks, $11 millions.

The Bank had petitioned Congress, in 1818, for an amendment to the charter to allow some other person than the president and cashier of the parent Bank to sign the notes; but the petition had been refused. This labor was very great, the circulation then being over $8 millions. The reason for not letting anyone but the president and cashier of the head bank sign the notes was that the variety of signatures would make the notes non-uniform, which was one of the evils the bank was intended to correct. The Senate authorized the appointment of special officers for this duty, but the House declined, chiefly, as it appears, on the ground that the big Bank would get too much power over the local banks. Smith of Maryland said that the officers could not sign more than fifteen hundred notes each day, in view of their other duties. The same petition was renewed in 1820 and again in 1823. In the latter petition, which was made the subject of a report of a committee of the House of Representatives, it was prayed that the part of the charter might be changed which provided that no director, except the president, should be eligible for more

317

than three years in four; that a law should be passed providing for the punishment of persons convicted of fraud on the Bank; that the Board might be authorized to appoint persons to sign notes of the smaller denominations at the parent bank; that the notes of the Bank might be made receivable by law in payments to the United States only at the bank or branch where they are made payable. The committee reported against the first point; in favor of the second and third. In regard to the fourth point, they say that the existing regulation operates as a practical prohibition to issue any notes in the western States and to a like prohibition to issue them to the South during six months in the year. They propose, therefore, that this request also be granted. The document is in fact an exposition of the difficulty in which the Bank found itself, with branches scattered all over the country, in each district of which there was a strictly local currency, while the notes of the national Bank were to be maintained at an equal value everywhere. This committee argue that if the notes of the branches also had only local circulation, specie would be drawn and transmitted when the exchanges so required, and that the expense of this would provide the required check and guarantee on the transactions. No action was taken.

The liquidation had reached such a point, in 1823, that the currencies of the different States were all substantially equal on the Atlantic coast, having all been brought to par. The Bank of the United States therefore yielded on the point about receiving branch notes; but it is a significant fact that those notes of large denominations were quoted at one-quarter of one per cent. discount at Philadelphia in 1824. The usage of the Bank in 1830 was to redeem all its five's everywhere, and generally any small amount anywhere.

It was a trifling incident, but an unpopular one, that the Bank of the United States, in 1823, reduced the rating of pistareens from twenty cents to seventeen cents; It was a necessary consequence of the restoration of the currency to specie value.

The directors of the Bank resolved, December 2, 1823, to "operate in exchange." In the next two years, the active capital was increased by the sale of $3 millions or $4 millions worth of stock which had been forfeited in the stock jobbing operations of 1818. In the same years it took government loans of $10 millions. Gouge asserts that this proceeding brought it and all the other banks in the country, in 1825, to the verge of suspension. It is certain that the crisis here preceded that in England and was not a direct consequence of it.

Raguet says that formerly the banks of the United States only discounted notes payable on the spot, and if for accommodation they discounted a bill payable at a distance, it was done on the same terms as if on the spot, no profit in the way of exchange being expected. The Bank of the United States began the business of dealing in inland bills of exchange, buying and selling bills on all points where it had branches upon terms which gave it a profit. He regards this dealing as mischievous for reasons which are connected with the expansions and contractions of the currency; that is, at different places the Bank makes money easy when it wants to sell bills and tight where it wants to buy them. He represents the Bank as trying to act as the arbiter of exchange. This had been claimed as a merit on its part by its friends. The suggestion is that the Bank creates and overrules the exchange and does not follow the market.

April 9, 1825, seven expresses arrived at Philadelphia from New York in one day with news of a great rise of prices in the markets of Liverpool and London. All prices advanced, especially cotton. In July the price of cotton fell 3d. a pound at Liverpool. This produced a crisis in New York with many failures. "Many of the banks were in great difficulties. Several of them broke, and such were the straits of the United States Bank that one of the directors talked publicly on the exchange at Philadelphia of the expediency of suspending specie payments." Biddle wrote that the storm passed over this country a few weeks earlier than over England. He had never felt any uneasiness about the banks of this country except on that occasion. October 1st, the government paid off a loan of $7 millions, nearly half of which was payable at Philadelphia, whereby the United States Bank was brought in debt to the local banks of Pennsylvania and New York. It sold its funded debt for nearly $2 millions, and some bank stock besides, and extricated itself by November 1. Two circumstances increased the difficulty: a demand for specie for the British army in Canada and a demand for specie to found a bank at New Orleans. "I went immediately to New York," says Biddle, "where I sought the gentleman who was preparing to draw specie from the banks of Philadelphia in order to send it to New Orleans, and gave him drafts on that city. These drafts were not given to protect the Bank itself, which was then a creditor of the Philadelphia banks for more than the amount of them, but they were employed to arrest from these city banks a drain which could not fail to embarrass them." He declared that he had met the panic by an increase of the loans of the Bank at that time.

The specie in the Bank of the United States in July, 1821, was $5.8 millions. It declined to $3.3 millions one year later. Then it increased steadily to $6.7 millions, January, 1825. In July it was down to $4 millions, and in the following January to $3.9 millions.

In 1827, the Bank renewed its petition with regard to the compulsion on the chief officers to sign the notes; once more in vain. This led to the revival of the use of branch drafts. They were drawn by the cashier of any branch on the parent Bank, to the order of some officer of the branch, and endorsed by the latter to bearer. They then circulated like bank notes. At first the denominations were five's and ten's. In 1831, twenty's were added. They were also payable at the place where issued. Binney, Wirt, and Webster gave opinions that these drafts were legal. The Secretary of the Treasury approved of them and allowed public dues to be paid in them. They were a most unlucky invention. Most of the subsequent real trouble of the Bank can be traced to them. Immediately upon their re-introduction, the "race-horse bills" reappeared,—that is, drafts drawn between the different places where there were branches, so that a bill falling due at one place was met by the discount of a bill drawn on another place. The name, which is said to have been invented by Cheves, was derived from the nimbleness which was required of the drawers to keep up with the system. The device largely robbed the Bank of the control of its own business.

The receipt of branch drafts at New York in 1828 was nearly $12 millions and in 1829 over $11 millions. The total receipt of them in 1828 and 1829 at Philadelphia, New York,

Baltimore, and Boston was over $37 millions. They became the medium with which the South and West paid for its purchases. Gallatin said of them that they "are of the same character, depend on the same security, and in case of failure, would share the same fate with bank notes. Though not usually included in the amount of the circulation of the Bank, we cannot but consider the average amount in actual circulation as making part of the currency of the country."

In December, 1827, the Bank of the United States was able, by putting out its branch drafts to stop the circulation of the notes of the Cape Fear Bank of North Carolina. To this operation of the branch drafts Gouge attributes in part the difficulties of 1828.

At the triennial meeting of the stockholders, in 1828, the enthusiasm was very great over the good management and prosperity of the Bank. The increase of the value of real estate at Cincinnati made it probable that the loss there would be recovered. The suspended debt was $7.1 millions. The whole anticipated loss was $3.1 millions, to meet which there were reserves, etc., for $2.9 millions. The domestic exchange business was $22 millions, on which the profits were nearly half a million. The circulation was $13.4 millions; the specie $5.8 millions; the loans $31.5 millions. Commenting on this report, Niles said: "The Bank now appears devoted to the purposes for which it was instituted, with much steadiness and great care, and, on that account, deserves well of the country," but he clung to his conviction of its unconstitutionality. He apprehends trouble from the multitude of five-dollar notes issued by the branches, many counterfeits on them being already in circulation. These are facilitated by the great number of different signatures. The last detail shows that he means branch drafts.

There was great popular suspicion and jealousy of the operations of domestic exchange at this period. The charges were thought to be unwarranted, which the Bank made for drafts between different places. If the great Bank secured through its branches, as it appears to have done, all the internal exchange business of the entire country, it would indeed, by promising to pay everything, never need to pay anything, but settle the whole by bookkeeping balances. It appears that it charged only such rates as might be considered a commission for the facilities thus offered. The best proof we have of this is in a statement of the inconvenience which was suffered, and the greater expense which was incurred, after it was destroyed. Wickliffe declared in the Senate of Kentucky, in 1838, that one purpose of chartering the Southwestern Railroad Bank, was to "redeem the trade of the South and West from the shameful brokerage and shaving on the exchanges practiced by the banks of the South and West since the fall of the United States Bank."

On the other hand Nathan Appleton affirmed that "The late United States Bank took care to charge the highest rates for exchange which the alternative of transporting specie would admit." Biddle acquired a very thorough understanding of all the movements of trade inside of the United States. In an Essay published in 1828, he describes some of these operations: "A merchant borrows from the bank and sends abroad $100,000 in coin or he buys bills from one who has shipped the coin. With these he imports a cargo of goods, obtaining a long credit for the duties, sends them to auction where they are sold, and the auctioneer's notes given for them. These notes are discounted by the banks, and the merchant is then put in possession of another $100,000 which he again ships and thus he proceeds in an endless circle, so long as the banks by discounting his notes enable him to send the coin and tempt him to do so by keeping up prices here by their excessive issues. The banks, therefore, begin by diminishing or withdrawing these artificial facilities, leaving the persons directly concerned in this trade to act as they please with their own funds, but not with the funds of the banks. The immediate consequence is that the auctioneers can no longer advance the money for entire cargoes; that they no longer sell for credit but for cash; that the price of goods falls; that instead of being sold in large masses they are sold slowly and in small parcels, so that the importer is not able to remit the proceeds in large amounts. This diminishes the demand for bills and for specie to send abroad. ... Time is thus gained until the arrival of the southern exchange which will supply the demand without the aid of coin and then everything resumes its accustomed course."

Upon this occasion it suited the Bank to stand off from the market, and Biddle made the following exposition of the policy which it had pursued. As we shall see, on other occasions, when it suited his purpose to adopt the policy of interference and paternal control, he found grounds for that as good as those he here gives for the let-alone policy.

He says that the exportations of specie in the winter of 1827-8, and the imports of goods were very large. The cotton bills were late in coming forward, so that the demands for payment fell on the vaults of the Bank. "Such an effect was to be averted without loss of time. The directors of the Bank of the United States, as was their natural duty, were the first to perceive the danger, and the Bank was immediately placed in a situation of great strength and repose." He thinks that but for the restrictions placed by the Bank of the United States on the local banks the latter would, within the previous six weeks, have been brought to the verge of insolvency. He says that the people are extragavant and contract debts imprudently. "The Bank of the United States is invoked to assume that which whoever attempts deserves the ruin he will suffer. It is requested to erect itself into a special providence, to modify the laws of nature, and to declare that the ordinary fate of the heedless and improvident shall not be applied to the United States. ... But if the Bank of the United States blends any sense with its tenderness, it will do nothing of all this." The most remarkable passage in the essay, however, is the one which describes banking on a mixed currency. The writer was a master of the art he described, and the literary merit is so high that the passage is fit to be incorporated in a text book of the subject. "The law of a mixed currency of coin and paper is that when, from superabundance of the mixed mass, too much of the coin part leaves the country, the remainder must be preserved by diminishing the paper part, so as to make the mixed mass more valuable in proportion. It is the capacity of diminishing the paper which protects it. Its value consists in its elasticity; its power of alternate expansion and contraction to suit the state of the community, and when it loses its flexibility it no longer contains within itself the means of its own defense and is full of hazard. In truth, the merit of a bank is nearly in proportion to the degree of this flexibility of its means." If a bank lends on long terms with renewals, its debts cannot be called in at once, while its notes are payable on demand. "This is the general error of banks who do not always discriminate between two things essentially distinct in banking, a debt ultimately secure and a debt certainly payable." If a bank which lends only on short business paper finds its coin called for, it lends less every day than what is paid in. "The operation proceeds thus: by issuing no new notes, but requiring something from your debtors, you oblige them to return to you the bank notes you lent them or their equivalents. This makes the bank notes scarcer; this makes them more valuable; this makes the goods for which they are generally exchanged less valuable, the debtor in his anxiety to get your notes being willing to sell his goods at a sacrifice; this brings down the prices of goods and makes everything cheaper. Then the remedy begins. The foreigner, finding that his goods must be sold so low, sends no more; the American importer, finding that he cannot make money by importing them, imports no more. The remainder of the coin of course is not sent out after new importations, but stays at home and finds better employment in purchasing these cheap articles, and when the foreigner hears of this state of things, he sends back the coin he took away. ... We therefore get back our coin by diminishing our paper and it will stay until drawn away by another superabundance of paper. Such is the circle which a mixed currency is always describing. Like the power of steam, it is eminently useful in prudent hands, but of tremendous hazard when not controlled, and the practical wisdom in managing it lies in seizing the proper moment to expand and contract it, taking care, in working with such explosive materials, whenever there is doubt, to incline to the side of safety."

This is the art of the "complete banker" of the period. It describes the bankers in full possession of an "elastic currency," and manipulating it to the full limit of its capacity of vibration. How could any business firm, which relied on bank accommodations, traverse ten years of it?

From 1820 to 1826 the Bank did very little business in New England, New York, or the South and West. From 1826 to 1832 it did a very large business in the Mississippi Valley, but still little in New England or New York. After 1832 its business was more evenly distributed over the country.

In 1830, the Bank of the United States began to draw bills on England to be negotiated beyond the Cape of Good Hope, thus diminishing the export of specie. This was one of the causes of the accumulation of silver. here at the end of 1829 and in 1830 and 1831.

In the early twenties the circulation of the Bank was $4 millions or $5 millions. Towards 1830 it increased to $10 millions. In July, 1830, the Bank had $12.1 millions in specie. Its usual full stock had been between $6 millions and $7 millions. In July, 1831, it held $7 millions, the minimum of the period at the end of the second decade.

The Government paid $3 millions on its stock note in the Bank in 1830, and the other $4 millions in 1831, so that after that it was a holder for value.

It is stated that the annual expense of the Bank in 1821 was about $300,000; in 1833, it was put at $500,000, including all the branches.

In 1829 Secretary Ingham expressed great satisfaction with the way in which the Bank made transfers of public money, and also with its arrangements for paying the public debt, as he said, in that year of commercial distress, "without causing any sensible addition to the pressure, or even visible effect upon the operations of the State banks." In the

President's message of the same year he said, with reference to the debt payment of the previous July: "It was apprehended that the withdrawal of so large a sum from the banks in which it was deposited, at a time of unusual pressure on the money market, might cause much injury to the interests dependent on bank accommodations, but this evil was averted by an early anticipation of it at the Treasury, aided by the judicious arrangements of the officers of the Bank of the United States." It was indeed in operations of this kind that Biddle was most skillful.